A European Management Model

A European Management Model

Model

Beyond Diversity

Edited by

Roland Calori and Philippe de Woot

Prentice Hall

New York London Toronto Sydney Tokyo Singapore

First published 1994 by
Prentice Hall International (UK) Limited
Campus 400, Maylands Avenue
Hemel Hempstead
Hertfordshire, HP2 7EZ
A division of
Simon & Schuster International Group

Typeset in 10/12 pt Sabon
by Mathematical Composition Setters Ltd, Salisbury, Wiltshire.

Printed and bound in Great Britain by T.J. Press Ltd, Padstow, Cornwall

Library of Congress Cataloging-in-Publication Data

A European management model : beyond diversity / edited by Roland
  Calori and Philippe de Woot.
      p. cm.
  'Derived from a study undertaken jointly by the European Round
Table of Industrialists (ERT) and by the Group École Supérieure de
Lyon in 1992'—P.
  Includes bibliographical references and index.
  ISBN 0-13-309592-4
  1. Management—Europe. 2. International business enterprises—
Europe—Management. 3. Executives—Europe—Attitudes. I. Calori,
Roland. II. Woot, Philippe de.
  HD70.E8E927 1994
  658'.0094—dc20   94-16794
                                                              CIP

British Library Cataloguing in Publication Data

A catalogue record for this book is available from
the British Library

ISBN 0-13-309592-4

   2   3   4   5   98 97 96 95

Contents

List of tables

List of figures

Acknowledgements

This book is derived from a study undertaken jointly by the European Round Table of Industrialists (ERT) and by the Groupe Ecole Supérieure de Commerce de Lyon in 1992 to examine management philosophies and practices in Western Europe. The study was initiated by Dr Bertrand Collomb, Président Directeur Général of Lafarge Coppée and Chairman of the ERT Working Group on Education until September 1992 and by Bruno Dufour, Directeur Général of the Groupe Ecole Supérieure de Commerce de Lyon. It was further encouraged by François Cornélis, Chief Executive Officer of Petrofina and Chairman of the ERT Working Group on Education since September 1992. We would like to thank them for taking this initiative and for their contribution to the work.

Many of the chapters of the book are based on the transcripts of interviews with 51 top managers of 40 large international companies with headquarters or major operating units in Europe. We quote these managers profusely in the following pages, and list their names, affiliations, and positions on pages x–xiii. Their ideas and experiences are the flesh of this work, while we provided the backbone. We are most grateful to them for their contribution and the warm welcome they gave us.

The interviews were conducted by members of the faculty of the Groupe Ecole Supérieure de Commerce de Lyon. Some also contributed chapters to this book, and are named therein. Patrick Banuls, Yves Livian, Philippe Sarnin and Murray Steele contributed by interviewing managers and analyzing transcripts. Peter Lawrence from Loughborough University Business School and Dominique Turcq from the Ecole des Hautes Etudes Commerciales agreed to share with us their expertise in the domain of comparative management and contributed to the second part of the book. Keith Richardson, Secretary General of the European Round Table, encouraged us to write this book; his support and suggestions were most helpful. We would like to express our gratitude to them all for their participation in this collective work. Caroline Walcot and Dominique de Garady from the European Round Table, and Renée Todeschini, Gisela Gröning, and Elisabeth Epinat from the Groupe ESC Lyon succeeded in simplifying the complexity of our long-term job. We wish to thank them all.

Managers who participated in the study

Companies and countries of origin	Names of managers and titles at time of interview
Agfa Gevaert NV, Belgium/Germany	André Leysen, Chairman of the Supervisory Board
Amorim, Portugal	Américo Ferreira de Amorim, President
Austrian Industries AG, Austria	Paul F. Roettig, Senior Vice-President of Human Resources
Robert Bosch GmbH, Germany	Hans L. Merkle, Managing Partner
British Petroleum, United Kingdom	Robert Horton, Chairman and CEO
BSN France	Antoine Riboud, Chairman and CEO Daniel Lefort, Directeur Général des Relations Humaines
The Coca-Cola Company, United States	Ralph H. Cooper, Senior Vice-President and President of its European Community Group
Fiat SpA, Italy	Umberto Agnelli, Vice-Chairman John Kirschen, Vice-President of Fiat Europe Vittorio Tesio, Director of Personnel Planning and Management

Ford of Europe (UK), United States	Bruce Blythe, Vice-President Strategic Planning
Fuji Bank (UK), Japan	Keisuke Yoshitomi, Director and General Manager
Furukawa Europe (Germany), Japan	Shigeji Matsuno, Managing Director European Operations Shigeru Suzuki, Managing Director
Hewlett Packard SA, United States	André Breukels, Personnel Director for Hewlett-Packard's American Division
Hoechst AG, Germany	Justus Mische, Member of the Board in charge of Personnel
Hoffmann-La Roche AG, Switzerland	Roland Berra, Head of Corporate Executive Resources
Itoh Europe (UK), Japan	Hiroshi Wakabayashi, General Manager Business Development
Lafarge-Coppée, France	Bertrand Collomb, Chairman and CEO
Lyonnaise des Eaux-Dumez France	Jérome Monod, Chairman and Président Directeur Général Marc Fornacciari, Director of Planning
McDonald's (UK), United States	Paul Preston, Chief Executive Europe
Mitsui and Co (France), Japan	Nobuyuki Shimizu, Président Directeur Général
NEC (UK), Japan	Kaneo Suzuki, Managing Director
Nestlé, Switzerland	Helmut O. Maucher, Chairman of the Board and CEO Herbert Oberhansli, Attaché Economique au Président
The Nokia Group, Finland	Simo Vuorilehto, President
NTT Europe Ltd (UK), Japan	Kageo Nakano, Managing Director

Petrofina SA, Belgium	François Cornélis, CEO
Philips, The Netherlands	Wisse Dekker, Chairman of the Supervisory Board John D. de Leeuw, Director Corporate Human Resources Willem H. J. Guitink Corporate Director of Management Training and Education
Pilkington plc, United Kingdom	Sir Antony Pilkington, Chairman
Pirelli SpA, Italy	Jacopo Vittorelli, Vice-President Gavino Manca, General Manager of Economic Affairs
Profilo Group, Turkey	Jak V. Kamhi, Chairman of the Board
Royal Dutch Shell, United Kingdom and The Netherlands	Ernest Van Mourik Broekman, Group Human Resources and Organization Coordinator
Saint-Gobain, France	Jean-Louis Beffa, Chairman and CEO
Schneider Group, France	Didier Pineau-Valencienne, Président Directeur Général Jean-Pierre Doumenc, Directeur Général de l'Institut Schneider du Management Didier Guibert, Directeur des Ressources Humaines, Jeumont Schneider
Siemens AG, Germany	Walter Schusser, Vice-President in charge of Personnel Management and Training Hans-Jörg Hörger, Director of Management Training
Société Générale de Belgique SA, Belgium	Viscount Etienne Davignon, Chairman
Solvay SA, Belgium	Baron Daniel Janssen, Chairman of the Executive Committee

Telefónica de Espana SA, Spain	José-Alberto Blanco Losada, Deputy General Director for Strategic Planning
Texaco (UK), United States	Bob Solberg, CEO
Titan Cement Company SA, Greece	Theodore Papalexopoulos, Deputy-Chairman
Trafalgar House, United Kingdom	Brian Goldthorp, Director of Personnel Trafalgar House Engineering Division
Unilever, United Kingdom and The Netherlands	Floris A. Maljers, Chairman of the Board
Volvo, Sweden	Pehr Gyllenhammar, Executive Chairman

The European Round Table of Industrialists

The European Round Table of Industrialists is composed of Chairmen and Chief Executives of some 40 major European companies who serve in a personal capacity in what can be truly described as an industrialists' think-tank. Their objective is to help the Commission of the European Community construct industrial strategies that will strengthen Europe's economy.

The ERT was created in 1983 because a number of industrialists believed industry was not sufficiently involved in the policy-making process of the European Commission. Pehr Gyllenhammar of Volvo, Wisse Dekker of Philips and Umberto Agnelli of Fiat, with the active support of Etienne Davignon and François-Xavier Ortoli, both EC Commissioners at the time, set up the group and invited 14 other industrialists to join them. Over the years the number grew to roughly 40. The membership, which is by invitation, changes slightly every year.

ERT members meet twice a year in plenary session to decide major policies and issues. Policy groups, chaired by individual ERT members and staffed by experts from ERT companies, study the issues chosen and make recommendations. Reports of particular importance are published by the ERT and circulated to the relevant decision-making bodies at European, national and international levels, as well as to other industrialists, interested organizations, the media and the general public.

ERT members also meet regularly with the President and Commission of the European Community and with the top officials of the government holding the EC Presidency to present and discuss ERT proposals.

Issues of particular and continuing interest to the ERT are the creation of the Single Market, the development of trans-European infrastructure networks, a more active working relationship between education and industry, lifelong learning, the development of central and eastern Europe and Russia.

The ERT organizes conferences on various topics, including a continuing series of seminars and job exchanges so that young managers can gain professional experience on the European level and, in 1991–3, a series of high-level seminars for senior managers in Poland, Hungary and the Czech and Slovak republics.

The Lyon Graduate School of Business

The Groupe ESC Lyon is a French 'Grande Ecole' with an international scope which specializes in business education, management development and research. It defines its mission as working closely with companies to develop tomorrow's managers and entrepreneurs, to contribute to innovation in management methods, and to be a melting pot of European and international business cultures.

In business education, the Group offers eight programmes: ESC Lyon (the initial graduate degree in business education), the Cesma MBA (a postgraduate, post-experience degree), four specialized Master of Science degrees and two Doctoral programmes.

Two divisions of the Group specialize in management development: the Centre de Développement du Management and the Centre des Entrepreneurs. Research is done in close cooperation with companies through the Institut de Recherche de l'Entreprise and through Chairs.

The faculty of the Groupe ESC Lyon includes 90 permanent professors, lecturers and researchers. It is a private institution, affiliated to the Lyon Chamber of Commerce and Industry.

List of contributors

Editors

Roland Calori (Hautes Etudes Commerciales – France, Docteur Habilité en Sciences de Gestion) is Professor of Business Policy at the Groupe Ecole Supérieure de Commerce de Lyon. He is also a business consultant in the domains of strategy processes and implementation of strategic change. He is the co-author of several books including *L'Action stratégique* (Editions d'Organisation, 1989), *The Business of Europe, Managing Change* (Sage, 1991), and *Diagnostic et décisions stratégiques* (Dunod, 1993). He has written numerous articles published in international journals in the field of strategic management (*Long Range Planning*, *Strategic Management Journal*, *Organization Studies*, *Harvard l'Expansion*, etc.). He is member of the editorial board of the *British Journal of Management* and of *Organization Studies*. His current research interests are in managerial cognition and integration mechanisms following cross-border mergers and acquisitions. He has coordinated the European Round Table–Group ESC Lyon study on which this book is based.

Philippe de Woot (Docteur en Droit, Docteur en Sciences Economiques) is Professor at the Université Catholique de Louvain where he teaches business policy and business ethics. He is a consultant to and board member of some European MNCs. He is the author or co-author of several books including *Management stratégique des groupes industriels* (Economica, 1984), *High Technology Europe* (Basil Blackwell, 1989), *Le Métier de dirigeant* (De Fallois, 1991). He has written numerous articles published in international journals on subjects related to his research areas: management of strategic change in turbulent environments, competitivity of European companies, top management role and attitudes. Philippe de Woot is a founding member of the Strategic Management Society and a corresponding member of the Academie Royale de Belgique.

Contributors

Tugrul Atamer (Docteur en Sciences de Gestion) is Professor, Head of the Business Policy Department of the Groupe Ecole Supérieure de Commerce de Lyon. He is the co-author of *L'Action Stratégique* (Editions d'Organisation, 1989) and *Diagnostic et Décisions Stratégiques* (Dunod, 1993). He has published several articles related to his research on the international dynamics of industries and international strategies.

Michel Berthelier is Director of the Centre de Développement du Management of the Groupe Ecole Supérieure de Commerce de Lyon. He is the head of Data Master a consulting firm in the domain of firm strategies and regional development. He has particular research interests in diversification strategies and development strategies of local authorities.

Bruno Dufour (ESSEC and Master in Economic Psychology) is Director General of the Groupe Ecole Supérieure de Commerce de Lyon. He is also Managing Director (and co-founder) of Francital-Ixeco (a textile group). He has published several articles on management issues, particularly related to his main research interests: the evolution of higher management education and the use of new information technologies in education. He is a fellow of the Creative Education Foundation (USA), and a member of several Academic Councils, among which: the ELEDA (European association for the development of new technologies in management education), the EFMD (European Foundation for Management Development), and the AACSB (American Assembly of Collegiate Schools of Business) International Affairs Committee.

Peter Lawrence is Professor of Comparative Management at the Loughborough University Business School in England. He studied at the Universities of London, Cambridge and Essex. He has held short-term posts in East and West Germany, France, Sweden, the Netherlands, Israel and the United States. His main interests are in the nature of management work and in management in other countries. He is the author/editor of 18 books, including *Managers and Management in West Germany* (Croom Helm, 1980) and *Management in France* (with Jean-Louis Barsoux (Cassell, 1990)). He is currently working on a book on management in the US.

Evalde Mutabazi (Docteur en Sociologie) is Professor in the Department of Management and Human Resources of the Groupe Ecole Supérieure de Commerce de Lyon. He is the author of several articles on intercultural management, the editor of a forthcoming book, *Réussir l'internationalisation: un défi humain et interculturel pour l'entreprise* (Eyrolles), and one of the contributors to *International Human Resources Management* (Prentice Hall, forthcoming).

Pancho Nunes (Docteur en Sciences de Gestion) is Professor of Business Policy at the Groupe Ecole Supérieure de Commerce de Lyon. He has published articles on the process of decentralization and networking in large companies. His current research interests are in the formulation and implementation of international strategies.

Michel Petit (Professeur Agrégé) is Senior Lecturer at the University of Lyon 2 and Associate Professor at the Groupe Ecole Supérieure de Commerce de Lyon. He has held fellowships in the Universities of Münich and Bielefeld in Germany. He is the editor of *L'Europe interculturelle: mythe ou réalité?* (Les Editions d'Organisation, 1991). His current research interests are in intercultural management and business negotiation.

Philippe Poirson (Maîtrise de Psychologie, DESS de Psychologie du Travail) is Director of Human Resources Development of the Groupe Ecole Supérieure de Commerce de Lyon. He is the co-author of several books in the field of human resources management, including *Human Resource Management in Europe* (Kogan Page, 1993).

Fred Seidel graduated in history and political sciences from the University of Marburg (Germany). He is Professor of History and Comparative Management at the Groupe Ecole Supérieure de Commerce de Lyon and head of the Intercultural Communication Department. He has published articles related to his main research interests: ethics in international business and history of business systems.

Dominique Turcq (Hautes Etudes Commerciales – France, PhD in Corporate Sociology from Paris University), is currently an Affiliate-Professor of Strategy at HEC and a Brussels-based consultant on international management. Previously he has held positions in the Sony Corporation and has been adviser to the French Ministry of International Trade and Industry. Dominique Turcq has written various articles on the Japanese economy and on international management, as well as several books including: *The Strategic Animal* (EHESS, 1985) which was awarded the Shibusawa–Claudel prize and *The Inevitable Japanese Partner* (Fayard, 1992).

Jean-Paul Valla is Director of the Institut de Recherche de l'Entreprise, the research centre of the Groupe Ecole Supérieure de Commerce de Lyon. He has written several books and articles on business-to-business marketing and interorganizational networking. He is a founding member of the Industrial Marketing and Purchasing international research group.

Etsuo Yoneyama (Maîtrise de Philosophie) is Professor in the Department of Intercultural Communication of the Groupe Ecole Supérieure de Commerce de Lyon. He is responsible for the 'Programme on Japan' launched by the Group. He is a co-author of *L'Europe interculturelle: mythe ou réalité?* (Editions d'Organisation, 1991). His research focuses on comparative management between Japan and Europe.

Foreword

Bertrand Collomb, Chairman and CEO, Lafarge-Coppée

This book has been published under the auspices of the European Round Table of
Industrialists. It is the result of an initiative by the ERT Working Group on
Education, which was taken up actively by the Lyon Graduate School of Business.
The project was undertaken with the aim of contributing to management education
and management development.

When one thinks about management in Europe, it is the image of diversity
which dominates. As our businesses become more international, we have to
understand diversity, tolerate it and learn from it. In order to create the necessary
interdependence between the units of our firms across Europe and across the globe
we also have to integrate diversity. Recognizing what we have in common, across
our borders, should help in communication and in teamwork. Do we Europeans
have our own special common ways of running a business? Are we different in this
respect from our principal competitors – the Americans and the Japanese? Is there
a *European* management model? How can we integrate the variety of management
practices?

Chief executives and company directors from major international companies
have been interviewed on these issues. Their views and those of the researchers who
contributed to this book suggest some answers. Europe is diverse, yet our common
European characteristics overcome these differences the moment we compare
ourselves to the United States or Japan. An orientation towards people, internal
negotiation, managing international diversity and managing between extremes
appear to be distinctive of management in Europe. In the past, the history of Europe
has deeply influenced our management practices, in the future, the ongoing
dynamics of European integration will probably accelerate their convergence
through a process of reciprocal learning.

Learning will be a key success factor in competing with our American and
Japanese counterparts and in the development of and cooperation with Eastern
Europe. Indeed we are faced with several major challenges. The social aspects of
European business management will probably have to adapt in order to survive the
current crisis. European firms will have to learn to put customers first, reach the
highest quality standards and involve people. To integrate diversity they will have

to develop knowledge flows between units which are geographically dispersed, stimulate horizontal networks and collective learning throughout the organization. Integration through people is at least as important as integration through structures and systems for those who believe that 'people make the difference'. Thus management education and development become priorities.

Management education should give more importance to basic sciences which help understanding in what is happening in and around organizations: Sociology, Psychology, Economy. Understanding is more important than 'techniques', there are some universal techniques but their use is dependent on the cultural context in which they are applied. Engineers and managers have to understand cultures, short seminars preparing individuals for expatriation are not sufficient, a deeper understanding is necessary and should be developed in basic and higher education. In practice this means intercultural groups of students, intercultural faculties and programmes and tight cooperation between schools and firms. Some leading European schools and companies have already started this radical transformation of business education, it is now time to disseminate such practices and strengthen the efforts. The ultimate challenge for Europeans is to understand each other better, in order to work together better. It starts with understanding their diversity, their unity and the process by which diversity will be integrated.

Introduction

When one thinks about management in Europe the image of diversity usually dominates, and the idea of a distinctive European style of management seems like wishful thinking. A wide majority of books on management practice in Europe show differences and insist on managing such differences. In fact, management in Palermo, London, Frankfurt and Helsinki are considered such different realities that some researchers and practitioners have reached the (apparently) paradoxical conclusion that the identity of Europe is to combine diverse cultures. But beneath such differences are there any *common* characteristics of management across Europe that distinguish it from management in North America or in Japan? If there are common characteristics, could they act as bridges between managers from diverse European countries, improving communication and helping them to tolerate diversity? Building on shared characteristics would strengthen European integration at the level of the individual, the firm and the broader society.

Some may dream of a European *model* of management, a system that would prove its effectiveness in world competition and that could be taught in the way the American and Japanese models were disseminated in most of the management schools across the world. We are probably far from a European model of management, but who knows? In his book *Head to Head* Lester Thurow, the Dean of the Massachusetts Institute of Technology, predicts that Europe could be the centre of the World Economy in the twenty-first century and praises the virtues of management structures and practices in Europe (although he does refer mainly to the German model). Working with its own management model could become a stimulating strategic goal for a Europe now suffering from 10 per cent unemployment.

If we can distil common European management characteristics, with a view to strengthening bridges and improving communication, what should firms, educational institutions and governments do with the knowledge? The present book was designed to give some answers to these questions. It is comprised of three parts.

Part I is based on interviews with 51 directors from 40 large international companies with headquarters or major operating units in Europe. Most of the companies are members of the European Round Table, and originate in 14 countries of Europe. But, to capture the foreigners' views of management in Europe, the sample also includes US and Japanese directors in charge of the European operations of their firms. The chapters in Part I show that, beyond the diversity of management philosophies, structures, and practices across Europe, there are some common characteristics which are the ingredients of a European model of management. Taking a dynamic perspective, and looking at both the past and the future, suggests that reciprocal learning from the best practices is the key to this evolution. In Chapter 1, Roland Calori proposes a categorization of European management systems; in Chapter 2, Roland Calori, Philippe de Woot and Jean-Paul Valla reveal the ingredients of a European model of management as perceived by directors; and in Chapter 3, Roland Calori and Fred Seidel discuss some historical factors which may explain the differences and commonalities, and present a scenario of future developments as seen by the chief executives who participated in the study.

Part II analyzes the positions and perspectives of US, Japanese and German firms involved in the international competition taking place on the European scene.

The chapters mainly show the cultural gaps that companies have to fill in order to work effectively in Europe. In Chapter 4, Dominique Turcq analyzes the strategies and practices of US firms in Europe; in Chapter 5, Etsuo Yoneyama shows that while the Japanese are strong in Europe, they still have to improve their management of human resources; and in Chapter 6, Peter Lawrence analyzes the recent combination of management systems in West and East Germany, and addresses the challenge of being at the interface between Western and Eastern Europe and developing a more integrated continent.

In the light of this international competition and managers' views, Part III analyzes the key issues of integrating people and organizations, and formulates some recommendations. In Chapter 7, Michel Petit, Evalde Mutabazi and Philippe Poirson, show why and how we should step from a *multi*cultural to an *inter*cultural Europe. In Chapter 8, Tugrul Atamer, Pancho Nunes and Michel Berthelier present case studies of six European companies which implemented change in order to integrate diversity. In Chapter 9, Bruno Dufour analyzes the views of top managers on the changes needed in the domain of education and the development of managers, and proposes some guidelines for institutions involved in these activities.

In the conclusion Philippe de Woot synthesizes the major challenges facing European firms: expanding the strategic base, integrating diversity, combining individual talents and fulfilling social responsibilities. These are basic conditions which will enable Europeans to work better together and improve their competitiveness in a world economy.

Part I

Beyond diversity: common characteristics of European management

Tout ce qui simplifie l'Europe par idéalisation, abstraction ou réduction la mutile. L'Europe est un *complexe* (complexus : ce qui est tissé ensemble) dont le propre est d'assembler sans les confondre les plus grandes diversités et d'associer les contraires de façon non séparable ... Nous devons considérer l'un dans le multiple et le multiple dans l'un, sans que l'un absorbe le multiple et le multiple absorbe l'un.
Edgar Morin, *Penser l'Europe*, Paris, Gallimard, 1987, pp. 25–6

The starting point of the study and the interviews for it was a simple question: 'Is there something like a European model of management?' Put this way, the question sounds simplistic and biased. Fortunately the answers could be more complex than a simple 'yes' or 'no'. A positive answer would be contrary to the current beliefs that management philosophies, structures and practices are diverse across the world and across Europe. But this view of management is comparatively new: in the 1950s and 1960s the universalistic view dominated. The contingent view and the success of comparative management (for instance Weinshall, 1977), the concept of national culture in the workplace (for instance Hofstede, 1980), and historical analyses of business systems (for instance Chandler, 1986) came with the multinationalization of firms. Confronted with cultural stress, managers began to think about adapting their domestic behaviour to foreign contexts. The success of Japanese firms in occidental markets in the 1980s strengthened the interest in comparative management, and books on management in Europe started to appear when it became clear that a unified market was in sight.

The original hypothesis was that management in Europe is diverse, but when compared to America and Japan, some common characteristics appear across Europe which together form the ingredients of an evolving management model. When we speak of management in this book we refer to three interrelated levels: management philosophy, structures and behaviour. We also based our work on the following assumption: directors in top management positions with international experience have a rich and comprehensive understanding of management across countries and regions, and, when properly interviewed, can communicate their knowledge. Using these managers as experts in this subject area, we analyzed their opinions and comments to obtain our results and *share their managerial knowledge*. Thus the study on which this part of the book is built does not fit into any of the three streams of academic research cited above, but rather is closer to expert consultation, and therefore completely original because of the group of managers consulted.

We interviewed 51 directors – the Chairman or Chief Executive and/or the Vice-President in charge of the organization and development of human resources – in 40 large international companies with headquarters or major operating units in Europe. The bias towards large international companies was to ensure that discussion would take place with individuals who had international experience and knowledge. To ensure that we obtained the widest possible range of viewpoints, we interviewed companies from 14 Western European countries. Top managers of the European operations for some US and Japanese companies were included in the study to give a 'foreign' view, and to complement the 'insider' perceptions of management styles in Europe. Table I.1 presents the samples.

On average, the interviews lasted for 1 hour and 40 minutes. The first part of the interview was unstructured, and managers were asked to express their views spontaneously on common European characteristics and on diversity. The second part of the interview was on the same themes but semi-structured. The third part was unstructured but guided by a few broad questions which focused on the future and managers' wishes in terms of education and development. All the interviews

Table I.1   Sample of companies

Location of European headquarters	Country of origin of the company (headquarters)		
	European country	USA	Japan
France	5	1	1
United Kingdom	5	4	4
Germany	4		1
Belgium	4		
The Netherlands	3		
Italy	2		
Switzerland	2		
Austria	1		
Spain	1		
Portugal	1		
Greece	1		
Turkey	1		
Sweden	1		
Finland	1		

N.B. Some companies have a double origin in Europe and are counted twice (for instance Shell is Anglo-Dutch).

were taped. The full transcripts (altogether about 2000 pages!) were then analyzed by themes and sub-themes to show differences and similarities.

Two possible sources of bias must be noted. As we interviewed top managers in large international firms, their views may reveal more international homogeneity under the influence of the philosophies, structures and practices of their companies. One could argue that in less international, small and medium-sized firms, the management style would be more influenced by national culture. The second source of bias may stem from the different standpoints that the interviewees may have chosen. When analyzing the transcripts we found we could identify three levels:

1. General principles and management techniques.
2. Culture-dependent management philosophies, structures and practices.
3. Business-specific and company-specific management practices.

Managers were free to comment on any of these levels. Those who had general principles and management techniques in mind had a tendency to support the thesis of a world-wide homogeneity (i.e. that management techniques are about the same everywhere in developed countries). Those who opted for culture-bound practices (the way techniques are implemented or the management of people) had a tendency to support the thesis of differences between nations or geographical zones. Those who referred to the management practices in their business or in their company biased their answers towards homogeneity or towards diversity, depending upon the homogeneity of their company across borders. These differences in standpoints may explain some of the differences in views regarding the degree of homogeneity and diversity in European and international management.

The picture which emerged from the transcripts was neither all black nor all white. Table I.2 summarizes the general opinions of the managers, classified in terms of whether European diversity dominates, European identity dominates, or universality dominates, both now and in the future.

The 'universalists' are the ones who believe that, in multinational corporations, management is the same all over the world and/or will become universal. They mainly argue that management *methods* and *techniques* are the same world-wide. Table I.2 shows that the dominant opinions in the sample are mixed. The same occurred at the level of the individual: no advocate of diversity denied the existence of some common characteristics and no advocate of European identity denied some degree of diversity.

The following chapters present the majority opinions of the managers interviewed. As a consequence they lose the richness of the realm of individual opinions. Marginal opinions may also be underestimated, but this is the natural drawback of any synthesis. Some readers may become annoyed by the frequent use of labels and stereotypes – for instance 'US management', 'the Germans . . .' – in the sense that we present here only simplified images of each national or regional community. This was done because it is easier to make world-wide comparisons when the level of complexity of each unit is reduced (at least for the period of the comparison). A closer look certainly shows, for instance, that the management of General Motors is very different to the management of Microsoft and that talking about 'the American style of management' is a huge simplification. However, most of the managers we interviewed were at ease with such simplifications. *When we had computed our analysis of the transcripts we found that each individual had only a partial view of the situation and of the perspectives. But we believe that put together, the views of the individuals in the 40 firms give a rich and reliable picture.*

Chapter 1 will first briefly review the literature on the diversity of management systems, comparing the US and the Japanese systems, and comparing European countries and regions. It will then focus on the managers' views of the diversity of management philosophies, structures and practices across Europe. Chapter 2 will delineate the common characteristics across Europe which were revealed by the study: an orientation towards people, internal negotiation, skills in managing international diversity and managing between extremes – the ingredients of a

Table I.2 General opinion profiles

Percentage of respondents	Now	In the future
There are (will be) common European characteristics	27%	45%
Mixed	26%	27%
Diversity dominates	40%	14%
Universality dominates	7%	14%

European model of management as compared to the US and the Japanese models. Chapter 3 will put these findings into the perspective of history and the future scenarios sketched by the managers we interviewed. Because we wanted to preserve the reliability of the opinions expressed and the images described by the respondents, as experts being consulted, this part of the book uses a great number of quotes from the interviews.

When thinking about management in Europe we have learned that one has to forget simplistic *either ... or* dichotomies. The results of the study show that in Europe, management philosophies, structures and practices are diverse *and* share some common characteristics, when countries are compared to each other and to the United States and Japan. The evolution will be towards some convergence of management, not only at the European level but also at the world level. Understanding diversity, the common characteristics, and the long-term trends in Europe can improve tolerance of other styles and the effectiveness of managers in contact with 'foreigners' in a world economy.

References

Chandler, A. D. (1986), 'The evolution of modern global competition', in *Competition in Global Industries*, Porter, M. E. (ed.), Boston: Harvard Business School Press, pp. 405–48.

Hofstede, G. H. (1980), *Culture's Consequences: International Differences in Work-related Values*, Beverly Hills: Sage Publications.

Weinshall, T. D. (ed.) (1977), *Culture and Management*, Harmondsworth: Penguin.

CHAPTER 1
The diversity of management systems

Roland Calori

The idea that good scientific management is universal spread when the US economy and American business schools dominated the world in the 1960s. Since then, recognition of the diversity of good management practices has grown, even in the United States. The dominant assumption now is that management philosophies and practices should fit the sociological context in which they are placed (Hofstede, 1993). The change in the dominant paradigm coincided with the success of Japanese firms world-wide and the differences that managers and researchers could observe between the US and Japanese systems. The contrast between the two systems is striking. It is presented briefly below before focusing on Europe, because comparisons with the two other zones of the triad helps in understanding specific European characteristics. We will first build comparisons from the existing literature, and then analyze and synthesize the views of the directors in our study.

1 Contrasting the US and the Japanese systems of management

The Art of Japanese Management by Richard T. Pascale and Anthony G. Athos (1981) was one of the most respected books – along with those of Ohmae (1976) and Ouchi (1981) – to describe the subtleties of the Japanese management system as an alternative to the dominant American model.

For Pascale and Athos the best firms are characterized by a fit between seven elements – the famous 7Ss: *s*trategy, *s*tructure, *s*ystems, *s*kills, *s*tyle, *s*taff (people) and shared *s*uperordinate goals. The Americans are similar to the Japanese in the way they manage 'hard' components of the 7Ss: strategy, structure and systems. The Japanese are different from the Americans in the way they heed and manage the soft components: skills, style, staff and especially shared superordinate goals. Their culture helps them value interdependence as a mode of relationship, whereas the Americans value independence. In Japan the 'self' is considered as an obstacle to development; individuals define their identity by the group to which they belong.

American society, on the other hand, is built upon the importance of the 'self'. The authors quote Takeo Fujisawa (co-founder of Honda): 'management in Japan and management in the USA are similar up to 95 per cent, and totally different on the remaining 5 per cent, the essential 5 per cent.'

Such differences have been commented upon extensively in further research. American management produces rational tools and strategic planning in a search for coherence whereas Japanese companies (such as Canon, Komatsu, Honda, NEC) define a simple, long-term 'strategic intent', create an obsession for winning and focus on careful implementation (Hamel and Prahalad, 1989). In the United States, business schools teach professional management: 'They have perpetuated the notion that a manager with net present value calculations in one hand and portfolio planning in the other hand can manage any business anywhere' (Hamel and Prahalad, 1989). Although Japanese managers go to universities, priority there is given to on-the-job training and in-company training programmes.

The individualistic orientation of Americans and the group orientation of Japanese have several managerial consequences: for instance, there is greater loyalty to the firm in Japan (lifelong employment). Similarly, the strongly shared group values allow decisions to follow bottom–up processes in Japan compared to top–down processes in US firms (Thurow, 1991). In the US, the focus is on managers rather than on workers, the core of the enterprise is the managerial class, the manager is a cultural hero. In contrast, the core of the Japanese enterprise is the permanent worker group, decisions are taken in group consultation sessions, control is achieved by the peer group rather than by managers (Hofstede, 1993). Japanese workers do not need an American-style manager to motivate them. At the level of the firm, the concept of interdependence vs. independence also produces different organizational formulae. American firms show a tendency to segment their operations into 'strategic business units', whereas Japanese firms show more horizontal integration around core competences (Hamel and Prahalad, 1989).

Chandler (1986) put these characteristics into an historical perspective. In the US, a corporate meritocracy emerged and a new class of professional managers developed. He described this management culture as 'managerial capitalism'. Delegation of responsibility could succeed only if top management retained access to information as a means of control. Thus divisionalized structures and sophisticated management systems developed. The Japanese cultural heritage fostered a form of management that Chandler called 'group capitalism'. The homogeneity of Japanese society, its isolationism during the Tokugawa period, and the influence of Eastern religions and philosophies contributed to emphasize group behaviour and interpersonal harmony. Within the organization such values took the concrete forms of lifelong employment, information-sharing and joint decision-making ('nemawashi' and 'ringi'). Language and cultural barriers made it difficult to integrate non-Japanese. This had the effect of encouraging Japanese companies to retain decision-making and control at the centre where they could be managed by those who understood the subtleties of the system.

James C. Abbleglen and Georges Stalk (1985) used a radically different perspective in studying the Japanese corporation and comparing it to the dominant

American model. They argued that market strategy and manpower strategy, *not* management style, made the Japanese world pace-setters. Japanese firms have a growth bias: 'Management with a bias towards growth have distinct mind-sets which include the expectation of continued growth, decisions and plans formulated to produce growth, and the unfaltering pursuit of growth unless the very life of the organization is threatened' (Abbleglen and Stalk, 1985). In this perspective, priority is given to the creation and ruthless exploitation of competitive advantage by creating value for the customer and superior quality.

Some recent studies seem to confirm this view. 'The world competitiveness report', produced every year by the World Economic Forum, ranks Japanese firms first in the following domains: product quality, delivery times, after-sales services and in-house training (while US firms lag behind, at around tenth place). This view is fully consistent with what Hamel and Prahalad (1989) defined as 'strategic intent': building layers of competitive advantage in order to achieve global market leadership in the long term. On the other hand, US companies are managed towards the maximization of profits and the short-term satisfaction of shareholders: managers are rewarded mainly on profitability targets and strategies are designed to improve return on investments.

Lester Thurow (1991) confirms this crucial difference in business logic: for the Americans the ultimate goal is profit, whereas for the Japanese profit is a means to build an empire and strengthen their company and 'Japan Inc.'. According to him, the two *systems* are fundamentally different: US society is oriented towards consumption and the welfare of shareholders, whereas Japanese society is oriented towards savings and investments. The percentage of savings on available income is more than twice as high in Japan as in the United States. During the period 1985–90, the Japanese invested 35.6 per cent of their GNP while Americans invested only 17 per cent. Lower interest rates in Japan do not affect savings and make cheaper capital available.

Thurow (1991) also points out dramatic differences between the roles played by government in the two systems and the consequences on the structure of industry. Apart from the induced effects of the US government's defence policy, the American system is characterized by pure liberalism. The Japanese government, on the other hand, has always participated in the elaboration of national industrial strategies, indirectly protecting some domestic industries, selecting priority sectors to develop in the long term, and funding research and development related to these domains. In the 1930s, the US government initiated anti-trust legislation in order to preserve free competition on the domestic market. In contrast, the Japanese government never completely dismantled the Zaibatsus, and conglomerates survived and developed under the form of 'Keiretsus', which are absolutely legal. Mitsui, Mitsubishi, Sumitomo, Fuji, Sanwa, Daï-Ichi and Hitachi together represent an *organized* economic structure. Share-swaps between the members of a Keiretsu guarantee cheap and stable capital, both of which are needed to elaborate long-term industrial strategies. Supplier–client relationships and transfers of knowledge within the Keiretsu enhance integration.

When one considers such contrasts between the two systems, it is clear that the 5 per cent difference mentioned by Takeo Fujisawa is essential.

Top managers' views

Although it was not the focus of our discussions, the directors we interviewed expressed their views on the characteristics of the US and Japanese management systems (as we tried to elicit distinctive European traits). Below we briefly report the images they had of the two dominant models and check their consistency with the analyses proposed by researchers. Figure 1.1 shows a synthesis of the US system of management, and Figure 1.2 shows a synthesis of the Japanese system of management as perceived by the directors of companies established in Europe.

First it is important to note the consistency between the descriptions given by the managers and by researchers, although the labelling of concepts differs slightly. European directors depicted US management in more positive terms than researchers did; apparently they still value some key characteristics of American society such as entrepreneurship, a concept and a reality resulting from the combination of individualism, profit-orientation, and competition. Competition was identified as a basic characteristic, perhaps due to the contrast with Europe, where firms and markets are more protected. The directors' image of Japanese management stresses the search for quality as a fundamental characteristic; they seem to be sensitive to this as a concrete competitive challenge, and to think that Europe still has to learn from the Japanese in this domain.

The comparative analysis of US and Japanese management has led some researchers to a wider comparison between an Anglo-Saxon 'individualistic form of capitalism' (represented by the US and Great Britain) and a 'group form of capitalism' (represented by Germany and Japan), in the terms used by Georges C. Lodge (1991). In the same vein, Michel Albert (1991) differentiates between the 'Capitalisme Anglo-Saxon' and the 'Capitalisme Rhénan' which includes Germany, some of its small neighbours (Austria and Switzerland), and Japan. This extended segmentation is based on constructs which are similar to the US vs. Japan comparison. According to these authors, the UK and the US share the same paradigm: liberalism, profit orientation, short-termism, domination of finance over industry, a shareholder orientation supported by an active stock market,

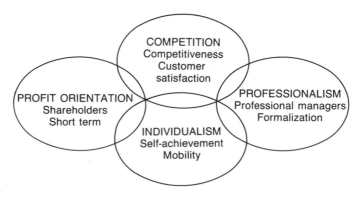

Figure 1.1   Characteristics of the US system of management

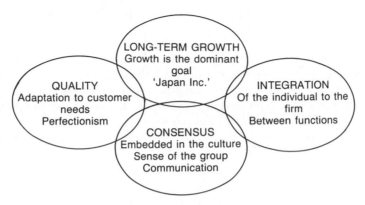

Figure 1.2 Characteristics of the Japanese system of management

individualism, and high mobility of personnel . . . in brief, the 'cicada'. Germany and Japan share similar paradigms: organized competition, long-term orientation, a stakeholder orientation, high investment, stable capital structures, a sense of community, and loyalty to the firm; in brief, the 'ant-hill'.

Indeed there are striking similarities between the UK and the US on the one hand and between Germany and Japan on the other. However, some inconsistencies appear. German firms definitely belong to an occidental clan where the 'self' dominates work relationships. The German manager is a specialist, whereas the Japanese manager is a generalist. The German social market economy, and the relationships between top management and trade unions, are basically different from Japan. The differences between American and British management are more subtle. Peter Lawrence (1993) has identified some of them. In Britain management is intuitive: systems, standard operating procedures and strategic planning are much less developed than in the United States. British management is pragmatic and discretionary whereas American management is more rationalistic. In the US conflicts are considered as normal and desirable in order to bring the toughest to the front. The British view conflicts as disruptive and a sign of failure. The best British brains do not seem to favour careers in business, whereas business and business schools have a much higher status in the United States.

Among the directors we interviewed, only a few referred to the dualistic typology between 'individual capitalism' and 'group capitalism'. For the reasons listed above, we believe it is too simplistic. However, it also suggests indirectly that strong differences exist within Europe, and more precisely between the United Kingdom and Germany.

2 The diversity of management systems within Western Europe

We will first review the literature proposing typologies of management systems within Western Europe, and then focus on directors' perceptions of European diversity.

Diverging conclusions from the literature

Several typologies of management systems in Europe have been proposed; the problem is that they do not really fit with each other. Laurent (1983) considers two opposite clusters of countries: France, Belgium and Italy where managers view the organization as political systems governed by hierarchical relationships and authority, and a cluster of northern European countries where managers view the organization as a network. Schneider and de Meyer (1991) also stress the difference between a Latin Europe (South) and northern Europe.

Albert (1991) contrasts the Anglo-Saxon model (the US and the UK) to the 'modèle Rhénan' (developed by the Germans), but does not characterize most of the other European countries. J. Simonet identifies four models within Europe: the German, the Latin (without France), the French, and the Anglo-Saxon (including Scandinavian countries). He differentiates by considering only two dimensions: the degree of formalization and the degree of centralization. This typology may please the French, who think they are unique, but they may be less satisfied when they discover that their uniqueness is depicted as a 'bureaucratie pyramidale'. Simonet's typology is inconsistent with the one proposed by G. Hofstede (1980). In his study of work-related values, Hofstede suggests the existence of four clusters: Scandinavian countries, the British, a Germanic group and a group including Latin countries and Belgium.

Finally, some authors, such as Todd (1990), argue that even national boundaries are too broad and that deep regional differences exist within countries in a patchwork Europe. It should be acknowledged that the micro-regional view is well based, and that considering the nation-states as the elementary units of analysis is a simplification. For instance, Hofstede (1980) found significant differences in work-related values between the German-speaking Swiss community and the French-speaking Swiss community. In one of the cluster analyses computed in this study, Italy appears in the same cluster as Germany. Surprisingly, the author comments on this result by arguing that the people and the firm in the sample belong to *northern* Italy, which could be closer to other Alpine countries than to the Mezzogiorno!

While considering nation-states as the unit of analysis is a simplification, it is an acceptable simplification because laws and education systems are designed at the level of nation-states. Moreover, comparative analysis between nation-states can always be refined and completed by a comparison between micro-regions.

One type of research compares actual management practices across European countries such as: professional profiles of managers, reward systems, training schemes, number of hierarchical levels, etc. For instance, the yearly reports of the Price Waterhouse–Cranfield Project (1991, 1992), present a comprehensive comparison which analyzes human resource management across 10 European countries: Denmark, France, Germany, Italy, Norway, Spain, Sweden, Switzerland, the Netherlands and the United Kingdom. Aggregate analysis of the 10 main dimensions of the data base shows that each country is characterized by a specific mix of practices, i.e. no cluster of countries emerge.

Organizational structures have also been compared. Horovitz (1978), for instance, studied French, British and German firms. The British prefer a flexible decentralized structure, with few headquarters staff, and a holding form of organization. In Germany the organization is more specialized (by function), the operational units have less autonomy, decisions are made by an executive committee, and coordination is achieved through numerous headquarters staff and planning. In France organizational structures are less formal than in Germany, but specialization by function and strong roles for headquarters staff are also preferred. The role of the 'Président Directeur Général' appears to be more decisive than in the two other countries.

Peter Lawrence (1993) suggests that the orientation of the managerial profile (generalist vs. specialist), and the degree of individuals' mobility between organizations are important dimensions which characterize the manager's job. The combination of these dimensions with a measure of various signs of formal authority and hierarchy (as suggested by Laurent, 1983) shows that each country is unique (cf. Table 1.1).

Another type of research has tried to capture work-related values which are ingrained in practices. The most comprehensive work of this type is the study completed by Hofstede (1980) in 53 world-wide subsidiaries of IBM. This research (based on questionnaires administered to thousands of employees) has elicited the following four dimensions which discriminate between national cultures in the work place:

1. *Power Distance* refers to the degree to which power differences are expected and, indeed, preferred by a society. A high score on this index reflects a societal belief that there 'should be' a well-defined order in which everyone has a rightful place; a low score reflects the belief that all people should have equal rights and the opportunity to change their position in society.
2. *Uncertainty Avoidance* refers to the degree to which the society willingly accepts ambiguity and risk. Nations characterized by high scores are risk-averse; they prefer certainty and security. In contrast, nations characterized by low scores are motivated by risk-taking and accept ambiguity.

Table 1.1 A comparison based on aspects of the manager's job (adapted from Lawrence, 1993)

	Generalism	Mobility	Hierarchy
Britain	+	+	−
Germany	−	−	−
France	+	−	+
Netherlands	+	−	−

3. *Individualism* and its opposite *collectivism* refer to the degree to which a society emphasizes the role of the individual versus the role of the group. In nations high on the individualism scale, every person is expected to take care of himself or herself and his or her immediate family. In contrast, nations high on collectivism show an emotional attachment to organizations and institutions. The emphasis is on 'we' and the greater good of the group.
4. *Masculinity* refers to the degree to which a society holds traditional male values, such as competitiveness, assertiveness, ambition, and the acquisition of money and other material possessions. A low masculinity score (or a high feminity score) reflects a more nurturing, caring value orientation, which emphasizes consideration of others.

National cultures in the workplace are ranked according to these four general dimensions.

From this study, we selected some results concerning European countries, and the positions of the US and Japan for purposes of comparison. Table 1.2 shows that four clusters emerge:

1. A Germanic group (Germany, Austria, Switzerland), mainly characterized by high masculinity and low power distance.

Table 1.2 A selection of results from Hofstede's study

	Individualism	Masculinity	Power distance	Uncertainty avoidance
Austria	2	1	4	2
Germany	2	1	4	3
Switzerland	2	1	4	3
Finland	2	4	4	3
Norway	1	4	4	3
Sweden	1	4	4	4
Denmark	1	4	4	4
The Netherlands	1	4	4	3
United Kingdom	1	1	4	4
Ireland	1	1	4	4
Belgium	1	2	2	1
France	1	3	2	1
Spain	2	3	3	1
Portugal	3	4	2	1
Italy	1	1	3	2
Greece	3	2	3	1
USA	1	2	3	4
Japan	2	1	3	1

Note: 1 signifies that the score of the country on this dimension belongs to the first (highest) quartile among the 53 countries studied.
 2 signifies that the score belongs to the second quartile.
 3 signifies that the score belongs to the third quartile.
 4 signifies that the score belongs to the fourth quartile.

2. A Scandinavian group (Sweden, Finland, Norway, Denmark) plus the Netherlands, mainly characterized by high individualism, low masculinity and low power distance.
3. An Anglo-Saxon group (Britain and Ireland) characterized by high individualism and masculinity, and low power distance and uncertainty avoidance.
4. A relatively heterogeneous Latin group (France, Spain, Italy, Portugal, Greece) plus Belgium, which is mainly characterized by high uncertainty avoidance and high power distance.

The work by Hofstede has been criticized as being reductionist, arguing that all cultures are too complex to be captured by questionnaires and a few dimensions. Other models for cultural analysis have also been proposed, such as that by Kluckhohn and Strodbeck (1961). In spite of its biases, however, the research on work-related values by Hofstede remains the most comprehensive international field study available on this issue.

The necessary complement to the research described above is provided by a third stream of research: *rich interpretive studies of a small number of cases*. The research carried out by Philippe d'Iribarne (1989) is a good example. He studied an American, a French and a Dutch plant within the same multinational company, and provided rich comparative descriptions of practices, beliefs and basic assumptions in the three locations. We will not attempt to summarize his findings here, as no summary would do justice to his descriptions.

The first two streams of research – comparative analysis of practices, and positivistic studies of national cultures – are limited by the variables they select and measure. Different variables produce different and sometimes inconsistent typologies. Rich interpretive research is limited by the number of cases that a researcher can study in a given period of time. We believe that analysis of the content of non-directive interviews with top managers is a viable research alternative for delineating management systems in Europe. Top managers have an integrated, holistic view of the categorization based upon their expertise.

Top managers' views: the diversity of management systems across Europe

When top managers talk about the differences in Europe and delineate geographical zones, the resulting maps are even more diverse than those produced by researchers. But when the individual maps are aggregated, the final typology of management systems is instructive. Such an integrative segmentation, as presented in Figure 1.3, gives a richer picture than 'flat' typologies; one can read the dendogramme at different levels of aggregation. In the figure, the deepest differences are shown at

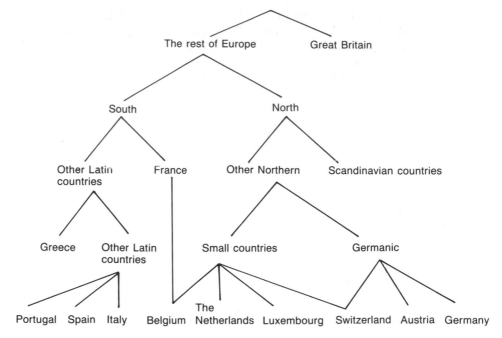

Figure 1.3 Typology of management systems in Europe according to top managers

the top. A first connection is absolutely striking: the correlation between this segmentation and geography. Four levels of segmentation are considered:

- At the first level of segmentation, the United Kingdom is an island separated from the rest of Europe. It was recognized that the UK is an exception to many possible common characteristics of management in Europe, and that British management is close to the American model of management.
- At the second level of segmentation, the north/south dichotomy of the European continent is mainly based on four dimensions:
  South more state intervention, more protectionism, more hierarchy in the firm, more intuitive (some say 'chaotic') management;
  North: less state intervention, more liberalism, more participation in the firm, more organized management.
- At the third level of segmentation, France is differentiated from other Latin countries mainly because it combines intuition and organization, and because the links between firms and a strong state are tight and based on a management elite produced by the 'Grandes Ecoles'. The correspondence with geography shows that more than two-thirds of France is above the 'olive tree line', which is considered as the real, but invisible, frontier between the north and the south.
  At the same level of segmentation, the northern group (which does not include the United Kingdom) splits into a subgroup of Scandinavian countries

and a subgroup of other northern countries (including Germanic countries and small countries like the Netherlands and Belgium). Management in Scandinavia is differentiated from management in Germany by being less oriented towards performance, more oriented towards the quality of working life, and less favourable to status differences between people.

● At the fourth level of segmentation, the German system is the one which has been best described and has become a model. The case of the small countries, the Netherlands, Belgium and Luxembourg, calls for some comments. They fall in the middle of the segmentation dendogramme. Because of their small size and history, they opened up earlier to foreign countries and influences, and managers now consider them the best illustration of a blend of practices prefiguring a European management model:

> I think they are influenced by German practices, the Belgians may also be influenced by French practices, while the Dutch are also influenced by British practices. These small countries are melting pots. They have been more sensitive to outside influences and have integrated these influences: because of the pressures against them, because of the small base they have for recruiting and because they were forced to go outside looking for markets.

> The best examples of European companies are Shell and Unilever, who have been operating under joint Anglo-Dutch ownership for, I don't know, fifty years, more perhaps, and I suppose they are the nearest to what you might call a European company.

Switzerland also belongs to this group, thanks to diverse cultural influences.

As Figure 1.1 shows, at the fourth level of segmentation Greece is differentiated from the other Latin countries, mainly because the present situation is considered as 'chaotic'.

Managers did not explicitly mention Ireland (which probably belongs to a broader Anglo-Saxon block, but which may also share some Latin characteristics).

Of course, this picture will not satisfy a careful analyst who will argue that Catalonia, the Basque country and Andalucia are different, that Lombardy and Sicily are two different worlds, that the Alsacians and the Corsicans have little in common, and that the Walloons and the Flemish in Belgium are not the same. He or she would be right; even the most global product, Coca-Cola, has to adapt to regional differences within countries in Europe and is advertised in two languages in Barcelona. Managers have to bear in mind all the levels of differences, but they also have to simplify complexity. From this perspective, we will consider the following three types of management in Europe which correspond to the two first levels of segmentation:

1. Anglo-Saxon.

2.   Latin.
3.   Northern Europe, using the German model as an example.

The United Kingdom, an exception in Europe

When you say European, you mean those who are not English?

This sentence from one of the interviewees briefly summarizes the general opinion that the United Kingdom is a case apart. Management philosophies, structures and practices in the UK are closer to the management characteristics of the United States, in the opinion of five of the directors we interviewed. For several others, the UK is (literally) 'somewhere in between' the US and the European continent:

> My first remark is: is there a European management culture? And I put a big question mark behind it... You could also defend the thesis that there is an Anglo-Saxon, and a continental management culture, because the British in many respects have management habits which are more related to the Americans than those on the continent. They are, may be, in a sort of in-between position.

Management in the UK has the following characteristics in common with US management:

- A short-term orientation (more than continental Europe).
- A shareholder orientation (whereas the rest of Europe has more of a stakeholders' orientation).
- An orientation towards trading and finance (the importance of the stock market is more developed than in continental Europe).
- A higher turnover of managers.
- A greater liberalism towards foreigners (e.g. the Japanese).
- More freedom for top management *vis-à-vis* the workers and the government.
- More direct and pragmatic relationships between people.
- More variable remuneration.

But management in the UK generally differs from management in the United States on the following points:

- Adversarial relationships with labour.
- The tradition of the manager as a 'gifted amateur' (as opposed to the professionalism of US managers).
- The influence of class differences in the firm.

Moreover the British management system differs from the US on the common European characteristics which will be described in Chapter 2: an orientation towards people, internal negotiation, managing international diversity, and managing between extremes. However, concerning some of these characteristics, the UK has *sometimes* been cited by the directors as a probable exception.

With regard to the importance of profits and social responsibility, and the principles involved in a 'social market economy', the UK appears to one of the managers interviewed like a separate case:

The British, like the Americans, are more oriented towards short term and quick financial profits than, let us say, the Germans... or even the European continent....

In Germany, in Sweden, in Denmark, and even in France, there are a lot of checks and balances against management freedom of actions, there are supervisors' reports, there are workers' representatives on the board and there is much more government intervention, so there are many other forces acting on European continental management than there are on British management. On the other hand, British management is much more beholden to its shareholders than European management is. We have to pay far more attention to the attitude of our shareholders... This is because our market structure is different. I mean in Britain something like 80 per cent of company shares are quoted on the stock market. I think in Germany it is less than 50 per cent, and in Italy it is less than 20 per cent.

Junk bonds could never have started in Germany, it is just impossible to imagine the Germans with junk bonds. I think the UK market and the US market have more of a trading nature than Europe, which has more of an investing nature.

There is a significant degree to which the United Kingdom recognizes social responsibilities, public responsibilities, less than corporations that I know of, that we operate, and that we own in the rest of the EC. I think that we in the UK are somewhere between the European ethos and the American ethos. This is a continuum and we are a little bit out to the side towards the Americans. And indeed, you will recognize that in the last dozen years, where we have had political direction of a certain kind, this has been something which the government as a whole encouraged. I think we recognize social and public interest less than we did a dozen years ago, because the government has led us to think that it is desirable to take less interest. We have gone back nearer to the Adam Smith concept... The very fact that the government announced its intention to terminate the existence of the National Economic Development Council only a week ago is an illustration of that. That was an institutional framework that the government set up in the 1970s, so that heads of firms and the state and trade unions and communities could meet together to regulate the social market economy... So I do think that we (the UK) are different.

Management in the UK is sometimes (for two managers in our sample) an exception to the second common European characteristic: internal negotiation. In this respect also, Thatcherism has changed the power balance between the unions and management. As to a third common characteristic of management in Europe – managing international diversity – the UK is recognized as having a more global vision in the sense that they have a wider concept based on the Commonwealth and the old empire; also British managers prefer to speak English in the foreign subsidiaries of their companies.

However, these opinions are expressed by a *minority* of interviewees. For the majority, the United Kingdom shares the common European characteristics that will be developed in the next chapter.

The Latin way of doing business

Compared to the common characteristics of management in Europe which will be developed in Chapter 2, Latin (or southern) Europe has the following specificities:

- More state intervention.
- More protectionism.
- More hierarchy in the firm.
- More intuitive management.
- More family businesses (especially in Italy).
- More reliance on an elite (especially in France).

State intervention takes several forms. First, the state owns and manages some industrial companies and financial institutions:

> In Italy, state-owned companies were created mostly before the war, in the 1930s, when there was the great economic crisis. Many companies were close to bankruptcy, and the state created an institute to control them and to avoid plant closures. In other countries, state intervention was carried out by nationalizations... In Italy, the state has operated as an industrial actor with a bias towards administrative [as opposed to entrepreneurial] forms of management...

In France, the state is more firmly based, and has originated industrial policies and several 'grands projets', such as the Minitel and the Train à Grande Vitesse. Ownership of the top financial institutions is also a way in which the state influences policies.

A second form of state intervention combines regulations and attitudes towards international competition, which may be biased towards protectionism. Protectionism has been mentioned in particular by the US and Japanese managers in our sample, the latter taking the example of EC policy towards Japanese imports and car-industry transplants. In this area, France, Spain and Italy have the most protectionist positions across Europe.

Japanese managers notice that in France offices are enclosed, whereas open plan is more frequent in the UK. This is one of the many symptoms of a stronger presence of hierarchy in Latin Europe compared to northern Europe. Other symptoms are the higher number of hierarchical, organizational levels and the lower degree of participation by personnel (compared to northern Europe, excluding the UK).

Management is more personalized and the concept of leadership is better accepted in southern Europe than in Germany or in Scandinavia. This management style is more inclined to intuition and to management by 'chaos': 'Especially in southern Europe, including France, the heads of firms are suspicious about structures and procedures. They manage by pressure, intuition and chaos. They don't pay too much attention to organization charts'. Linking this view with the above-mentioned administrative style of state-owned companies gives a dual picture of management in southern Europe.

Certain characteristics are linked more specifically to some of the southern countries. In Italy, there are far more family businesses based on family ownership. As a consequence, the heads of some big firms personalize the company and management may be more paternalistic than in the north. 'I think the style of X[1] was not very different from ours. The only thing was that we were, apparently, more paternalistic than X... Z was the owner of the whole town, public libraries, hospitals, primary schools, nurseries... everything was in the hands of Z who managed it for the benefit of the whole town, not only for its employees'.

A final trait of management in southern Europe is particularly developed in France: the importance of *the elite* and of the *Grandes Ecoles* which educate this elite. These alumni, with diplomas in hand, are hired to become the 'cadres dirigeants' of both private and state-owned companies: 'The French believe that they can manage any firm when they come out from l'Ecole Polytechnique or from l'Ecole Nationale d'Administration. In Germany, it is radically different; one has to go through a whole career in the company. Reaching the top depends on the person's abilities and success in the firm'. In addition to these specific Latin structures and practices, the countries in southern Europe share the common characteristics of management which will be developed in Chapter 2.

The German model

In the case of management in Germanic countries, some authors and a few managers use the word *model*, probably considering that German management is consistent and has proved successful enough. Michel Albert (1991) writes about 'le modèle Rhénan' with admiration.

In the broader zone that we defined as northern continental Europe (Germany, Austria, and to some extent Switzerland), the German model is close to the Scandinavian management style and to management in the small countries (Benelux), and is by far the most visible style. According to the directors we interviewed, the German model is based on three cultural and structural characteristics:

1. Strong links between banks and industry.
2. The balance between a sense of national collectivity and the Länder system.
3. The system of training and development of managers.

The model can be described by the following five components:

1. The system of co-determination with workers' representatives present on the board.
2. The loyalty of managers (and employees in general) who spend their career in a single firm, which then gives priority to in-house training.
3. The collective orientation of the work-force, which includes dedication to the company, team spirit and a sense of discipline.
4. The long-term orientation which appears in planning, in the seriousness and stability of supplier–client relationships and in the priority of industrial goals over short-term financial objectives.
5. The reliability and stability of shareholders, influenced by a strong involvement of banks in industry.

The system of co-determination, ironically implanted in the German steel industry by the Allies after World War II, certainly is a source of social cohesion and effectiveness:

> The Conseil de Surveillance (Aufsichtsrat) is composed of 50 per cent workers' representatives and 50 per cent representatives of the shareholders. Decisions cannot be blocked because the President, always named among the representatives of the shareholders, has a casting vote. This is important, parity would be disastrous. Before the Council meets, the representatives of the shareholders meet and prepare decisions and the representatives of the workers meet and prepare decisions, then the President checks if there is an agreement or not. Most of the time, there is harmony in the Council, but negotiations have taken place before. And on both sides people work hard. The workers have internal structures and are very well informed about the company. They circulate information from the top down and from the bottom up. They understand the difficulties of the company, they defend their interests but also understand the collective interest of the company. I often see real entrepreneurs among these workers, people who know what they want and who certainly are proactive and constructive... in many other countries where there is no system of co-determination, the top management makes decisions that are far from practical and is then surprised at the reaction of the workforce.

Co-determination is strengthened by the German system of a single trade union which allows easier negotiations. It seems that co-determination creates intense communication flows rather than a method of sharing power. Similar systems exist in the Netherlands and in Scandinavian countries.

The second characteristic of the German management system, loyalty to the company, may be related to participative processes, to the priority given to in-house, on-the-job training and to the team spirit in German firms.

In Germany the link between the firm and the employee is very strong, in both directions. There is a tendency to keep employees as long as possible, sometimes lifelong. The precondition for lifelong employment is strong and effective training and personal development effort by the company, both basic training and complementary training. Investment in this domain is considerable. Employees demand such support so that they can increase their knowledge and skills and keep close to the state of the art. In our firm, links with employees are very tight. The average number of years of employment is 17... In Germany people spend their career in the firm and are promoted from within... However, the geographic mobility between sites of the same firm is not so marked; people do not like to leave Bavaria for northern Germany, or Hesse for Bavaria...

When common European characteristics of management philosophies, structures and practices were evoked, Germany appeared to be an exception to the general rule of low formalization:

The Germans write a lot... they work hard but for every one working there is somebody writing in a little book!...

If I invite the President of X (a big German group) to speak, three months before the meeting his secretary is already impatient to know how long he should speak... If no answer has been received one month before, they start to panic. The British prepare their speech two days before, and the French the week before, but the slides are ready at the last minute. When I hear the President of X talking about management in his group, there seem to be quite formal procedures, procedures that work well, by the way. We try to organize procedures but they do not work well because of our culture.

When the low customer orientation of the Europeans is discussed, Germany also appears to be a case apart for a minority of the directors interviewed.

Some similarities emerge between the German and the Japanese models of management: the loyalty of managers based on in-house training is common to the two countries. The long-term orientation is common to the two countries. However, important differences are also noted. It is true that the stability of financial resources is common to the two economies, but this stability is based on these different structures:

● the involvement of banks in industry (and vice versa) in Germany;
● the Keiretsu structure in Japan.

The participation of workers is common to the two systems but:

● it is based on negotiation in Germany;
● it is based on natural consensus in Japan.

The collective orientation of the work-force, team spirit and a sense of discipline are common to the two systems, but:

- in Japan, the individual is overshadowed by the group;
- in Germany the individual still defends his/her self-interest and originality.

Finally, German managers are 'specialists' (of a given function) whereas Japanese managers are 'generalists' who are developed through internal job rotation. For these reasons, directors do not agree with Albert's assertion that the 'modèle Rhénan' is very similar to the Japanese model (1991). Another argument is that the German model shares some characteristics with the rest of Europe, which differentiate management in Europe from that in Japan. This point will be developed in the next chapter: an orientation towards people, internal negotiation, managing international diversity, and managing between extremes.

3 Concluding comments

It is tempting to view management philosophies, structures and practices in Europe as if they were stretched between three poles, as presented in Figure 1.4:

- Anglo-Saxon management to the west.
- the German model to the east and Japan to the far east.
- the Latin model to the south, based in the Mediterranean countries where occidental philosophies were born.

This is a simplified but reliable image of the diversity of management in Europe. Some believe that it is a benefit for Europe to find such diversity in such a small geographic area, and that it offers Europeans opportunities to learn complementary skills and attitudes more quickly, so that they can be more effective in a world market where two extreme models – the US and the Japanese – now compete with each other. But, citing this diversity is akin to seeing the bottle as half empty (a bottle of wine or beer, depending on whether you live in the south or in the north of Europe). There is also the view of the same bottle half full of some common

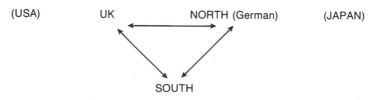

Figure 1.4 The stretching forces in European management

European management characteristics. Just as statistics now show that the consumption of wine is tending to grow (relative to beer) in northern Europe, a region of brewing tradition, whereas the consumption of beer is tending to grow (relative to wine) in southern Europe, a region of wine tradition, the existence and development of common characteristics can also be reasonably expected.

The segmentation of management styles made by the directors in our study identified a cluster of 'small countries' (the Netherlands, Belgium, Luxembourg and Switzerland) as being characterized by international openness, a combination of unity and diversity, and a 'blend of practices prefiguring European management'. Study of management in the 'small countries' would be instructive with regard to an emerging European model. For instance, management in the Netherlands has been analyzed by d'Iribarne (1989) and by Lawrence (1991). d'Iribarne describes the Netherlands as a consensual society, examining facts with objectivity, moved by a desire for discussion and conciliation, with an aversion for any form of pressure from external authority. This search for pragmatic compromise between the members of a community has been described as 'Pilarisation' ('Verzuiling', cf. Lijphart, 1975). Lawrence (1991) also notes the following characteristics: mutual adjustment and cooperation, restraint, humility, heedfulness to civic values, modesty, pragmatism, informality, and a recognition of the importance of the quality of life. Most of these characteristics seem to be necessary ingredients in a process of international integration. In the past, the 'small countries' have demonstrated their ability to cooperate: in 1922 Belgium and Luxembourg created the Union Economique Belgo-Luxembourgeoise', and in 1948 the Netherlands joined them to form the Benelux. So the smaller countries may well be the best source of inspiration for building distinctive managerial skills in the integrated Europe of the future.

Notes

1. X, is a US company which merged with the Italian company whose director is speaking here; Z is another Italian company.

References

Abbleglen, J. C. and G. Stalk (1985), *Kaisha, The Japanese Corporation*, New York: Basic Books.
Albert, M. (1991), *Capitalisme contre Capitalisme*, Paris: Seuil.
Chandler, A. D. (1986), 'The evolution of modern global competition', in Porter, M. E. (ed.) *Competition In Global Industries*, Boston, Mass.: Harvard Business School Press, pp. 405–48.

d'Iribarne, P. (1989), *La Logique de l'honneur, gestion des entreprises et traditions nationales*, Paris: Editions du Seuil.

Hamel, G. and C. K. Prahalad (1989), 'Strategic intent', *Harvard Business Review*, May–June, pp. 63–76.

Hofstede, G. H. (1980), *Culture's consequences: International Differences in Work-related Values*, Beverly Hills: Sage Publications.

Hofstede, G. H. (1993), 'Cultural constraints in management theories', *Academy of Management Executive*, 7, 1, pp. 81–95.

Horovitz, J. (1978), 'Allemagne, Grande Bretagne, France: trois styles de management', *Revue Française de Gestion* 17, September–October, pp. 8–17.

Kluckhohn, F. and F. Strodbeck (1961), *Variations in Value Organizations*, New York: Row, Peterson.

Laurent, A. (1983), 'The cultural diversity of Western conceptions of management', *International Studies of Management and Organization*, XIII, 1–2, pp. 75–96.

Lawrence, P. (1991), *Management in The Netherlands*, Oxford: Basil Blackwell.

Lawrence, P. (1993), 'Through a glass darkly: towards a characterization of British management', paper presented at the '*Professions and Management in Britain*' *Conference*, University of Stirling, Scotland, August.

Lijphart, A. (1975), *The Politics of Accommodation, Pluralism and Democracy in The Netherlands*, 2nd edn, Berkeley: University of California Press.

Lodge, G. C. (1991), *Perestroïka for America*, Boston, Mass.: Harvard Business School Press.

Ohmae, K. (1976), *The Mind of The Strategist: The Art of Japanese Business*, New York: McGraw Hill.

Ouchi, W. A. (1981), *Theory Z: How American Business Can Meet the Japanese Challenge*, Reading, Mass.: Addison-Wesley.

Pascale, R. T. and A. G. Athos (1981), *The Art of Japanese Management*, New York: Warner Books.

Price Waterhouse–Cranfield Project on International Strategic Human Resource Management (1991, 1992), Report, Price Waterhouse and Cranfield School of Management, UK.

Schneider, S. C. and A. de Meyer (1991), 'Interpreting and responding to strategic issues: the impact of national culture', *Strategic Management Journal*, 12, pp. 307–20.

Simonet, J. (1992), *Pratiques du management en Europe, gérer les différences au quotidien*, Paris: Les Editions d'Organisation.

Thurow, L. (1991), *Head to Head*, Cambridge, Mass.: MIT Press.

Todd, E. (1990), *L'Invention de l'Europe*, Paris: Le Seuil.

CHAPTER 2
Common characteristics: the ingredients of European management

Roland Calori, Jean-Paul Valla and Philippe de Woot

Of course if we only look at Europe from within there are differences between countries in the way firms are managed. But if we look at Europe as a whole from outside, comparing it with Japan and the US, then it looks different and relatively homogeneous.

A systematic analysis of the *spontaneous*[1] answers from the directors in our study shows that there *are* some common characteristics of management in Europe in terms of philosophies, structures and practices. Four major traits emerge:

1. Orientation towards people.
2. Internal negotiation.
3. Managing international diversity.
4. Managing between extremes.

And two minor traits complement the picture:

1. Product (engineer) orientation (vs. customer orientation).
2. A more intuitive and less formalized management.

These characteristics are common to the European zones that we identified in Chapter 1. Of course, there are some nuances and sometimes an exception (but that confirms the rule, as the French say optimistically). Moreover, each characteristic is distinctive of Europe in the sense that it differentiates Europe from the United States or from Japan or from both.

These descriptive characteristics are not strong enough or consistent enough at present to form a model as such. The term model implies the notion of proven success (and this has not yet been demonstrated at the world level). However, the common characteristics are *bridges* on which the integration of European diversity could be built.

1 Orientation towards people

Compared to their US or Japanese counterparts, European firms share a common inclination towards the fulfilment of individuals, caring for people and social responsibilities. This is partly based on the notion that 'profit is not all' and also on the 'Social Market Economy' system (which mainly differentiates Europe from the US).

Fulfilment of people

The Europeans are focused on people, on the individual:

> We consider that people are an integral part of the firm. Of course we work for profit, but also for people. In the United States, profit dominates everything, and people are considered as a resource that you can take and leave. This is a major difference. Now you could say that the European philosophy is close to the Japanese. I don't think so. There is a fundamental difference between the two. Europe is an individualist society whereas Japanese society is based on the collective. Fernand Braudel argued that it comes from the different agricultural systems. The oriental system is based on the culture of *rice* which requires teams of people, whereas our system is based on the culture of *cereals* which can be achieved by individuals. You know that what counts in Japan is to belong to a group... group enthusiasm. You start the day with a nice song celebrating your company. I do not see our people singing in the yard: 'We are a good company'; they wouldn't do that!

> The European culture has always been more humanistic... For instance, sanctions are often dissimulated, we take great care of people, we always try to avoid shedding blood, as we say here...

European firms tend to give more freedom to individuals, and this attitude seems to be valued by Japanese managers:

> In Japan the managers are selected among the thousands of people who have been recruited and trained for a long time. They are trained according to the needs of the firm, and training shapes people's minds towards homogeneity. This system does not respect the personality of the individual. On the other hand, in Europe managers are hired and in-house training is less developed; they take managers as they are, with their personality, and they respect their personality. As a consequence of their training, Japanese managers may lack originality. This is not true for Japanese entrepreneurs, but it is true of managers in general, whereas in Europe, even management in big firms is more personalized.

Compared to Japanese and US companies, European management allows individual differences and cultural differences within the firm; *conformism* is less strong, marginals and outsiders are tolerated. The difference between Japan and Europe seems to be clear, but there is also a difference with the US. Contrary to the superficial image, US firms are conformist; the use of first names hides strict relationships between people, and conformity seems to be the rule:

> American society makes me think of 'Easy rider', this movie from the sixties where two 'easy riders' cross the country on their motorcycles. America is the country of democracy and freedom, but the two guys do not reach their destination. They are killed by two truck drivers who don't like 'easy riders'.

This freedom given to the individual in Europe may be a strength, a source of motivation and innovation, but it may also be a weakness if individualism impedes teamwork. The Japanese might teach Europeans the art of team-building.

Europeans also put a greater emphasis on leisure. They want a better 'quality of life' and more time for leisure, whereas the Japanese are still ready to sacrifice themselves for the good of the company and for their nation. American managers also seem to be less demanding than the Europeans: 'With the emphasis on self-achievement and competitivity, I see American managers taking only 20 days a year for holidays. This, the Spanish managers at least would never accept, they want more!' Attention to the individual may lead to the adaptation of a function to the skills of the people:

> In our firm, we do adapt functions to the individuals and it is the right way to do it. First, we define functions according to the needs of the company. Then we adapt the definition of the function and tasks to the skills of the people; we do not stick to the schemas.

However, according to one American manager in our sample 'US companies and European companies are slowly converging to a middle point' as far as orientation towards people is concerned. And according to one Japanese manager, there is a recent tendency towards more personalization in Japanese firms.

Caring for people relates to particular attitudes towards employment. Before firing people, European firms take precautions. Several systems are used to reduce the negative impact of dismissals: outplacement, early retirement, training, etc. This contrasts with the US attitude of 'hire and fire'. One may argue that social regulations may explain such practices, they do not explain everything. Even in Switzerland, where there are no regulatory barriers to firing people, 'cela ne se fait pas' (it is not done).

These aspects of managerial philosophies, structures and practices may be rooted in the humanistic tradition of Europe, and even more deeply in ancient Greek philosophy channelled through the Judeo-Christian paradigm. This is not the right place to discuss these deep influences. But at a more visible level orientation towards people is also based on the notion of the social responsibility of firms and on the 'Social Market Economy' system.

Profit is not all

Profit *is* the fundamental aim (of the majority) of big European companies, but economic and social criteria are *both* important in Europe: 'you cannot have profit without fulfilling social responsibilities' – they are linked together.

> In the US the ultimate aim is to *maximize the return to the shareholder*; this is coupled to a much higher social mobility of people. Since return has to be maximized in the short term, one can react to human resources issues, considered as cost elements, much more drastically than in other continents. In Japan, on the other hand, again driven by the history of the country, the prime interest is the welfare of the country and, derived from it, the *welfare of the company*. In Europe, I suppose there is an element of both. In the first place, there is a much stronger history of social protection of the individual, not only in terms of the strength of union power, but also of the political support for social legislation. On the other hand, there is also an emphasis on shareholder return. As a substantial part of European industrial investment came from the States, US priorities have permeated through the European industrial scene... The background of social protection means that you get more adherence of people to their companies than in the States... On the whole, European management tends to have a longer-term view of the health of the company, combining profitability with social acceptance.

In Europe the balance will depend on whether the firms are public or not. Firms that are public cannot neglect their shareholders.

Social solidarity could well be a European characteristic leading to a compromise between efficiency and solidarity. European social protection systems are certainly more developed than in the US and in Japan. Japanese companies aim at long-term growth, and profit may be considered as a means to achieve growth; on the other hand social disparities are still marked:

> Of course Japanese companies take great care of their titular personnel, but there are still deep disparities between the titulars and the non-titulars, in the big international Japanese firms only about 50 per cent of the employees are titular. Moreover, subcontractors' personnel do not have the same social treatment as those at Matsushita, Toyota or Mitsubishi.

The European combination of economic and social factors often results in a social market economy system, which was first developed in Germany and takes various forms in most European countries.

Social market economy

In a social market economy firms take a *stakeholders'* approach more than a *shareholders'* approach. From this perspective, the difference between the American system and the Japanese system is found more in the *relative importance of the categories of stakeholders* with whom managers of firms have to deal. Compared to the United States and to Japan, the role of the trade unions and the role of the state are more marked in Europe. European managers certainly spend more of their time in negotiations with powerful trade unions. With regard to the role of the state, the comparison with the US is relatively clear, while the comparison with Japan is more subtle:

> America believes in liberalism; half of the people, the rich ones, find it advantageous; the other half who believe in the system hope that their children will get rich thanks to the system. The Europeans are not really liberal, they are more social-democrats: they believe that the optimum is the result of a combination of liberalism and regulatory mechanisms.

Of course in the US there are regulations and firms actively lobby Congress. The difference comes from the fact that in Europe there is a tendency for the stakeholders to sit around the table to try to reach a mutually acceptable objective and to design industrial policies.

> For important issues, the Chancellor invites the heads of the most important firms to a meeting – let us say Daimler-Benz, Siemens, Thyssen, Hoechst, BASF, etc. – the Presidents of the BDA [the body of employers], the Presidents of the BDI [the German Association of Industries], the heads of the most powerful labour unions: DGB, IG Metall, etc. They discuss important issues which require concerted effort and agreement; they manage by round table.

In Japan there certainly is a concerted effort between the MITI and the heads of firms, but the labour unions are not really partners in negotiations at the top; and 'somewhere all these organizations are only one . . . they reach consensus naturally'. The final word on the negotiations with stakeholders in Europe comes from the top manager of an Italian company: 'For instance, if you have to close a plant, in Italy, in France, in Spain or in Germany, you have to discuss the possibility with the state, the local communities, the trade unions . . . everybody feels entitled to intervene . . . even the Church!'

The structures and the techniques of social relations and regulations vary across Europe but the philosophy is the same.

> In Germany we have the system of co-determination. You don't find it in Spain, in France or in Italy, and certainly not in the UK. On the other hand, in Spain there are strict limitations on employee dismissals; in Italy the Labour Office influences recruitment . . . The practices vary but the *philosophy* is the same: social responsibility.

British managers may not recognize this characteristic; actually, the United Kingdom is perceived as an exception to the principles of the social market economy – especially after 12 years of Thatcherism. British liberalism is closer to the north American system; the UK profit orientation also is typical of the Anglo-Saxon style of management. But the United Kingdom is *not* an exception to the basic characteristics described earlier, i.e. the importance given to individuals, to their fulfilment, to the amount of leeway they have, to the personalization of management. And the old labour union tradition is also still strong.

2 Internal negotiation

In European firms negotiation not only takes place with 'external stakeholders', but also inside the firm between different levels of management and the employees, and between the headquarters and the units. In US firms, the decision-making power is in the hands of the boss. Decision-making is quick, top–down, without the necessity to convince, stepping quickly to implementation; the values of the company are the values of the top management team. In Japan decision-making is more complex. It takes place in a consensual mode; the boss has power but uses it 'in a delicate way'. Some ideas come from the shop-floor, but when decisions are taken at the top, everyone agrees. In Europe, the top management has power, but it has to consult, to discuss, to negotiate, to convince: 'There is a need for independence, authority is questioned. The decisions coming from the top are criticized. People start to involve themselves only after a lot of discussions, dialogues and information.'

The European managers were first forced into dialogues due to the strength of the labour unions, in order to avoid or to manage labour conflicts; this took a great deal of managerial time and effort. The context of 'class struggle' in Europe may have played a role in the past, but over the years this factor has ebbed away. After World War II, the system of co-determination was implanted in Germany. Similar systems exist in the Netherlands and in Scandinavia. Today dialogue with the labour unions has become a *natural* component of management everywhere in Europe.

However, there are differences in the nature of the social dialogue within firms across Europe. In France and in Italy, there is more 'confrontation', in Germany more 'consensus and social engineering'; in Scandinavia it is based on 'the naturally egalitarian view of the society'; in Britain it may come from 'the sense of guilt which the ruling classes felt after the war'. To some extent the UK may now be an exception to the principle of management dialogue with unions, because Mrs Thatcher changed the power balance.

In many companies and countries, the principle of dialogue has been enlarged:

> It is not so much a dialogue with the union leaders; it is a dialogue with particular people representing the employees, not all of them are union

leaders. They are employees of the company. I invited employees to sit on our board and we were the first major company in Sweden to do so. That was my invitation, not a law; the law came afterwards, in the mid-1970s. We did this in 1971, because I believed that the employees should be part of the decision-making: at the top and at the bottom and all the way through.

Even more than old ideological factors or regulations, some common cultural roots have led European managers to use dialogue and negotiation. Managers need to *convince* people in order to obtain their *involvement*. The European educational systems may develop a need for individual responsibility, a need to defend one's own interests, and a need to debate and to find a *rational* answer.

> When I think of my time in Holland, when I used to be responsible for dealing with the staff council, it was an interesting combination of a group of people who were all committed to the health of the company but who were also representing their particular interest groups. I always had the feeling then that they had a very real wish to be properly informed of what really was going on and what the objectives of the company were and how employees could play a role in achieving these objectives. It was a combination of bargaining and of a need for information to get involved.

There is a subtle but important difference with Japan:

> Japanese industry has always worked with the consensus model inside the company. I have very often participated in the process and it hardly ever happens that if an idea is put forward by management, it is changed after the confrontation process. Moreover, in Japan, the idea has always been that if a person is consulted, then it is that person's responsibility to give some added value. But in Europe, for instance in Holland, the works' council wants a consultation not so much in order to give added value, but because they want to be consulted, they want to be informed, they have to be concerned.

As a result, it takes more time to get things done in Europe than in America or in Japan. In order to avoid endless debates or resistance to implementation of an idea, European managers need particular skills:

- the capacity to explain and to convince people;
- 'diplomatic' aptitudes;
- a leadership style more than skills in management technique.

This does not mean that European heads of firms are more leaders than managers. The term 'leader' encompasses other aspects, such as vision coming from the top. It does not fit with the need for negotiation and it is not accepted in northern Europe (Germany and Scandinavia). Internal negotiation may take some time, but this form of participation in decision-making is a condition for a quicker and more effective implementation.

3 Managing international diversity

European managers have an ability to recognize diversity and a particular skill for managing international diversity:

> European business leaders are better equipped to deal with cultural diversity, geographical diversity, than most American managers. I don't think that that would necessarily hold for the Japanese. If you look at, for instance, Canon Europe, they have about 450 Japanese managers running the business in Europe, they are Japanese, they have been imported from Japan and they have learned to deal with diversity. I mean that is the weakness of the American businesses.

To some extent, Europeans like diversity. At least they respect it: 'a European without a passport is not a European'. By plane in one hour, a manager will cross several frontiers in Europe. European firms have been forced to look outside at other *different* markets, and to develop a culture of working abroad because of the small size of each domestic market. The large American domestic market explains the more domestic view of American firms in the past. The domestic strength of US multinationals partly explains their 'US' view of the world, illustrated by the concept of an 'international division'. Of course some US multinationals, such as Hewlett Packard, have developed a more differentiated view of foreign geographic markets, and the gap with Europeans is narrowing; however, the gap still exists. Some American managers recognize it:

> I think European managers have a high degree of adaptability and flexibility. Let us take an example, I have worked a lot with Finnish managers. It is remarkable how Finnish managers adapt to the European market, for the simple reason that their home market is too small. Look at the Dutch – you know, Unilever, Shell, Philips – historically they have worked across boundaries. I think the Americans, and I am talking *in general* now, still are very much focused on their own market.

Actually the best examples of the European attitude towards geographic and cultural diversity come from the smaller countries: 'The smaller countries, the Netherlands and Belgium, because of the pressures against them, because of their small domestic markets, because of the small base they have for recruiting, developed superior skills in international management and in dealing with diversity.'
  If we look at a product like photographic films, for example, Kodak sells 55 per cent of its production in the US, Fuji sells 65 per cent of its production in Japan and

Agfa Gevaert sells 3 per cent of its production in Belgium. Agfa Gevaert was thus forced to become European and to make Europe its domestic market. It now sells 55 per cent of its production in the EEC. For Agfa Gevaert, the first step to becoming a truly international business was to become European.

The difference with Japan is more subtle. Japan has a large domestic market but was also forced to export. On the one hand, the Japanese are learning diversity: 'I think that about 20 000 Japanese every year come to German universities ... They develop their knowledge of foreign languages, at least to be able to read it.' On the other hand, the Japanese still seem to have a preference for global products which capture common global characteristics of markets, as well as a tendency to export their management style to foreign countries. The Europeans have more respect for foreign cultures and for foreign management styles.

Respect for foreign cultures and decentralization

European firms accept the risk of intercultural management. When doing business abroad, they tend to respect the host country, and when they acquire companies abroad, they have a higher tolerance of that firm's culture:

> They are less imperialistic than the Americans and the Japanese, who have a tendency to export their models.

> We have gone through quite a number of acquisitions since 1980. We bought some major operating companies in France, in Holland, in Spain, and most recently in Germany, Austria and Sweden. What we have done with those companies is to make sure that we operate them as companies specifically fitting the rules and the culture of the country they are in. For instance, we have been very careful that the board's structure reflects the legal requirements, the culture of the countries in which they operate and what we consider to be good business practice there. We have been very keen to see that the top management of the company reflects the nationality of the country in which they operate. So if we have a company in France, we would expect the top management to have a strong French team. Now I do not mean to say that all the jobs would be occupied by French nationals, but we would have a strong, distinctive requirement for French management. In Holland, Dutch management, etc. ...

European companies have a tendency to put nationals at the head of foreign subsidiaries with a smaller number of non-locals to add international flavour, reciprocal learning and some coherence with the corporate culture.

On the other hand, the Japanese have a tendency to reproduce the Japanese management ethos and their corporate culture. US companies try to reproduce their corporate culture via the authority of the top management and by procedures.

> Some American companies were heavily criticized in the 1970s because they exported their US policies abroad. In our company, and I think that it is true for most European firms, when taking part in foreign countries where we are established, we always felt and behaved in line with and integrated with national customs. In other words, we want to be in France as a French firm, in Brazil as a Brazilian firm ... The attitude of American firms may have changed a bit in this direction. But, for example, there are a lot of Japanese companies in Germany which do not have a workers' council and they don't care much about creating one.

The European tendency to adapt to foreign management practices and markets leads to more decentralization of foreign operations.

Decentralized operations

The oil industry offers a good example of the European tendency towards decentralization. The oil industry is not purely global (in the sense of standardized products and services); rather it is worldwide, and one has to adapt to local markets and local political contexts:

> We have always tended to give the local operating companies a high degree of autonomy. And that autonomy was not only reflected in the formal levels of financial decisions, but also reflected in the way that particular markets were and are being approached, retailing strategies, strategies for lubricants, product positioning. Our tradition may be decentralized. I would say that the Americans followed a much more centralized approach. With them it was control not only in terms of costs and expenditure and salary development and the like, but also in terms of marketing. They used much more of a centralized approach towards their European subsidiaries.

Decentralization does not mean that corporate culture is weak; the corporate culture can be strong but also allow variants. Decentralization may lead to the acceptance of multi-localization of strategic functions like research and development. This, for instance, is typical of some European firms involved in the pharmaceutical industry, 'which have R & D centres in the US, in the UK and in Japan, complementing the home-based R & D'. In this respect, some foreign operations become 'Centres d'Excellence' for the whole group. Such strategies lead to a form of 'partnership' between the headquarters and the units, more than domination by the headquarters of the units. Of course, there are exceptions, but this characteristic of European management can be viewed as a general trait on average.

The differences in this area between the United States, Japan and Europe now seem to be narrowing, with US and Japanese multinationals tending towards more decentralization of their international operations. This trend could mean that the European ability to manage international diversity is a competitive strength.

However, some of the managers in our study argued that the Europeans are not as good at integrating as their competitors.

The need for integration of international operations

It may be that the Japanese *refuse* to differentiate their strategies and their management, and focus on global products for their international development:

> They [the Japanese] do not differentiate their consumers' electronics, but they are ready to do it if necessary.

> My view is that the Europeans are better equipped to deal with diversity, but this may also lead to weakness. That is, the Americans and the Japanese are much better focused than we are. So we may have drowned ourselves into the heart of diversity.

Whether geographical differentiation of products is a strength or a weakness partly depends on the type of product: whether it is potentially global, such as electronics or pharmaceuticals, or more multi-domestic, such as food or retail banking. However, even in the food business, the global approach can lead to excellent results, as demonstrated by Coca-Cola and McDonald's. It seems that Europeans are not so good at (purely) global strategies, where it is necessary to capture the common characteristics of markets and design the same product for the whole world. At least this is the view of some Japanese managers: 'If you do not focus on potentially global products and if you do not capture the common characteristics of the different markets, the growth in worldwide market share and the chances to become the leader are limited.'

Another issue is organizational integration. Too much differentiation may lead to duplication and higher costs:

> Excessive differentiation and decentralization in the past has been a terrible mistake. We now run our European division from Brussels. We have one office and we run the whole of Europe from there. Now it has been a hell of a fight and you know Paris did not like it, and Hamburg did not like it, and Vienna did not like it, and I have to tell you London did not like it either. I mean, I run the corporation worldwide from London, but the operations for continental Europe are now run from Brussels. But of course, the savings are enormous. Instead of having 12 head offices, you just have one. Instead of having 12 research centres, you have one. Instead of having 12 strategies, you have one ... When I took over I inherited an organization that was designed to have 12 businesses in 70 countries. And when you looked at it, those 12 businesses were really three. And when I looked at the 70 countries, I could say we really had three and a half regions: America, Europe, the Far East and Africa.

According to this logic, the supreme skill may be to reconcile differentiation *and* integration. Then the question is: are European firms better at reconciling differentiation and integration?

Are Europeans better at reconciling differentiation and integration?

It may be particularly relevant to consider the opinion of US and Japanese managers on this issue. The general idea is that European firms are better at dealing with differences but that they still have improvements to make regarding integration.

> The successful companies will be those, in my view, that have a European concept, European direction, but don't forget that the consumer in Toulouse is not the same as the consumer in Berlin . . . That is, the ones who will do both: integration and differentiation . . . Among European managers, only the successful ones who learned to deal with a more complex environment, only those may be superior to the Japanese or the Americans.

But this hypothetically superior skill in reconciling local responsiveness and global integration is limited to the European region:

> As far as the European market is concerned: yes Europeans are better; especially firms from continental Europe. But it is a necessity of the market and a matter of experience. With time and sufficient experience, Japanese managers will be as good on the European market. In any case, it is a key factor to succeed in Europe.

Some European managers agree that *inside* Europe, they may be better than the Japanese and the Americans in reconciling differentiation and integration, but *outside* Europe, they are not.

> Unity in diversity is the old motto of the Dutch Republic. You know we were a Republic of the United Provinces until the takeover by Napoleon. The United Provinces was a big structure, a bit like the Swiss cantons, and all the seven provinces had their own peculiarities, that was the diversity. But still we had to operate on a number of issues as one country, that was the Unity.

Most of the international European companies followed the route from high differentiation to a balance between differentiation and integration:

> Nowadays, we are moving towards more integration. You can see that from the evolution of our organization. For instance, in some businesses we recently changed the organization from the simple coordination of four countries, to an organization with a European sales director for the business. During the last few years, the business dimension has become more important than the geographic dimension in our organization.

The unification of Europe certainly triggered such reorganization, and will continue to encourage it. The integration process, however, is done *through people* more than through structures and procedures.

Integration through people

Basically, international management of people in Europe has been marked by differentiation, for instance in the way employees are paid and rewarded. Differences will probably persist in some domains despite the integrated market, even in some US companies in Europe, who, in general, have the reputation for homogenizing their personnel practices:

> We have a whole portfolio of incentive programmes to be adapted to different markets, in particular concerning the sales-force. We do differentiate in this domain, whereas in the United States we have a uniform system. Here the way we reward or compensate sales representatives in Spain is very different to what we do in Finland or in Germany. It could be a difference between individual compensation and team compensation, it could be a difference between a flat salary and a salary with an incentive portion, depending on the sales channel and the geography ... This is because conditions, standards of living, are very different, taxation is different, social security is different. So for a long time we will see people being compensated nationally, according to the market-place.

> However, integration through people will take other forms:

- Requiring the ability to speak several languages.
- The international rotation of managers.
- International training programmes where the corporate culture is spread and strengthened.
- Reciprocal learning.

Sharing the same language appears to be the first condition for integration through people. In this domain, Europeans may have a competitive advantage in Europe, in particular Dutch, Swiss and Scandinavian managers. The British, on the other hand, have a tendency to focus on English, as their 'survival' abroad does not require the knowledge of foreign languages. Paradoxically, the domination of English as an international language is working as a factor of European integration.

> Integration through people has a double objective. The first is to homogenize the corporate culture at the European level. The second is to develop people by giving them the opportunity to learn, to work in a different environment and to enrich their personality. The key factor in personal development is to give people the opportunity to confront different social and cultural environments: and this also works as part of

integration. Differentiation is preserving some social and cultural specificities of the subsidiaries, on top on the shared values and the common identity.

The ultimate aim is 'to make the *whole* company stronger', to 'make use of French or British or German talent', to integrate through integrative people and reciprocal learning.

Given the relative diversity of management philosophies, structures and practices in Europe (as noted in Chapter 1), the European territory may be particularly favourable to personal development through confrontation of different environments. The result of such confrontations may be a more balanced management style between extreme management models. In fact, our study shows that the fourth common characteristic of management in Europe is this tendency to manage between extremes.

4 Managing between extremes

Management in the United States and Japan are often considered as two extremes on the basis of several characteristics, as noted in Chapter 1. For instance, the long-term growth orientation of the Japanese is the opposite of the short-term profit orientation of the United States.

'Europe is in between' was a typical remark in the study interviews. If there is a European style of management, it is 'halfway' between the US model of management and the Japanese model. This common European characteristic emerges in three dimensions of management:

- The relationships between the individual and the firm.
- The time frame (short term vs. long term).
- The balance between individualism and a sense of collectivism in the workplace.

In the present study, top managers were asked to position European firms, US firms and Japanese firms on scales representing variables corresponding to these dimensions. The results are presented in Figures 2.1–2.5. Of course, there are exceptions and the positions of some of the European countries themselves are sometimes dispersed (dispersion is mentioned on the figures).

The relationship between the individual and the firm shows up in the employee's loyalty to the company and in the relative importance of in-house training.

> The Americans are far less loyal, less wedded to their company; they have a much more individualistic view of their career; management changes very easily. You can hire and fire. Chief executives move with no problem between competitive companies. They see themselves as

assets, if you like, which are fully marketable. In Japan, it is the absolute opposite. As we all know, they don't rehearse, they jog for life – great company loyalty. And Europe is somewhere in between, perhaps more pragmatic.

However, attitudes in Europe ranged from the Germans, with lower staff turnover, to the British, with a high staff turnover.

Attitudes are partly related to employees' fidelity to their work: 'At Siemens the managers know something about electronics.' 'Everyone to his trade' or 'shoemaker stick to your tools', as the Germans say. Linked to loyalty to the company, the relative importance of in-house training or 'apprentissage' in the firm also distinguishes between the US, Japanese and European systems. But here, the differences between Europe and the US are less clear, and again, the practices in Europe range from the Germans, who give great importance to in-house training, to the British, who by comparison have relatively little in-house training.

On average, Europe is in the middle between the US and Japan. A manager from an Anglo-Dutch company summarized the positive effects of the professionalism of managers and of commitment to the company.

> In the first place, our company recruits and develops with the purpose of a full career. We recruit extensively in Europe at universities, and bring people to training programmes and job development programmes until they can be considered to be full professionals in their particular disciplines. The general characteristic is that a strong identification with the company is being pursued, so that people feel there is a common interest building up between the objectives of the company and their personal aims. And on the whole, people feel that a full career in our

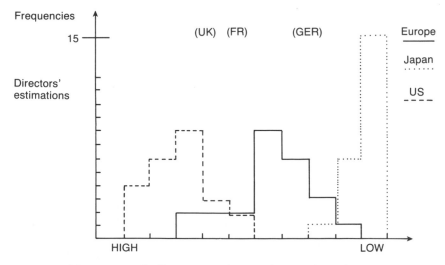

Figure 2.1 Staff turnover of executives and employees

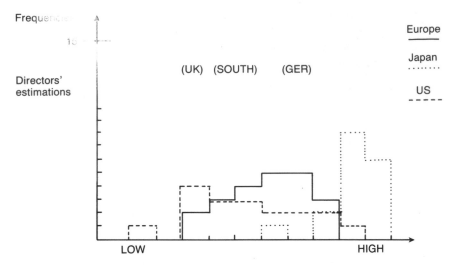

Figure 2.2   Importance given to in-house training

company is worthwhile, rather than using it just as a stepping stone towards something else. In-depth professional excellence is extremely important in our industry.

The time perspectives used by firms and managers can be estimated by considering the time scales allotted to strategic decision-making and investments and the stability in relationships between suppliers and clients. Figures 2.3 and 2.4 summarize the

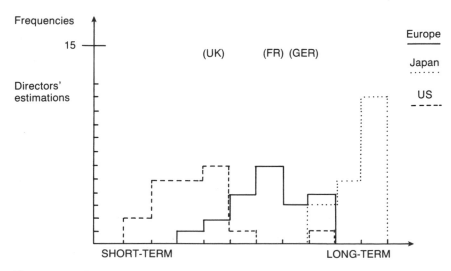

Figure 2.3   Time-scales allotted to strategic decision-making and investments

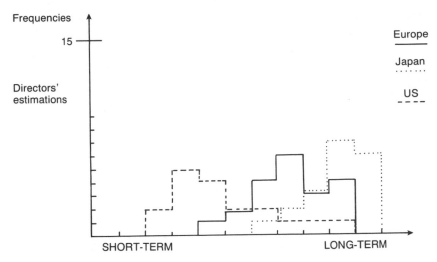

Figure 2.4 Stability in relationships between suppliers and customers, contractor and subcontractor

position of Europe between Japan with a long-term orientation, and the US with a short-term orientation. As far as strategic decision-making is concerned, European countries range from Germany and France at one extreme, to the UK at the other.

'Europe, at least the big international firms in Europe, have a philosophy between the Japanese, long term, and the United States, short term.' Japanese companies are growth-oriented, sometimes at the expense of short-term profitability. Their shareholders are 'insiders' and the strategies of firms contribute to the long-term power of 'Japan Inc.'. US companies are pushed to short-term profits by their shareholders, who tightly control the top management. In Europe, there is a relative stability of shareholders, which explains the balanced position:

> Of course I take care of the price per share, but not only that, in the sense that I have the support of some powerful and stable shareholders. I know that if the price went down, they would not sell, they have agreed on our long-term strategy. Actually, they supported us when the price went down.

> The heads of US firms in the cement industry have treated the business as a 'cash-cow' and they delayed investing in their companies ... the Europeans did not react like that to the tensions on the market.

European management also seems to be in the middle between *individualism and team spirit*. The Japanese clearly have a strong collective orientation and team spirit. American firms are spread on the scale, but there is a tendency for individualism to be dominant as Figure 2.5, illustrates. There is not much difference between the US,

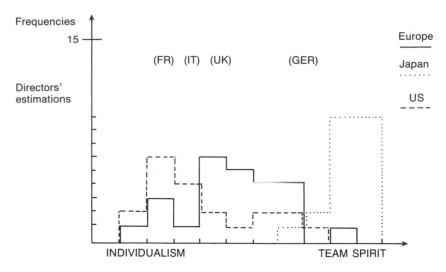

Figure 2.5 Individualism versus team spirit

southern Europe and the UK on this scale. Positions may be blurred because of ambiguity regarding the term individualism:

> The Americans also work in teams. They are ready to fight for collective challenges – look at their attitude in the Gulf War. They are generous; for example the close relations between alumni and their university. But the Americans are individualistic in their work: their career, their money, their personal achievement. The Europeans give the impression of caring more about the collective but they also are individualistic in the sense that they want to preserve their personal autonomy. Nuances are important in this matter.

Northern countries, and in particular Germany, seem to be more different from the Americans on this score. In fact, the challenge for the Europeans is to *combine* individualism with team spirit:

> This is the concept of 'Employee Involvement' and 'Management Commitment'. We can learn to modify our individualism. The sense of collectivity will never be as strong as in Japan; there it is natural. In Europe, we try to involve people, to find a balance between private life and commitment to the firm.

If European firms, on average, are 'in between', there are signs that north American companies are tending to move towards a more balanced position. There are also weak sociological signals showing that the Japanese may be slowly spreading towards a more balanced position, searching for more individual fulfilment and innovation in the firm.

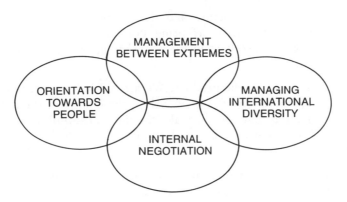

Figure 2.6 Common characteristics: the ingredients of European management

Considering the four major common European characteristics described in sections 1 to 4 and the nuances surrounding them, one cannot consider yet that there is a European *model* of management. However the four characteristics are consistent with each other, and seem to be valued by managers. Although the positive characteristics may have some 'shadow' sides to them which are not as desirable, they are, nonetheless, the first ingredients of a European management model.

In the following section, we add two minor characteristics which were fairly common but appeared less systematically in our study and which were not really valued highly by the directors when viewed in relation to management in the US and in Japan.

5 Minor characteristics

Two minor characteristics common to management in Europe emerged from the comparison with the US and Japanese models:

● Product orientation, i.e. the domination by engineers of marketers.
● A more intuitive and less formalized management.

Product orientation

This characteristic has two aspects: a positive side – brilliant engineers designing wonderful products, and a negative side – a lack of customer orientation and uneven skills in marketing.

Again, this is a general picture and there certainly are exceptions. British companies are not characterized as being dominated by engineers, and some European companies are excellent in their marketing. But the myth of the 'good product' is still strong:

> We are very focused on the product. We are old industrial countries.
> We have an old tradition of craftsmanship, the quality of the product,
> and I am convinced that we can make the most beautiful products in
> the world. If the client does not understand it ... well, it is because the
> client is ... stupid ...

Of course there are sectors where technical ability is a key factor in success, but even in these activities, customer orientation is also a key factor. 'The Japanese are the best in launching quality products with excellent marketing. Whereas we Europeans have been handicapped for a long time because our firms were managed by engineers making beautiful products and then passing them to the sales department ... The Japanese start from the market.' The particular skill of the Japanese may well be their capacity to *integrate different functions*: marketing, R&D and manufacturing.

The difference with the Americans is more subtle, American firms look for simple products and processes:

> The Americans have always been more market-oriented but they always
> find simple technical solutions. Let me give you an example: gearboxes.
> In Germany, or in general in the European car industry, the habit is to
> manufacture gears in a very clean way, so that all impurities are
> eliminated. The Americans found that when you use the gearbox,
> impurities fall by themselves. They just put a magnet under the housing,
> and the impurities are attracted by the magnet. It works well, it lasts for
> a long time. But a European manufacturer would never accept such a
> solution.

However, this raises the issue of *quality,* which may be different from innovation or technical sophistication. The Japanese built their international development on quality and marketing skills.

> We produce industrial plaster and we sell it to ceramic producers all
> over the world, including one Japanese company. The Japanese sent us
> back a load, saying 'we can't use that, it makes bubbles'. Incredible, no
> other client ever complained. They found out what was wrong: 'there is
> copper in your plaster'. Copper in the plaster! How can it be possible?
> We finally discovered that one of our suppliers was sometimes using
> detonators with copper wires in his quarry. You can just imagine the
> few grammes of copper wire lost in the middle of 20 tons of
> plasterstone! Anyway, the Japanese client was the only one who noticed
> it. It shows the Japanese demand for quality.

In general, European firms are less good at marketing than their Japanese counterparts and less customer-oriented than their American counterparts. In

America, the customer is the 'king': 'You notice it in hotels, shopping and everything in the States.' The Americans did not invent marketing, but they developed it at a far more rapid pace. Japanese cars or Japanese videos are the best illustrations of the combination of an obsession with quality and marketing skills.

The lower status of marketing in Europe appears in the composition of top management teams.

> The United States has developed marketing systematically and you will often find at the head of US firms some people from marketing. The heads of British firms more often have a financial background; the heads of German firms a manufacturing background. Among the heads of French firms, you often find engineers or civil servants from the Ministère de l'Economie et des Finances ... In the domain of marketing, we still have to learn a lot; the Japanese are also ahead of us.

It is useful to try to explain why the Europeans may have 'the worst of both worlds: being neither customer-oriented nor quality-oriented'. Some top managers argue that there was less competition in the European market compared to the US market, which is characterized by tough competition on prices. In Japan, domestic competition is quite strong and Japanese firms had to learn quality and marketing in order to be competitive before they began to sell to foreign markets. Skills may develop under competitive pressures. The Japanese and US managers in our sample share this view: 'the Europeans are too proud of their products', 'there is not enough competition'. But they also acknowledge that there are brilliant exceptions in Europe (especially in the areas where marketing is a condition of survival) and they notice that European firms are changing towards more customer orientation. European unification and increased world competition certainly influence such developments.

More intuitive and less formalized management

In general, management in Europe is less formalized than in US firms. Here the difference with Japan is more subtle. The use of the written versus the oral form of communication, and the use of procedures are two symptoms of formalization.

> In Europe we don't especially care for formalization. For instance, in our firm for a long time we did not have any formal procedure for the approval of investments. However, we felt that we knew what we were doing. We had objectives, we had discussions, but no procedure was written anywhere. We still prefer dialogue to procedures.

> In comparison with competitors in the US and in Japan, our Group has many fewer written rules. It is sometimes a cultural shock for the managers we transfer between continents. The American managers coming to Europe have the impression that the system is chaotic. The

Europeans going to the States find written responses and documents on practically any issue.

I noticed this when we took over Union Carbide's European operations in 1979, the tremendous amount of written rules that they had for every contingency.

In our company, our philosophy, our standards are communicated by people rather than by written instructions.

Differences can be found especially in the area of management of human resources: e.g. promotion plans and personnel appraisal systems. Quality charts, value statements and codes of ethics are also more frequent in US companies, which may be due to the weight of legal constraints there. The Japanese seem to have both written rules and oral communication. The consensual mode of management may replace written formalization. In the case of Japanese firms, the *ritual* of decision-making (Nemawashi and Ringi) can also be considered as formal. 'I know Japan well enough to say that they write everything, but they do communicate everything to all the people concerned, and they also discuss a lot.'

In Europe, however, there are exceptions. German firms have the reputation for more formalization and more written rules. A few managers in our sample noticed that there are differences between the north of Europe (more formalization) and the south of Europe (more 'chaotic'), and that the overall picture is moving towards more formalization. This is especially true in the south: 'There are more and more written procedures at Fiat.'

Formalization has the advantage of clarity, and the disadvantage of rigidity; finding the right balance is a challenge. It seems that Europeans, in general, rely more on agreement, dialogue and conviction, on *experience* and the *sense of responsibility* of people:

I don't think that we give so much importance to written rules. When the issue is uncertain, experience and what we call in Germany 'human wisdom' play the major part ... Talking about procedures makes me think of portfolio analysis which, 10 years ago, was considered a rational procedure in German firms ... We were very happy to get rid of this tool.

Experience and empiricism refer directly to intuition, a preference for improvisation in order to seize opportunities. 'In Europe there is more empiricism. If a nice opportunity is offered, it does not matter if the documents do not fit exactly with the standards, or with the rules in the manual, we will take the opportunity if we are tempted.' It is possible that some European companies may have invented 'chaos management' in the terms used recently in the vanguard strategic management literature: 'Some Japanese transplants in Europe are more productive that some Japanese plants in Japan ... This could prove that the sense of chaos is not necessarily a bad thing.'

This review of common management philosophies, structures and practices across Europe shows that European firms have some distinctive characteristics compared to US and Japanese firms: an orientation towards people, internal negotiation, managing international diversity, and managing between extremes (cf. Figure 2.6). We also mentioned that, according to the directors in our study, some of the differences between the three zones are becoming blurred, especially in multinational corporations which are in direct contact with the three continents.

A minority of the directors we interviewed argued that the gap between European, American and Japanese multinationals is already narrow. The *methods* and management *techniques* are the same: 'Top managers were trained in the same kind of schools and universities in the US and in Europe: in Fontainebleau, in the London Business School, in Stanford . . . everywhere they deliver the same concepts.' Europeans have learned organizational models from the US (the divisional organization) and from Japan (horizontal relationships between business units). All multinational groups are now organized according to the same general principles.

Another argument is that the characteristics of the industry may be a better predictor of management style than the country of origin. It is true, for instance, that the oil industry demands different structures and management practices than, say, the clothing industry. However, within a given industry, some differences still emerge between the three zones of Europe, Japan and the United States.

According to a third argument, the best companies have already learned common management practices: 'The real difference is between the best companies (wherever they come from) with the best management practices and companies with "mediocre" management practices. Management in the world and in Europe is homogeneous at its best.' Indirectly, this argument advocates global reciprocal learning. But if we except the 'best' multinationals in 'global' industries, differences do exist between the three zones.

Finally, the dominant opinion is the following: management methods, management techniques and organizational charts may *look* the same, but there are still some differences in the way they are applied in different contexts. Diversity is rooted in sociological and political differences which will not be erased easily. 'Because of the global nature of multinational business and the global nature of key issues in general, those differences are gradually narrowing down . . . Yet you still have differences because you don't change a culture, you don't change the whole system in ten years.'

Considering the three pictures of management that we have drawn for each of the three zones (cf. Figures 1.1 and 1.2 in Chapter 1 and Figure 2.6 in this chapter), it is instructive to identify the perceived currents of reciprocal learning in the past. From the Americans, both the Europeans and the Japanese learned *professionalism* and *competition*. From the Japanese, both the Europeans and the Americans learned *quality*[2] and *integration*. Japanese and American interest in European management is more recent. The transfers of managerial skills which seem to take place now will be presented in the following chapter, which analyzes the dynamics of the European systems.

Notes

1. Answers to the non-directive first part of the interviews, confirmed *afterwards* by the responses to some of the hypotheses that we had formulated.
2. In fact, the methods of total quality were invented in the United States, Japanese firms applied them with such success that they were transferred back to the West.

References

The literature on common characteristics of management across Europe is embryonic. First, some authors like Lester Thurow (1991) have a tendency to assimilate management in Europe to management in Germany. Our study demonstrates that such an assimilation is misleading. Second, some other authors elaborated upon the concepts of 'unitas multiplex' and 'dialogique' initiated by Edgar Morin (1987). According to these (see for instance Simonet, 1992) the identity of Europe relies on its diversity, and the 'dialogique' (pluralism, reconciling apparent opposites) should become a typical European characteristic. The concepts are fine but no concrete analysis of management implications (structures, practices) is provided. Also some aspects of the 'dialogique' (reconciling apparent opposites) seem to be shared with the Zen philosophy in which some aspects of Japanese management are rooted.

Finally, some consultants like Herbert Henzler are publishing their views on the subject based on their work experience. Such sources provide useful material for building hypotheses but they carry the biases of any non-systematical investigation.

Henzler, H. (1992), 'La Renaissance de l'Eurocapitalisme', *Harvard l'Expansion*, Winter, pp. 48–59.
Morin, E. (1987), *Penser l'Europe*, Paris: Gallimard.
Simonet, J. (1992), *Pratiques du management en Europe, gérer les différences au quotidien*, Paris: Les Editions d'Organisation.
Thurow, L. (1991), *Head to Head*, Cambridge, Mass.: MIT Press.

CHAPTER 3

The dynamics of management systems in Europe

Roland Calori and Fred Seidel

In the previous chapters we have described the diversity and the common characteristics of management across Europe. Such a description is useful, but to formulate strategies for improving management practice one needs to understand the dynamics of management systems. This chapter contributes to such understanding by looking first at the past, and then at the future, taking both an exploratory and a normative view.

The historical perspective is based mainly on analyses made by historians. The prospective scenario presented in Section 2 is based entirely on the predictions made by the executives in our study. Both the historical perspective and the prospective analyses converge towards a systemic view of the dynamics summarized in Figure 3.1. According to this view any change in the 'business system' is linked to changes in the whole society. Put another way: a business system naturally tends to fit with the society in which it is embedded. Also in this perspective, the influence of truly *multi*national firms in contact with different societies, and the influence of the European Community transforming some national structures into supranational structures, drive business systems towards international convergence.

1 A historical perspective

Management philosophies, structures and practices belong to broader sociological, political, economic and technological systems. Their dynamics can only be understood through the dynamics of the whole system, in which they influence and are influenced by other subsystems. An integrative historical approach, viewing the European system within the world system, would be a daunting challenge. This section will only scratch the surface of some aspects of European history which could explain some of the common characteristics and some of the diversity of management in Europe.

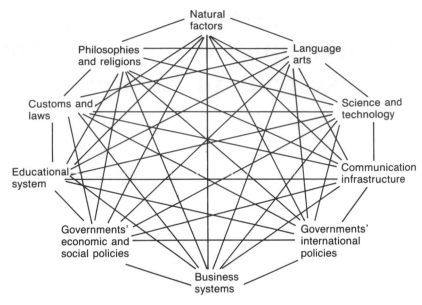

Figure 3.1   Political and cultural determinants of management systems

Let us start with an example of management in the Netherlands, borrowed from d'Iribarne (1989) and Lijphart (1975). Management in the Netherlands is described as: consensual, cooperative, moved by a desire for discussion and conciliation, based on objective facts (cf. Chapter 1).

The Utrecht Union (1579) was an agreement among provinces; it was not forced by any prince. The motto of the Dutch Republic was 'Unity in Diversity': in order to put a check on the Spanish domination, the seven provinces united but kept their sovereignty and their own governments. The federal body was formed with delegates from the seven provinces, with one vote given to each province and a rule of unanimity for all important decisions. This system required long discussion processes and mutual accommodation. At about the same point in time, religious tolerance and religious freedom became tenets of the Republic, although the Protestants outnumbered the other groups by far. The French domination of the Netherlands (1795–1813) abolished the federal system but political principles remained. In the second half of the nineteenth century, pluralism was the rule within the Dutch political institutions (Catholics, Protestants, orthodox, liberals and socialists). The system has been described as 'pillarization' (verzuiling), since the Dutch society is formed of several pillars (zuilen), each having its own rights, and together they support the structure of the nation. The country has to be governed by unanimous agreement among the pillars, and pragmatic trade-offs are sometimes necessary to reach such agreement (Lijphart, 1975). The experience of political accommodation, pluralism and democracy in the Netherlands probably influenced the management system of Dutch enterprises (d'Iribarne, 1989).

Understanding the historical roots and determinants of modern management systems increases tolerance of other systems and generates humility, but it also opens new horizons because it highlights some potential factors of change in the future. When trying to explain commonalities and differences in management across Europe we did not expect to find a correspondence with eras of European history. Actually the correspondence is striking:

- The common trunk of management practices is mainly rooted in philosophies, religions and arts which developed from the ancient Greek civilization to the Renaissance (which, to some extent, was inspired by antiquity).
- The diversity increased with the emergence and development of powerful *nation-states* across Europe (1650s–1950s). The emergence and development of modern firms (the successive industrial revolutions) coincided with an exacerbation of the divisions and conflicts between the nation-states. During this period the history of Europe is a history of differences.
- The creation of the European Economic Community and its more recent developments towards integration and a Union started a new era of convergence in Western Europe, so some barriers are now being lowered.

'Our common roots'

The Greek heritage is the first substratum in which European cultures and political systems developed. Five centuries before Christ, the rule of dialectics was established in the Athens Agora. According to this principle the dialogue should be maintained between adverse conceptions. Diverse and adverse conceptions should coexist, and no concept should be dictated by force. Democracy as a political system, managing international diversity and management through internal negotiation are all based on the same ancient principles: the dialectics of Socrates and Plato, Aristotelian logic and Aristotle's view of the unity and diversity of the universe.

The Roman domination of Europe contributed to improving communication infrastructures, and to spreading legal principles and Christianity, especially in the south of Europe. Christianity is the second pillar of European culture. The orientation towards people found in European modern enterprises may be related to Christian values. Charlemagne, King of the Franks, annexed northern Italy, Bavaria, Saxony, and Frisia, and was crowned Emperor by the Pope in 800. The Holy Roman Emperor developed Christianity and schools across his empire. The crusades, organized by the papacy between the eleventh and the thirteenth centuries, were signs of the existence of some European unity against the 'infidels'. The crusades and the Inquisition also demonstrated a fundamental opposition between Greek philosophy and Christianity. After the schism between the Catholic Church and the Orthodox Church (1054), and the Reformation which divided Europe into two zones in the sixteenth century, Christianity was no longer a source of unity. The south of Europe remained Catholic (Italy, Spain, Portugal, part of France, Bavaria and Austria) while the north became Protestant (Germany, Switzerland, England, the United Provinces and Scandinavia).

In the view of Max Weber capitalism originated in the Protestant ethic; professional success is interpreted as a sign of God's choice, and work is valued as an asceticism. Luther and Calvin, who recommended reading the Bible, contributed to more widespread literacy. The origin of the first industrial revolution in England and in northern Europe could be related to this religious substratum.

From the thirteenth to the sixteenth century, European networks developed between tradespeople, between scholars, and between artists. Genova, Pisa, Venice, and the delta between the Scheldt (Escaut), the Meuse, and the Rhine became poles of intense interregional economic activity. Italian bankers settled down in London, Paris, Bruges and Madrid. In the thirteenth century, the universities began to establish a network of knowledge, with students and professors travelling between Paris, Bologna, Oxford, Salamanca, Heidelberg and Prague (Morin, 1987). The invention of printing contributed to the Renaissance in the fifteenth and sixteenth centuries.

The Renaissance spread across Europe. Artists and scholars became cosmopolitan and polyglots: Erasmus lived in the United Provinces, in France, in England, and in Switzerland and visited Italy. During the Renaissance the European elite returned to the ancient Greek philosophy of dialectics and logics. The first signs of Humanism also emerged, for instance with the 'De Dignitate Hominis' from Pic de la Mirandole (1486).

Humanism can be considered the third pillar of European culture. The basic concepts are that man deserves freedom, and freedom is a condition of the fulfilment of individuals. Humanism broke with both Christianity and Greek philosophy in the sense that it put Man at the centre of the universe. In politics, Humanism led to Habeas Corpus and to the 'Déclaration des Droits de l'Homme et du Citoyen' (1789). The impact of Humanism was at its height in the nineteenth century, but some derived forms were produced later on: on the one hand hedonistic individualism and on the other hand humanitarianism. The different aspects of orientation towards people found in modern European enterprises (caring about people, fulfilment of the individual, social responsibility, as well as some perverse aspects of individualism in the work place) may all be rooted in the humanistic tradition. Edgar Morin (1987) recalls that European pluralism and humanism has hidden the most horrible inhumanity (colonial wars, extermination), and suggests that the European identity relies upon a second order concept: a 'dialogique' where contradictions can coexist. Morin also gives a more concrete explanation: the development of humanism coincided with the formation of powerful nation-states which generated a new religion, patriotism, and its perversion, nationalism.

The first industrial revolution and the emergence of the modern enterprise *coincided* with the exacerbation of rivalries between nation-states. In this environment deep differences between business systems formed during the nineteenth century and the first half of the twentieth century.

Nation-states and the modern enterprise

In the view of Braudel (1982) Europe is made up of several civilizations which share only a sense of freedom (albeit, sometimes at the expense of neighbours). Ethnic or economic *regions* across Europe existed long before the emergence of nation-states. The Basque Country and Catalonia are extreme examples. In the twelfth century the harbours of northern Italy and Flanders shared similar business cultures, while other regions were still in a feudal system dominated by agriculture. The emergence of some powerful kingdoms slowly rubbed away differences between micro regions but generated a new segmentation between broader states. The ways in which these kingdoms were formed created an administrative heritage which still remains today. A comparison between France and the United Kingdom is instructive.

The United Kingdom was created in the seventeenth century, when the English monarchy played a crucial role in federating England, Scotland, Wales and Northern Ireland. As England was a small country protected from invasions by the sea, from the twelfth century the central state was able to control this territory. The English monarchy was also able to impose its justice on the nobility without interfering in the internal affairs of the feudal lords (the Magna Carta). Thus the English nobility was pacified early thanks to loose control and to a natural protection from invasions. The democratic and liberal tradition of British society developed from this integrative process characterized by a subtle mix of centralization and decentralization (Elias, 1975). Recent comparative research on management structures shows the tendency of British firms towards decentralization, while the French are more centralized.

The creation of the French state followed a different route and was constrained by different environmental conditions. French royalty extended and asserted its strength from a central starting point, Paris, over a larger and larger territory. At a time when travelling was difficult, the large size of the country and its penetrable land frontiers increased the risks of separatism and invasions. Moreover France was and has always been a land of immigration (in the Middle Ages, during the Renaissance and during the twentieth century), mixing diverse ethnic communities. In order to cement the French State, Louis XIV invented 'la Société de Cour' to attract nobles to Versailles around the 'Roi Soleil'. His minister, Colbert, increased the control of the state over the economy, set up protectionist barriers based on mercantilist theories, and developed 'les manufactures d'Etat'. French political and administrative centralization increased further during the revolution by the 'Jacobins' with their ideal of 'centralized democracy', and under Napoleon. With this administrative heritage, the conditions were set for the emergence of relatively centralized French firms during the industrial revolution which followed.

Industrial revolutions in a world of nation-states

Whitley (1992) analyzes the history of 'business systems' and considers two sources of influence:

1. Institutions which form the cultural base of a society (such as the family, the church, etc).
2. Institutions which influence the proximate environment of the firm, such as political systems, and the financial and labour markets. Here the role of the state

is crucial as it defines the rules of the economic game and designs the education system and communication networks.

In this discussion, we will focus on the second source of influence. Given the difficulty of multiple comparisons, we will also focus on three countries – the United Kingdom, France and Germany – as they have been found to illustrate the diversity of management systems across Europe (see Chapter 1).

The modern enterprise emerged in the nineteenth century, a period dominated by Great Britain, which became the economic *model*. Building on the strengths of its technological skills and extensive colonial empire, the UK had by far the highest share of world trade: 27 per cent in 1820, and 22 per cent in 1850, when the volume of total world trade had tripled (Rostow, 1978). In 1842 Great Britain began reducing customs duties on imports, including agricultural products. By 1850 agriculture's share of the GNP had gone down to 20 per cent and the political influence of the traditionally protectionist agricultural sector had dramatically decreased. At the time, France and Germany were lagging behind and following more protectionist policies. Industrialization had developed in a few regions: the north of France and the Ruhr in Germany. At the time Germany still had not achieved its national unification.

Between 1880 and 1914 the positions of the three countries changed. Britain maintained its leadership in international trade (although its share decreased to 16 per cent) but it was no longer the world's industrial leader. The United States – in part thanks to its high demographic growth and its large domestic market – became the world leader in industrial production, and Germany became the European leader. France still lagged behind. It had been particularly affected by the economic depression of the 1870s and 1880s. Two of its most dynamic provinces – Alsace and Lorraine – had been annexed by Germany after the 1870 war, France's large agricultural sector had proven its lack of competitiveness and manpower mobility towards the industrial sectors was low.

The unification of Germany in 1871 under the German Empire created a large domestic market to sustain the development of heavy industries (coal, steel), and also of the new industries of the second industrial revolution: chemicals, electrotechnology, and later on automobiles. Thanks to its strong scientific base, Germany led the second industrial revolution in Europe. The growth of Siemens and AEG in electrotechnology, Bayer, Hoechst and BASF in chemicals, are examples of the development of a large number of German firms during this period.

The emergence of new industries during the second industrial revolution went hand in hand with the development of communication infrastructures, means of transportation and banking systems. The evolution required a strong technological base and led to an increase in the size and complexity of firms. As a consequence the need for more structured organizational forms and more professional management increased. The leadership role of German firms during the second industrial revolution developed some typical German management practices as described by Chandler (1990): more professional, scientific and specialized than British or French management.

At the beginning of the twentieth century, 40 per cent of the large firms in France belonged to the textile industry, most of the big British firms belonged to consumer goods industries, while in Germany the concentration was particularly strong in the knowledge and capital-intensive new industries. For instance in 1913 Siemens and AEG together held around 75 per cent of the German electrotechnology market. But the 'cartelization' of German industry during this period was even more distinctive. Contrary to the situation in the Anglo-Saxon world, where governments had set anti-trust regulations, the cartelization of German industry was welcomed by the state: it shaped an '*organized* managerial capitalism' in Chandler's words (1990). The cartelization started in the mining and steel industries, and spread to other sectors after World War I. According to Feldenkirchen (1988), by 1925, Germany's total production of coal, iron, steel and glass, and 80 per cent of its production of chemicals were cartelized. Diverse agreements were set up: pricing policies, organized production accords and agreements concerning customer targets. German banks were also involved in the process of *organizing* the German economy, to support the growth of the capital-intensive new industries. The banks encouraged and influenced the development of professional management in order to control the profitability of their investments. For instance Dietrich (1991) shows how the Deutsche Bank contributed to unseating the Mannesmann brothers from the head of Mannesmann AG between 1893 and 1900.

According to Chandler (1990), British and French capitalists hesitated to delegate managerial responsibilities and to hire professional managers. Moreover, British and French families were slow to venture into the capital-intensive new industries and to open their firms to the capital of financial institutions. In Germany wage-earning managers in industry modelled themselves on the best civil servants, and became 'civil servants in the private sector' (Kocka, 1981). German firms hired graduates from the newly formed Handelshochschulen. During this same period, the status of the managerial class remained low both in France and in Great Britain. The French developed the system of 'Ecoles Supérieures de Commerce' but the supply and demand of 'cadres' was relatively small, while the British did not make much effort to develop education in this domain. In 1913, Britain was still suffering from a rigid class system and depended increasingly on its colonies. France was still predominantly a protectionist rural society, resistant to modernity; its upper class was not tempted to venture into business. Germany had been leading the second industrial revolution and was starting to feel the social consequences: urbanization, proletarianization, and a growing socialist opposition. One should not underestimate cross-border regional similarities, for instance between the north of France, Wallonia, and the Ruhr in Germany. However, the broad picture shows that in the three countries different types of business systems formed during the first and second industrial revolutions.

With the constitution of unified modern states in Germany and Italy, Europe had become the 'Europe of Nations'. Economic power had become the basis of political and military power. Inevitably states increased their intervention in the economy, in order to protect firms and markets, and to forge the various weapons they needed to be great powers. All of these factors reduced the contacts between the different business systems.

Nation-states and business systems

From 1880 to the 1950s state intervention took several forms: social protection, international trade policy industrial policy, and education. The social protection system established by Bismarck in Germany – health in 1883 and pensions in 1889 – was certainly the most advanced and comprehensive in Europe. Bismarck's aim was to prevent social troubles and to circumvent the rise of socialism. The state intervened directly by requiring firms and employees to participate in funding social protection. The system thereby introduced the sense of social responsibility into the business community. In Britain, where social protection was private, and in France, where a mutual insurance system and a state system coexisted, the legislated participation of firms came much later.

Before World War I the differences in international trade policies among the three countries intensified the differences in their economic development. The absence of protectionist measures in the United Kingdom opened the British market to German products in the new industries. Faced with increased international competition, British firms turned to the Commonwealth. The moderate protectionism in Germany protected its new industries but also allowed it to maintain good commercial relationships with other European countries, in order to export the products of its second industrial revolution. France had the highest foreign trade tariffs (20 per cent on industrial products and even higher duties on agricultural products). This policy maintained a large agricultural sector and restrained productivity gains.

The 1914–18 war and the 'war economy', directed towards military imperatives in all three countries, dramatically increased the influence of the state on firms. Even after the Treaty of Versailles the state influence remained in the form of protectionism and industrial policies. In order to reduce social disorder and manage the economic consequences of the war (reconstruction and inflation due to government debts), nation-states maintained protectionism and sought economic self-sufficiency giving rise to autarkical ideologies.

One consequence of that protectionism was an increasing gap between the accelerating growth of industrial production and the low growth of world trade. In particular, international trade between European countries diminished in terms of percentage of GNP, whereas it had increased regularly in the period before the war. The more favourable economic situation between 1924 and 1929 and the World Economic Conference of 1928 did not change the trends which led to the economic depression of the 1930s.

Forced to focus on their low growth domestic markets, firms reacted through concentration and cartelization. Mergers and cartels developed in *all* the European industrial countries. For instance in Great Britain the steel industry concentrated and joined the international steel cartel in 1935. The German chemical industry grouped into the gigantic IG-Farben in 1926. The small and medium-sized businesses which characterized French industry reorganized into industrial groups through share swaps, but the production plants remained dispersed (Caron, 1988). Governments facilitated the concentration process directly or indirectly through their investments in the domain of national infrastructures. Great Britain abandoned its liberal policy, but began to be influenced by American management at the end of the 1920s when US multinationals established positions in the UK. For instance in the car industry General Motors acquired Vauxhall and built one of its bigger plants in Dagenham (UK).

In 1914, 35 per cent of British exports went to its Empire, in 1938 that share had risen to 50 per cent. French exports to its colonies rose from 19 per cent of total exports in 1929, to 28 per cent in 1938. In that same year, 70 per cent of German exports went to other European countries, but the share of German exports to the Balkans (under German influence) represented 14.8 per cent, having doubled between 1929 and 1938. The reorientation of international trade towards different zones of influence outside Europe did nothing to encourage contacts between the business systems and restricted the opportunities for reciprocal learning. Management structures and practices were confined to their respective zones of influence.

In the world of heightened political and economic tensions between states which existed until the end of World War II, the history of European business systems could only be one of differences.

Adding education to the picture

States design educational systems. In this domain, starting from the common point established during the Renaissance, the nation-states took diverging routes. France typically used its educational system as a means to strengthen its national identity. The 'Grandes Ecoles' founded by Napoleon at the beginning of the nineteenth century provided an elite of civil servants. In the 1880s 'l'Ecole Républicaine' aimed at developing patriotism. Based on an egalitarian ideology, 'l'Ecole Républicaine' gave priority to 'general education' over professional education – a major difference with the German system, where professional education was emphasized earlier in the curriculum. 'L'Ecole Républicaine' based its course content on the dominant positivist philosophy of the end of the nineteenth century, adopting the hierarchy of knowledge established by Auguste Comte: theory at the top, practice at the bottom. A simple comparison between French and British textbooks shows that the French developed deductive thinking whereas the British developed inductive thinking. The consequences on the working class and the management class in the twentieth century are clear:

● The pragmatism of British managers.
● The French tendency to rely on an elite, and the gap between 'les cadres et les non-cadres'.
● The specialized and technical orientation of the Germans.

The educational systems and the business systems strengthened each other. For instance, German firms were able to find the well-trained work-force they needed to sustain their high growth during the second industrial revolution. Paradoxically the French egalitarian system based on 'general education' produced a lower class of manual workers who felt they had failed in the competition for noble occupations. As an indirect consequence, the origins of the managerial class differed radically between the two countries: 24 per cent of German managers began as workers against less than 1 per cent in France; 50 per cent of senior French managers ('cadres supérieurs') came from the upper middle and upper class in France against 33 per cent in Germany; 46 per cent of senior French managers came from 'l'Enseignement Supérieur' (mainly from the 'Grandes Ecoles') against 16.5 per cent in Germany (Noiriel, 1992).

The managerial class was formed with the emergence of modern enterprises. The first business schools founded in Paris, Antwerp and Leipzig at the beginning of the nineteenth century had a limited impact. It was the increased capital intensity, technological intensity, size, and complexity of firms, plus the involvement of financial institutions, which created the need for professional managers who could be responsible for operations in place of owners–shareholders. The evolution was particularly marked in Germany, as would be expected given the leadership of German firms in Europe during the second industrial revolution. Chandler (1990) describes the German administrative heritage as '[organized] *managerial* capitalism'. The more recent dual system of 'Aufsichtsrat' (supervisory board) and 'Vorstand' (executive committee) in German firms is partly based on this administrative heritage. From 1875 onwards, German 'Handelshochschulen' contributed to the training of the German managerial class. Later on, in order to build on the high prestige of the universities in Germany, business training programmes were absorbed into faculties of economics under the form of 'Betriebswirtschaftslehre'. There students would follow a scientific education, but without practical training for managerial jobs. Firms recruited graduates with a rigorous scientific outlook and functional specialization. It was then considered the role of the firm to develop in-house the individual's managerial skills. Thus the matrix of today's German managers was formed 60 years ago.

In France the managerial class developed later than in Germany, mainly because France was lagging behind in the two industrial revolutions, and firms were smaller and/or dominated by families. However several 'Ecoles Supérieures de Commerce' were created as early as the 1870s. The number of students remained relatively small, given the small size of the market and the selective recruitment policy of these schools, which copied the system of the 'Grandes Ecoles d'Ingénieurs' established by Napoleon. The curriculum was diversified and pragmatic, oriented to the development of 'generalists' (and as such radically different from the German system). The matrix of the French manager was therefore also ready 60 years ago, with the hierarchical gap between managers and a poorly trained work-force predetermined by the elitist educative system. Business programmes only began to be integrated in French universities in the 1960s (much later than in Germany), and the elitist view of the Grandes Ecoles remained strong.

Because the technologies of the first industrial revolution did not require highly trained workers and technical staff, the United Kingdom was able to achieve its leadership without developing professional management. In the UK 'personal capitalism', as defined by Chandler (1990), lasted into the first half of the twentieth century: British company owners recruited members of their family and friends, who could be trusted and who belonged to the same class. There were no business schools in 1930; the interest in teaching business only arose after World War II, in some polytechnics, and in the universities. As the influence of the American firms established in the UK was strong at the time, the British adopted the American standards in teaching business administration.

Other countries in northern Europe, especially the Netherlands and the Scandinavian countries, had built educational systems similar to the German one. The south of Europe lagged behind with some exceptions (like the north of Italy with the Bocconi University). In the 1960s, the economic domination of the United States, its professional managers and famous business schools of higher education began to pervade all European countries to a differing degree.

The transition to a world scope

After World War II the military and economic domination of the US was stronger than ever. Its intervention in Western Europe avoided repetition of the scenario of division which had followed World War I. However, while the political division of Western Europe decreased, the whole world was being divided into two antagonistic blocks: the capitalist West dominated by the US and the communist East dominated by the USSR. The frontier between the two blocks cut Europe in two. This impervious separation allowed space for the expansion of socialist economies and Soviet administrative practices as far as East Germany. For a variety of reasons – including the threat of military domination from the East and the threat of economic domination from the US – some of the countries of occidental Europe decided to cooperate. The Netherlands, Belgium, Luxembourg, France, Germany and Italy formed the European Economic Community under the Treaty of Rome in 1957. We will not list here the successive stages which have resulted in an enlarged European Community (12 states), with associate members, and an increasingly intense cooperation which was recently formalized by the 1993 Single European Market and ratification of the Treaty on European Union.

The cooperation between states created the basic structural conditions for increased contacts between their business systems, first through open international trade policies (from the reduction of custom duties to the mutual recognition of norms within the EC), and second by improving communication infrastructures. European firms became more international, restructured and started to learn from the best foreign practices.

The long-term project of integration which had been envisaged in the 1950s was probably stimulated by the threat of Japanese competition in the 1980s. European states started to harmonize their monetary, economic and social policies, began to support technical cooperation (e.g. the Esprit, Eureka and Race programmes), to encourage contacts between educational institutions (e.g. through the Erasmus and the Human Capital Mobility programmes), and to harmonize some of their regulations. The heads of European firms often anticipated the events, as in the case of the 1993 Single Market, in order to be ready when the barriers went down. The growing power of multinationals in terms of employment and technological knowledge also influenced governments and European policy-makers in various ways, e.g. to reduce the constraints on businesses and shape Europe-wide industrial policies. Basically the principles in the 1985 White Paper which set out the Single Market programme demonstrated a further step towards liberalism within the EC. However, the EC's attitude towards third countries remained ambiguous (following the principle of reciprocity) and left room for negotiations. The business climate in Western Europe narrowed the gap between European management structures and practices. The development of business worldwide between North America, Europe and Japan also narrowed the gap between the three continents. Television programmes and mass international tourism developed thanks to improved means of communication, increased leisure time and higher purchasing power. More and more people learned to understand (if not appreciate) the cultures beyond their own frontiers.

While this extremely brief review of trends during the past 45 years is very superficial, we include it here to show that the *whole system* changed (cf. Figure 2.6), and the *whole economic policy* changed from pure rivalry to the acceptance of some cooperation. Such changes created the dynamics of *convergence* between countries and business systems. The recent fall of communism and the division of the Soviet empire means that the basic conditions for narrowing the gap between the West and the East are also now set.

On the other hand, the Eastern countries, after 45 years of imposed convergence and cooperation among themselves, may enter a period of local conflicts and divergence. Unfortunately the hypothesis of convergence may be limited to the countries of the triad and a few new countries which will be able to catch up with their economic and social development. Nowadays, the real division of the world may be between the rich and the poor. New trade blocks may form among the rich countries. Thurow (1991) predicts the coexistence of three trade zones, corresponding more or less to the three zones of the triad, and world trade will be negotiated between the three zones.

2 A scenario: future changes in management systems

Now that big international firms are under fewer political constraints, they have more power to shape the evolution of business systems. The heads of multinationals have a comprehensive view of management philosophies, structures and practices. They will make decisions according to their preferences and the challenges they expect to face. Given the power of their firms, the implementation of their decisions will shape the system. This section is based on the views of these influential experts.

Using a 10-year horizon we will describe below the views of the directors interviewed on:

- The changes in the socio-political context in which business operates.
- The dimensions of the homogenization of management in Europe.
- The dimensions of the homogenization of management world-wide.

and the two main challenges:

- learning.
- people involvement.

A distinction will be made between 'exploratory' components of the scenario ('what may happen': *will*) and 'normative' components ('what top managers would prefer': *should*).

The context is changing

In Europe the social market economy *will* remain, and social welfare *will* be respected, but the relative importance of stakeholders *will* vary:

- the influence of governments and unions *will* decrease;
- the influence of the EC, of local authorities and of ecologists *will* increase.

We *should* not overregulate Europe and overprotect individuals. This sort of 'mixed economy' *will* be a European reality. A balance between the power of private firms and the power of national governments and the EC *should* be respected. The social market economy *should* follow a German style rather than a Scandinavian style.

The implementation of the Single European Market *will* make small and medium-sized businesses face stiffer competition. The unification and harmonization of the market *will* take place, but a majority of managers want more: they want the Europeans to enact the Maastricht Treaty terms and to create a federal Europe. However, it *will* be hard to remove nationalism and cultural integration will take a very long time. Increased travel across Europe and international TV channels *will* contribute at least to a higher tolerance of different cultures.

Directors want a harmonization at the European level of laws related to business:

> Now we talk about the 'Comité d'Entreprise Européen' in industrial relations. We talk about the 'Société Européenne' which has been encouraged for years but which could not be achieved because of differences in the systems of participation in decision-making. The issue should be solved one day. Now if we want to establish a firm in

different European countries, we have to register in each country. This idea of the 'Société Européenne' is an important step forward, it *will* simplify business and help the harmonization of social policies.

Since the war, we have had the Anglo-Saxon system of the 'Board of Directors' and the German double system of 'Aufsichtsrat' and 'Vorstand': The French can choose any of these ... There are important differences linked to these different systems ... We need a common European business law.

The reciprocal learning within Europe *should* be built on some harmonization of the basic educational systems which are now often incompatible. (These aspects will be developed in more detail in Chapter 9.)

There *will* be more women in business in Europe. Many signals point in this direction: demographic patterns, the cost of education and training, the rise in single parent and dual income families, and companies need to hire the very best recruits available. Nowadays less than 3 per cent of senior managers are female. The Nordic countries are far ahead, with 75 to 80 per cent of women working outside the home and more than 10 per cent of senior positions held by women. The rest of Europe *should* learn from Scandinavian countries and break through the 'glass ceilings' which prevent women from rising to the upper echelons. Companies today are seeking managers who demonstrate skills which used to be considered 'softer' or more feminine: the abilities to communicate, listen to others, work well in teams, support others, direct through encouragement rather than fear, use intuitive as well as analytical thinking, and reach good compromises through positive negotiation.

Environmental issues *will* be of major importance everywhere in the world. Managers *will* have to pay much more attention to ecological issues, not only under the pressure of ecological groups or political parties, but also under the pressure of public opinion. In northern Europe, ecology *is* becom*ing* a 'religion'. Some firms *will* use the ecological argument in their differentiation strategy. In Germany, the concept of 'Social and Ecological Market Economy' *will* spread. Top managers *should* consider ecology in order to preserve or improve the quality of life. More broadly, managers *should* pay more attention to business ethics.

Environmental issues are going to be important to every manager with responsibility. Managers will be forced into it, although the smart companies are anticipating and they are moving ahead. A company like Du Pont, for example, is showing leadership in how they are going to cope with environmental issues. It is very smart, before you have the politicians and the works' council and society on your back, to be able to show proactive leadership in that area.

There is an indirect link between the ecological challenge and the challenge of Eastern Europe, considering the ecological risk in these countries.

The development of Eastern Europe is a challenge both for the West and for the East. Top managers are optimistic on the possible developments in the East.

They all hope for a healthier situation in Central and Eastern Europe. The majority think that Eastern Europe brings and *will* bring market opportunities, that Western European firms *should* seize these opportunities, and that the East *will* learn from the West.

However a minority of managers think that the contact with Eastern Europe *will* also rejuvenate some of the West's management practices:

> The centre of Europe has moved to the East. There is a new combination, a bit of Eastern Slav philosophy permeating, it could change the management style towards 'Gemeinschaft, Gemeinschaft ist mehr als die Wahrnehmung gemeinsamer Interessen', the sense of community with a common spirit.

> Eastern Europe will have an enormous impact on us because it is potentially a very large market and it is a natural market-place for us to fill. Now the impact on British management is the need to develop its own pedagogic skills. If you want Eastern European firms to be your clients or to be your partners, there is no possibility of that working effectively unless you educate them ... I mean the Russians do not need to be trained in terms of their technical knowledge, they need to be trained in management, in the basics of management. We will have to develop our pedagogical skills in this perspective.

German firms *will* be the most proactive in Eastern Europe:

> When you are a neighbour, you see things better and you are linked emotionally. The fact that Siemens opened its first office in Moscow five years after the foundation of the Soviet state, that it installed a telegraph line between London, Berlin, Moscow and Vladivostock, created a common history, traditions, even if some links have been broken by wars ...

In order to face the challenges in Eastern Europe and to share high risks, Western European firms could be pushed to cooperate and to follow the 'strategy of the parrot, moving with its beak and its feet'. But the Europeans are not the only ones interested in Eastern Europe, the Americans *will* take positions, for instance Coca-Cola is sending good Coca-Cola people there to develop the business.

Inequalities in the future may causes crises. Eastern Europe *will* be unstable for some years and the disparity with Western neighbours may create population flows. Europe *will* have to live with unemployment, and even increases in current levels, due to the necessity of rationalizing international operations. Firms *will* have to live with slow growth. Finally the gap between northern Europe and southern Europe may raise problems. It *should* be one of the priorities of the EC to reduce it and to help the weakest countries: Greece, Portugal, Spain and the south of Italy.

European firms operating in this context *will* be faced with increased US and Japanese competition. Their management philosophies, structures and practices *will* and *should* slowly converge at the European level, but a world-wide convergence of management styles *will* and *should* also take place.

Slow convergence in Europe: learning from the best practices

There *will* be some convergence in Europe but it will be *slow*, 'It will take time. The Germans took 70 years to achieve their customs union between 1818 and 1888!'. A common system *will* take one or two generations but under the pressure of international competition and thanks to the policy of the EC, there *will* be a convergence.

> The three models, the Anglo-Saxon, the German and the Latin could be reconciled. I think the long-term evolution shows that the gaps are narrowing. There are two conditions for this homogenization to take place: first, that the unification of the European market is achieved; second, that the media are less controlled by national governments. Anyway there will remain some specificities, in particular in the management of human resources. Also we must not forget a fourth model: the original combination of Slav philosophy and capitalist practices which is now emerging in the east of a 600 million people Europe.

> There will be some harmonization. Slowly, there will be an osmosis between systems: the French won't change, the German won't change, but they will adapt good practices from their neighbours.

Hopefully management *will* draw on the best characteristics of each culture. Europeans *should* and *will* learn from each other, enrich themselves from differences and integrate the best practices: 'We should integrate the German preoccupation with ecology, their ability in implementing solutions. They are the best at achieving three-year plans! We should integrate British pragmatism and preserve our French skills in designing architecture.'

The 1990s *should* also see the end of the domination of US culture in European schools of management, enabling them to be more realistic, to recognize European specificities and to mobilize European talents: 'Europe is so different from the US. We were wrong to apply the methods, the teaching material, the Harvard Business Schools and all that. The Germans never did it really; the French watched. But now I think the time of the Anglo-Saxon domination of management education is over.'

Some managers think that the German model of management could replace the US model in Europe. Given the economic success and power of Germany as well as its development in Eastern Europe, this is a plausible scenario. However, the pure alignment of Europe on the German model would be difficult in southern Europe and very unlikely in the UK. Other managers are attracted to the Dutch management system. A scenario of cross-fertilization is more probable and preferred.

As a result of this process of convergence, the resulting European picture *will* be more harmonious and still differ from the American and the Japanese models. This prediction also corresponds to the wishes of the majority of the directors interviewed:

- We *should* get the best from other cultures and practices.
- We *should* strengthen common characteristics in order to be more effective across borders.
- But we *should* also preserve some of the richness of diversity:

> Some level of cultural differences from nation to nation in order to give our children the richness, the variety of cultures.
>
> Do we have the right to change people in their culture, in their tradition? We must remain Austrians, you must remain French. What we need is to think European: the French must think European, the Austrians must think European, the Germans must think European, the Czeks, the Slovaks ... We do not need to unify everything.

One of the best signs that a European management identity is forming *will* be the multinational composition of top management teams: 'Look at the Germans now – they have foreigners in some top management teams. Look at Volkswagen – that is new for Germany. In Belgium you have had foreigners at the top of firms since the twelfth century. In Germany, it is new and you will see it more and more.' Simultaneously the gap between the three zones of the triad will narrow.

Slow convergence world-wide

There *will* be a convergence of management systems and styles across continents, especially between Europe and the United States.

> I think Europe is going more towards where the US has been, and the US is going more towards where Europe has been. Pretty soon they will be in the same place I think ... I don't know about Japanese management ... I think you are going to have more of a global harmony in management approaches among successful companies because they do talk to each other. They do go to Davos. There was a symbolic round table at Davos last year with Morita of Sony; Carl Hahn of Volkswagen and Don Keel, the head of Coca Cola on the same podium.

The notion of *model* will be questioned. The geographic base *will* no longer be a determinant of success: 'Successful companies will be the ones which will share the following characteristics: focus on customers, motivated and skilled personnel, the ability to implement.' The distinctions *will* blur and the convergence *will* be led by international companies. In the public sphere, world-wide TV broadcasting (e.g.

CNN is now broadcast all over the world) and intercontinental journeys *will* contribute to a slow homogenization of life styles. This 'universalist' view is typical of US top managers but it is also shared by several European managers in our sample. Japanese managers do not voice their opinion on this subject.

The Europeans *should* have a world-wide vision and take a world-wide position in the triad. They *will* have to face East/West and North/South challenges. European firms *should* learn from both the US and from Japan. As a consequence, international firms from the three continents *will* become more similar to each other.

Reciprocal learning

The ability to learn *will* be one of the two main success factors in the following decade. Reciprocal learning *will* develop between firms from European countries and between firms from the three zones.

Within Europe, the continent *should* learn from the British:

- The importance of profit.
- Skills in finance.
- A liberal world-wide vision of business.

From southern Europe firms based in the other countries *should* learn:

- Some 'sense of chaos' and intuitive management.
- Skills in designing new products.
- Negotiation of industrial policies.

From northern Europe, European firms *should* learn:

- Participative systems of management.
- A zeal for quality and manufacturing skills.

From the German model in particular, the others *should* learn about:

- Close relationships between banks and industrial firms.
- Close relationships between the individual employee and the firm, which increase a company's ability to implement strategies.

From the Scandinavian model European companies *should* learn about:

- A less hierarchical structure.
- An emphasis on harmony in the workplace.

And from the small countries, the others *should* learn about:

- Their international view of business.
- Their ability to learn from other systems, and to communicate in foreign languages.

Elements of the diversity in business systems world-wide are reproduced in Europe, in a small geographical area, and opportunities to learn from diversity have to be seized.

Reciprocal learning *should* also continue between the three zones of the triad. Figure 3.2 summarizes the flows of knowledge, skills and values in the workplace, as perceived by the directors interviewed. It is interesting to listen to US and Japanese managers talking about what *they* learn from Europe.

> Our European division brought something to our operations and divisions in Japan and in the US ... Well, simple things sometimes, for instance variable working hours. People can decide when they start. This was experimented with in Stuttgart in the early 1960s and was transplanted across the world and now today one of the company's values is variable working hours.

> Each culture, American, European, Japanese has positive and negative aspects ... In Japan we must learn the positive aspects of European firms, such as respect for the personality of individuals, the adaptation of strategies to particular regions ... maybe also a bit of individualism.

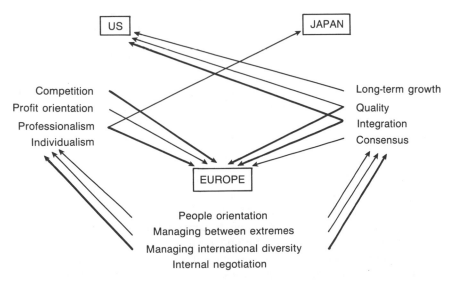

Figure 3.2 Reciprocal learning between the three zones of the triad

> We are based in Germany, our challenge for the German subsidiary is to improve the communication between the local employees and the Japanese ... to make our own model, mixing the strength of the two.

The Western way of living may become increasingly attractive to the younger generations of Japanese and management practices *will* probably be affected by such sociological changes.

> The interpreter spoke perfect American. The President of the company ... well, he was about 80 years old, and during the meal he fell asleep. So I was talking to the interpreter, a nice Japanese lady, married, with a child. Her husband's salary was not enough; the grandparents were taking care of the kid. When I asked her where she had learned American, she told me: at Columbia University. Then I asked her, 'Would you like to go back there?'... You should have seen her eyes! ... 'Oh yes!' ... In Japan there is a growing movement for emancipation which will change many things. It will not be a revolution, it will be slow. (Their culture is against revolutions.) But it will change.

On the other hand, the United States *will* influence Europe, demonstrating that 'economic performance is an absolute condition for being able to fulfil your social responsibilities.' Europe *should* also learn entrepreneurship ('flair' and 'courage') from North America, the European rates of creation of new businesses are far below the American rates. European managers *should* also learn geographic mobility.

From Japan, European firms *should* learn several things, but mainly the capacity to integrate. 'Now the tendency in our group is towards integration, and this is a key challenge. In this domain, the Japanese are the best: they know how to integrate the different functions in the firm – the dialogue between marketing, research and manufacturing.' Integration also refers to integration of people and team-building. In many industries, the Japanese still are ahead of Europeans in terms of quality control. Europeans *should* progress in this domain. They *should* also strengthen their skills in managing purely global businesses and sharpen their marketing abilities towards more customer-orientation. But direct learning from the Japanese is and *will* be difficult because of problems of language, and also because Japan is a completely different society with a particular sense of hierarchy and of collective harmony. It will be hard to transfer things directly from them. European firms will have to *reinvent*.

> I will tell you a little story. I took my board of directors to Japan for a visit a year ago, and among other people, we went to see the Chairman of the Stock Exchange. I have a godson who was finishing up his PhD at the University of Tokyo, who speaks perfect Japanese. He is bilingual. He came along with me and pretended to be my bag carrier, and we had three-quarters of an hour exchange of courtesy between myself and the Chairman of the Stock Exchange, and they provided the interpreter. As I walked out of the room, I said to my godson, 'Wasn't

that an interesting experience?' He said, 'Very interesting indeed. Do you realize that when you spoke, you were translated by the interpreter to the Chairman of the Stock Exchange in the language of obeisance. And when he spoke to you, he spoke to you in the language of dominance?' ... This little story tells you that it is not easy to learn the subtleties of a foreign culture, in which the management practices are embedded.

It *will* be difficult to copy the Japanese because their system is based on their sense of collectivity, whereas the European is basically individualistic. 'In order to balance individualism with mobilization for the company, we *created* the concepts of "Employee Involvement" and of "Management Commitment". In Japan consensus is natural; here you have to create it, you have to involve people'.

Before moving to the second main challenge of involving people, it is instructive to look at the image that the Japanese have of management in Europe. From the exterior signs which Europeans give, Japanese managers see a picture of a highly *hierarchical system* with:

- a tendency to function in a strict vertical hierarchy;
- authoritarian top managers, with a personal leadership style;
- isolated individual offices (instead of open-plan offices);
- managers who seldom visit plants and workshops.

This image of a rigid hierarchy depicted by some foreigners should alert European managers who want to develop 'employee involvement'. It may not be possible to dissociate such involvement from other organizational styles and characteristics: horizontal functioning, participative management, open offices and managers on the shop-floor.

Involvement of people

The aim of involving people in a company is to achieve convergence between the aims of the individual employee and the organization, to achieve a balance between efficiency and solidarity, to make profit *and* to enable the personal fulfilment of employees: in brief, to develop *enthusiasm for work*. Employee involvement is composed of four ingredients:

1. Communication.
2. Teamwork.
3. Less hierarchy.
4. Initiatives.

Improving internal communication is the first step:

> We need information and consultation. The works councils are going to
> have a greater influence in European companies. We use them in a very
> positive sense in the reorganization we are doing in Europe. We do
> involve the works council, and once we have agreement with them, then
> obviously we can move much quicker in implementation . . .

> You have to feel the pulse . . . what is happening and what needs to be
> changed. Feel the pulse, get unfiltered information. Of course, you can
> discuss things in the top management team, but they have a lot of biases
> and filters. So you have to go directly to the receptionist . . . have a
> coffee and ask how things are going, and you get a completely different
> picture. So we spend a lot of time on that. We like to get information
> from our employees as much as we can, and we like to give employees
> as much information as we can. If the receptionist should ask me, 'How
> are we doing in computers? What is our market position? What is our
> strategy?' we would answer, we would *explain.*

But communication is only the first step in developing employee involvement.
Team-work is the second step, and harder to achieve. European firms *should*
develop team-work:

- between functions;
- between different levels in the hierarchy;
- between people belonging to different cultures.

> We have to form teams; it is a condition of survival we cannot live with
> our deep-rooted individualism. Do we really teach team spirit at school?
> Do families with an only child teach team spirit? I am afraid our society
> produces lone wolves. But I think that basically European children have
> nothing against teams.

Managers sometimes criticize elitist educational systems, at least some French do.
Management schools and companies themselves have to correct the tendency to
individualism, to explain to employees that the company aims at team performance
more than at developing 'stars', and to recruit people who want to integrate
themselves into teams. This view questions the myth of the visionary leader at the
top, and also emphasizes the importance of top management *teams.*

The participation of people in decision-making is the third step and a necessary
condition for flexibility and creativity at all the levels in a hierarchy. The strong need
for individual fulfilment in Europe should help to involve people more in decisions.
Finally, initiatives and innovations *should* come from the bottom and the middle,
as well as from the top. Information technology could help the front line in taking
quick decisions and actions while being connected to databases.

Such principles are put into practice in several companies represented in this
study, for instance at Nestlé with the concepts of 'Employee Involvement' and

'Management Commitment', and at Unilever with the concepts of 'Project Teams' and 'Extended Head Office':

> If I look at our own organization, we have had more changes in the last six to eight years than in the fifty years before. We have survived such changes because our people increasingly understood the need to be flexible in our organizational behaviour. That has led us into two new directions: 'project teams' and what I would call 'the extended head office'. Now 'project teams' means that you say to a group of people (I will define the group in a minute): a) think of a new toothpaste which is b) good for good health and c) will be launched in the whole of Europe as soon as possible.
>
> You then appoint, say, six people of all disciplines: production, product development, marketing, accounting, research, and you tell them to set about and do that. They are not people who have ever worked together. Some of them may have, some of them not. They are supposed to speak to everybody who could make a contribution to the project and then report to a project director.
>
> Project teams mean you use people who are not normally doing this, although they should know something about it, but you use the creativity of a group of people. You have a mixture, six people, usually four to six nationalities, they work at four to six different locations, they have different backgrounds.
>
> The project team can be about a major issue, but it may also be a small issue, in which case you have a different level of team. The international, multi-disciplinary project team is in my view a very important thing for the future. We have a number now, and so far it works well ...
>
> The second direction is the extended head office. Of course, we have a number of people in the head office who control, or decide, or whatever. But we also want to involve people in operating units in top decision-making. We have, for instance in Brussels, a central organization for detergents, and a central organization consists of three full-time members and four or five part-time members who are working in the various countries. But they come to Brussels once a month for the decision-making process. So we have a head-office which consists of full-time head office people, but also people in the operating units who do nothing but participate in the head office decisions. That is the 'extended head office'.

The executives in big international companies aim at improving the flexibility of their firms through reciprocal learning and employee involvement. Smaller firms have a reputation for being more 'flexible'. We believe that this reputation is only partly true. Small firms do demonstrate operational flexibility; thanks to their size they may be quicker in their reactions. But the real issue is strategic flexibility, the ability to change. Here the mice are not better equipped than the elephants.

In the following chapters, particularly in Part III, we will address some of the challenges raised by the directors in our study. Nowadays management techniques seem to be mastered, most of the challenges ahead relate to the development of more intangible managerial skills.

References

Braudel, F. (1982), *L'Europe*, Paris: Arts et Métiers Graphiques.

Caron, F. (1988), 'Cartels et fusions en France: 1914–1945', in *Wettbewerbsbeschränkungen auf internationalen Märkten*, *Zeitschrift für UnternehmensGeschichte*, Beiheft 46, p. 185.

Chandler, A. D. (1990), *Scale and Scope*, Cambridge, Mass.: Belknap.

Dietrich, Y. (1991), *Die Mannesmannröhrenwerke 1888 bis 1920*, Wiesbaden: Steiner Verlag.

Elias, N. (1975), *La Dynamique de l'occident*, Paris: Calmann-Levy.

Feldenkirchen, W. (1988), 'Concentration in German Industry', in *The Concentration Process in the Entrepreneurial Economy Since the late 19th Century*, *Zeitschrift für UnternehmensGeschichte*, Beiheft 55.

d'Iribarne, P. (1989), *La Logique de l'honneur, gestion des entreprises et traditions nationales*, Paris: Editions du Seuil.

Kocka, J. (1981), *Die Angestellten in der Deutschen Geschichte 1850–1980. Vom Privatbeamten zum angestellten Arbeitnehmer*, Göttingen: Vandenhoeck & Ruprecht.

Lijphart, A. (1975), *The Politics of Accommodation, Pluralism and Democracy in The Netherlands*, London: University of California Press.

Mathias, P. and Postan, M. M., (eds) (1978), *Cambridge Economic History of Europe. The Industrial Economies. Capital, Labour, and Enterprise – Part I: Britain, France, Germany, and Scandinavia*, Cambridge: Cambridge University Press.

Morin, E. (1987), *Penser l'Europe*, Paris: Gallimard.

Noiriel, G. (1992), *Population, immigration et identité nationale en France : XIXie – XXie siécle*, Paris: Hachette.

Rostow, W. W. (1978), *The World Economy, History and Prospect*, Austin: University of Texas.

Thurow, L. (1991), *Head to Head*, Cambridge, Mass.: MIT Press.

Whitley, R. (ed.) (1992), *European Business Systems, Firms and Markets in their National Contexts*, London: Sage.

Part II
'Foreigners' and 'neighbours' on the European scene

An isle is emerging that is bigger than a continent, the Inter-Linked Economy of the Triad (the United States, Europe, and Japan), joined by aggressive economies such as Taiwan, Hong Kong, and Singapore ... It is becoming so powerful that it has swallowed most consumers and corporations, made traditional national borders almost disappear, and pushed bureaucrats, politicians, and the military towards the status of declining industries.

Kenichi Ohmae, *The Borderless World: Power and Strategy in the Interlinked Economy*, London, HarperCollins, 1990, p. xii

The world may not be borderless yet, but Europe's boundaries are permeable to foreign direct investments and they are moving in the East. American direct investments since the 1950s and Japanese direct investments since the 1980s have led to the coexistence of US, Japanese and European companies on the European scene. If we take the perspective of the European insiders, it is useful to understand the strengths and weaknesses of the 'foreigners' from the two other zones of the triad, particularly in terms of administrative and managerial skills. Considering the differences found between the American, the Japanese and the European styles of management (cf. Part I) a closer analysis of American management and Japanese management *in Europe* will assess their responsiveness and the extent to which they have learned from the experience of managing in Europe.

In Chapter 4 Dominique Turcq studies the management of American companies in Europe. He shows that American firms have adapted their home model to the minimum extent necessary to handle the complexity of the European market. Many may have difficulties in adopting a stakeholders' approach, which is typical of doing business in Europe. Chapter 5 by Etsuo Yoneyama analyzes Japanese management in Europe. Typical Japanese business policies seem to fit the European context, but the gap between the two business cultures raises problems in managing managers.

The frontiers of Europe have also moved in the East. The transformation of Eastern European practices is a major challenge for both Eastern European companies and Western European firms which plan to develop in these markets (cf. Chapter 3). In Chapter 6 Peter Lawrence analyzes the encounter between German management and East German companies after unification. He discusses the main problems that East German managers have to deal with in transforming their management practices and in competing with their Western counterparts. Other Eastern European 'neighbours' hope and expect to do more and more business with the West. Some will eventually become insiders in an extended Europe, some will join the triad. But they are already on the European scene now.

CHAPTER 4

Is there a US company management style in Europe?

Dominique Turcq

The hypothesis that there is a European model of management, as is defended in other chapters of this book, implies – as in a mirror effect – that there is an American model of management (as well as other national models, such as a Japanese one). The purpose of this chapter is to raise issues on the existence and performance of 'home culture-rooted' management models, like the US one and the European one, in the relatively homogeneous business environment of today's Europe. The chapter does not go as far as testing the fit and the interaction between a management culture and its prevailing business environment, but is a step in that direction. It opens some questions for further research,[1] namely on the sustainability of a model when transplanted into a different environment, and on the superiority of some models against others in a changing environment. One could argue that the US model could not succeed as such in a fragmented Europe but could be more successful than any European model in a unified and largely deregulated Europe. However, we do not intend to *prove* any one model's superiority, nor even to prove the existence of models; rather, we question the potential success of some management characteristics when confronted with a new and fast-changing business environment.

In summary, this chapter[2] suggests that US companies operating in Europe do not follow what could be called the European approach to management. US companies, as a whole, tend to export their home-base management model and adapt it in an incremental way and only to the minimum extent necessary to handle the increased complexity of the European market.

After having summarized some key aspects of the assumed models of European and American management in Europe, the second part of this chapter will outline the European business environment in which both European and American companies have to operate, i.e. a single but not yet an integrated market. The third part will use a few examples of management situations which reveal similarities in the practical implications of this economic environment on management issues for US and European corporations. The fourth part will develop the hypothesis that US and European responses differ more in their ways of dealing with the changes needed to adapt to a fast evolving environment than in the direction of these changes.

Finally, a few hypotheses will be raised on the competitive potential of some specificities of the US and the European approaches.

1 The European and US approaches to management: a quick overview

The European management model

Compared to US and Japanese management, the European management approach has its own distinctive characteristics. However, although commonalities exist, there also exists a great diversity of management characteristics within Europe that should be briefly discussed before covering the common underlying themes. European management differences have been fitted roughly into four classifications, two of which – the British and Germanic approaches – are clearly at opposing ends. The other two, splitting continental Europe into a northern and southern section, rest between these two extremes. This division varies by study and can include France and Belgium in either the southern or the northern group. Of course, these classifications tend to be stereotypes at best and it should be recognized that great ranges of management personalities and approaches exist even within countries. In general, the UK approach is viewed as being the most similar to US management characteristics and the German approach is regarded as having the greatest involvement of labour as well as a rigid equality in decision-making. (For an overview, see Chapter 1 of this book and the Groupe ESC Lyon Report for the ERT, 1993.)

On aggregate one can assume, for the sake of simplicity at this level of analysis, that the European management approach is more homogeneous when viewed from the outside and compared to the US and Japan. From a methodological point of view we observe here a typical 'fractal' framework, where the further one goes into elements that appear homogeneous at a distance, the more one discovers new segmentation lines. If one looks at the European model, the variety between nations could appear as a major differentiating line; if one looks closer at a particular nation, new lines will appear – such as the size of corporations, the regions in which they operate, the industries they are in, their age, etc., which can all be considered as radical differentiations leading one to consider the previous aggregation as grossly exaggerated. Compared to the US and Japan, the resulting image of the European Management model, as we will refer to it, is argued to be firmly founded on a strong social market economy approach to business and society. European firms play, apparently more consciously than their American counterparts, an active role in the community, government, and employees' lives. Moreover, European businesses, characterized as having a strong employee orientation, encourage internal negotiation on critical issues, and therefore more complex, more *political* decision-making processes, as opposed to the (stereotypical) US top–down decision-making style. Finally, because Europe consists of many countries with strong cultural differences, European managers may have a stronger ability, unlike their American counterparts, to manage international diversity and to manage between cultural extremes. Although there is varying sensitivity to these issues by Europeans as a whole, the Groupe ESC Lyon Report for the ERT (1993) finds that these characteristics are distinctive enough to differentiate Europe from the United States and Japan (cf. Chapter 2).

It would be misleading to consider the strong employee orientation of European companies only as a tendency to involve people from all levels of the corporation in significant decisions. In many countries, and especially in Germany, this is required as a part of corporate governance. The focus also goes much farther than simple involvement of people; it can go as far as to elevate the fulfilment and care of individuals above the profitability of the firm, based on the notion that 'profit is not all'. This is not to say that European managers ignore profitability, but that they believe that 'you cannot have profit without fulfilling social responsibility' (Groupe ESC Lyon Report for the ERT, 1993).

The significant differences between the European management approach and the US or Japanese approaches tend to exhibit themselves, first, in the involvement in the decision-making process of a greater number of people from various levels inside and outside of the firm; second, in the 'social involvement' concept; and third, in the *relatively* lower emphasis placed on profit. These three characteristics could also be applied to the Japanese model, but in a very different set of detailed elements on which this chapter will not elaborate, like lifetime employment, the Keiretsus' role in economic and social dynamics, or the role of shareholders in profit-sharing. The differences between a US and a European model can be explained in a relatively simple (even if slightly caricatured) framework stating the importance given to a variety of stakeholders to business interests in Europe relative to the United States.

Stakeholder versus shareholder management

The relative importance of shareholders versus the other stakeholders to corporate governance has never been as clear-cut in Europe as it is in the United States. In the US, shareholders are commonly assumed to be the most important, if not the only, influence over corporate decisions. And even in cases in which the role of others has been admitted, the common *normative* approach, as taught in most business schools, is to say that only the interests of shareholders *should* have a predominant influence.

Europeans with a 'social market economy' philosophical background have always felt uncomfortable with this approach. The importance of labour unions, banks, governments, and others is well established and accepted in the European way of managing any business. Furthermore, wide differences exist in the way corporate governance systems in different European countries take stakeholder interests in consideration, and these differences will continue to exist even after completion of the Single Market. One of the key obstacles prohibiting progress towards the definition of the European company statutes is the relative importance given to stakeholders as opposed to shareholders in the different European nations. This division is particularly evident between the UK, which is closer to the US model, and Germany, where legally trade unions are deeply involved in decision-making at the highest level of corporate governance. In Europe, shareholders are but one stakeholder among many.

Surprisingly, despite the greater influence of other stakeholders on their operations, European business executives have tended to use informal, *ad hoc* methods to analyze or understand stakeholders. Furthermore, we believe that they have systematically underestimated the importance of such an analysis. Instead they have relied on past history, intuition, experience and sometimes governmental or legal directions to guide their efforts.

The recent massive changes in the underlying fabric of European business has brought to the forefront the need to understand and manage better the variety of constituencies and stakeholders that operate in Europe. The Single Market, increased deregulation, and privatization waves have changed the roles that national governments play in protecting and directing businesses on their national soils. The influx of Japanese and American companies with 'European' perspectives and interests creates new competitive pressures that are forcing companies in Europe to adjust. The opening of Eastern European markets and production bases has led to a major rethinking of business system configurations. Furthermore, the spread of formerly *national* European companies into the international arena has created great potential for mistakes, as 'obvious' national approaches are not appropriate in a new environment. Companies very successful in their home European environment have proven unable to manage successfully the same business in the next country; examples abound in the banking, consumer goods, and distribution sectors. European companies have to adjust their stakeholder management skills to changing stakeholder environments.

The importance of stakeholder management contributes to the differences between European and US management approaches. In sum, stakeholder management issues are a central strategic concern of European top management and should, at least, be recognized as potentially significant for US companies operating in Europe. Our belief is that companies should manage their stakeholders in such a way as to gain competitive advantages in the European market. This is a critical issue for European companies, as they are highly aligned and dependent on strong national stakeholder relationships. It is also critical for US or Japanese companies in Europe since, if it is true that they had, until today, less chance to build their presence by relying on local networks, their future development and growth may depend on their ability to be better insiders.

Apparent specificities of US management in Europe

Probably the most obvious characteristic distinguishing management of US companies in Europe from European companies is that among the US companies there seems to be no clear distinctive management pattern related to European-specific factors. In fact, US managers' avoidance or ignorance of issues relating to distinct national differences or to the relation of stakeholders within Europe to business operations or investment decisions suggests that US corporate behaviour is not closely related to local national environments. Any European company, on the other hand, has to give at least a major consideration to its home base, and often differing considerations to other markets on the continent, depending on variables such as cultural proximity, languages, historical business links, and unique stakeholder constituencies. A US company's major responsibility lies clearly with its share-holders, who are predominantly located in the US. Any other responsibilities are considered to be of a much lower degree of importance.

A second distinction concerns the assessment of Single Market strategic opportunities for both European and US companies. For European companies the issue is whether or not they can ever truly make the shift from 'national-companies-with-non-integrated-Single-Market operations' to 'pan-European-companies-with-integrated-Single-Market operations'. For US companies the issue is whether a strategy *anticipating* or *depending upon* an integrated Single Market is the correct strategy. US companies generally tend to see the European market as more integrated than it really is.

A third distinctive characteristic, clearly on the long-term strategic front, is whether a European corporation's ability to manage stakeholder relationships better is a key factor to success, and, similarly, whether the apparent reluctance of US companies to manage these relationships is a liability or an asset. Answering this is fundamental to determining a course of action for improving the competitive position of either European or US companies operating in Europe.

2 A single but not yet integrated European market

Although the European Community has adopted significant measures to create the Single Market programme of 1992, the European market-place is far from fully integrated due to many factors:

- The diversity of people and societies reflecting centuries-old cultures, traditions and legal systems.
- The heterogeneity of national macroeconomic structures, including monetary policy instruments, the role of banks, and tax regulations which are converging only on very long-term trends.
- The watertight character of business communities and of national elite networks which are functioning under different rules and practices and which are only marginally interconnected.
- The numerous disparities in the webs of local structures and systems surrounding corporations and partially determining their behaviour, like education, taxation, hiring and firing systems.

Society: The most vital aspect of a community, its people, represents perhaps the greatest gap between Europe's ambitions of becoming an integrated market and its present reality. The most fundamental dividing factor is the existence of different languages – more numerous in reality than the mere number of official languages – which stifle cross-border activity and significantly increase difficulties in a range of activities, from complex negotiations and contracts to simple purchase agreements. Language also acts as a cultural barrier making it difficult for individuals to move and integrate freely into other countries, and for corporations to transfer skills when these are closely linked to communication with people (such as on-the-job quality management). Other barriers to the free movement of people include largely different taxation systems, incompatible social security systems, the necessity of maintaining expatriate status for employees *within* Europe, and the existence of different visa or status policies for non-Europeans. Significant factors affecting the integration of cross-border corporate activity include the substantially different labour pool structures, different consumer taste preferences, and cultural habits, all of which affect the ways in which investment decisions are made, business is conducted and tasks are performed.

Economic structures: The second significant barrier to achieving an integrated Single Market is the relative reluctance of the highly independent national European states to progress towards macroeconomic cohesion. Industrial and monetary policies remain national, leaving different currencies and largely different multinational infrastructures, particularly in telecommunications and railways. Corporations operating in the multinational European environment must also adapt to different structures in chain economics, for example differing bank and institutional investor roles, the existence of different distribution channels and purchasing mechanisms, as well as differing stock market and financial market regulations.

Business communities: A third significant factor preventing Single Market integration is the series of well-insulated links between national business communities and government, which are dominated by elite networks with little cross-border influence or interaction. European industry organizations tend to be confederations of national organizations with mostly vertical structures and little interdependence or inter-group decision-taking. Few pan-European industry federations exist with a centralized function for determining federation goals and means; this, therefore, makes the decision-making process for any pan-European federation a search for unanimity and consensus among members with potentially conflicting objectives. This is a difficulty faced not only by European industry federations but also by the greater European Community as difficult Community decisions, which can be to the detriment of one nation, must be reached among often uncompromising members. Until the European nations are willing to sacrifice their individual interests for the advancement of the Community as a whole, the national governments themselves will remain the major players responsible for changes and will continue to be inclined towards national preferences. Thus, firms will continue to lobby vertically to their own governments for special interests. Additionally, the strong links between national business and political communities, particularly through 'old-boys' networks, will encourage businesses to favour local sourcing, expansion plans and alliances, further impeding the integration process.

Rules on business practices: Finally, corporate activity is heavily inhibited by slowly converging and nationally oriented regulations and controls that effectively prohibit efficient, well-integrated multi-border operations. The costs, financial and other, created for example by multiple taxation regulations, legal structures and financial disclosure requirements is a considerable disincentive to cross-border investment as well as a competitive disadvantage for firms with pan-European operations. Additionally, there are significant differences, legally and culturally, in the relationships between management, shareholders and stakeholders. The differing relations between these constituencies, their relative influences and the resulting effect on individual and collective risk-aversion significantly influence corporate decision-making to differing degrees in the European countries. The well-known example concerns differing involvement of and responsibilities towards employees. However, similar major differences appear in responsibilities towards creditors in the case of bankruptcies (the relative weight and power of the various creditors varies largely between countries) and in legal responsibilities towards consumers or in relation to ecological damages.

Due to these remaining national differences in laws, regulations, culture and customs it will be many years, if ever, before Europe is effectively as fully integrated as the United States is considered to be.[3] These remaining barriers to full integration constrain corporate operations in many ways. For those firms seeking broader European markets, market access remains more difficult than in an integrated market, best practices are hard to transfer across borders, and strong market differences require more than incremental adaptation. For those firms seeking to make Europe a strong pillar of global competition, these tangible and intangible barriers remain significant obstacles to gaining the best combination of resources, which is fundamental for maintaining global competitiveness. Finally, economies of scale, conceptually anticipated to provide significant cost savings and synergies, have been more painful to realize and less significant than originally anticipated in the Cechini report and in the planning departments of major corporations operating in Europe.

The fundamental managerial challenge

These existing cultural, societal, governmental, technical and operational barriers to a fully integrated Single Market present significant challenges for pan-European business operations. Virtually every company with operations or sales in more than one European country has had to at least consider the implications of the Single Market on its business activities.

The most evident impact has been the potential for improved scale economies and the elimination of redundancies through rationalizations and restructurings. A shift to pan-European operations should theoretically benefit production, warehousing and logistics planning due to harmonization laws and the elimination of border controls. In addition, the marketing function could be affected positively for companies with the opportunity for pan-European branding or packaging following the standardization of product lines.

However, this search for strategic coherence can lead to increased (and sometimes excessive) centralization and a weakening (sometimes a loss) of contact with local market demands. Herein lies what appears to be a paradox of the European Single Market: the elimination of physical borders between countries has *increased* the transparency of significant cultural and societal differences that affect all business activities in every country. Thus the elimination of borders and physical barriers to trade has sometimes increased, rather than eliminated, the need for a presence of local managers to manage autonomous local markets. A lack of recognition of local specificities of customers, regulators, employees and competitors could lead to operational inefficiencies, strategic mismanagement, lost market opportunities and eventually severe losses of local market share. This is the fundamental complexity of the European situation and results in the critical need to manage sensitively and effectively the trade-off between economies of scale and a fully responsive multi-local presence. More than ever, companies operating in Europe must be able to gain simultaneously the advantages of being continental and those of being responsive to local opportunities and constraints. The right balance has become the key factor for success.

As the development of Europe's Single Market has progressed, US firms, like other major companies operating in Europe, have begun to reconsider their European strategy in terms of organization and operations in order to obtain an optimal balance. In particular, as firms cease viewing Europe as several separate national markets, organizations are being restructured along product-line divisions as opposed to national divisions. Firms are rationalizing production and logistics operations, centralizing 'common' functions such as finance, R & D and marketing, while decentralizing decision-making responsibility from corporate headquarters to product-line managers with cross-border responsibilities and to local sales and service offices. In this way, firms are able to leverage gains in those areas that can most benefit from rationalization with the costs of those functions or tasks that must, by nature, remain decentralized and close to local markets. Both Levi-Strauss and Coca-Cola are examples of US companies for which the management of this trade-off is considered successful.

Levi-Strauss is in the dynamic and diverse fashion market for which awareness of changing demographics and faster changing consumer tastes are critical (Levi-Strauss Annual Reports, 1990; 1991, and *Business Wire*, 12 February, 1992). In order to manage local customer differences, Levi's European operations are organized on a country-by-country basis, with each unit fully empowered to take responsibility for customer financing, sales and distribution in their own markets. Levi's European headquarters coordinates pan-European production, merchandising and advertising to capitalize on economies of scale. Additionally, Levi-Strauss has a world-wide information system that is used to control production and inventory levels to take advantage of flexible, cost-effective production alternatives. Such an information and communication system is considered a key to successful pan-European as well as pan-global operations.

Coca-Cola has also managed to balance the need for 'insiderism', or a local market presence, with economies of scale by building a few pan-European alliances for bottling and distribution infrastructure, while still relying on local or regional networks and maintaining close-to-the-field multi-local marketing and account service representatives (Coca-Cola Annual Reports, 1990; 1991, Sellers, 1990; and Friedman, 1992). Coca-Cola's multi-local emphasis allows for increased adaptability to local markets with very different buying and consumption characteristics. Although building economies of scale in production is essential for cost purposes, managing local market differences and aligning merchandising tasks to different markets is vital to Coke's strategy for new and developing markets. This is a good case illustrating that the European vs. local split is not relevant if done at the function level. Coca-Cola's marketing function is obviously split into tasks, some of them being very European – such as brand management, advertising and production – and some being extremely local or sublocal like specialized merchandising campaigns. Coca-Cola's President, Donald Keough, was quoted as saying, 'The key to growth in Europe is better selling right there where the cola meets the customer. That means closer relationships with retailers, bolder merchandising, cheaper prices and faster delivery' (Sellers, 1990).

The management philosophy of a Levi-Strauss or a Coca-Cola is not new or revolutionary: US firms are following their traditional American management and decision-making approach of organizing operations into as large an area as possible without losing touch with local market needs. US firms have transferred this management approach to Europe, adapting it only as much as necessary to handle the remaining complexities of a single but not yet integrated European market. For example, realizing that largely different consumer tastes and buying habits require greater attention to local markets, US firms tend to have more local sales offices and increased decentralization of responsibility to these offices than in their US home market.

Differing perceptions to the degree of European integration

A manager's view of European integration appears to influence his or her decision-making. The impact of the European Single Market on a company's operations is largely dependent on the manager's perceptions of the degree of integration (actual or potential) of the Single Market or the perceived level of impact of the Single Market on business operations. Thus, it is not only the reality of the level of European Common Market integration that affects business decision-making. This could, as a hypothesis, explain some elements of the differing approaches of

European and US managers to European management. For example, if American managers perceive Europe as more integrated than their European counterparts, then this could explain the US tendency to use a cross-border management model, as opposed to the European tendency to maintain a network of separate country division managers with less interdependence and communication. US companies tend to use business strategies that would more readily adapt to an integrated market than their European counterparts. The 'Europe' of a Coca-Cola should be quite different from the one of a Pernod-Ricard with its strong French base and bias, or the one of a German packaged food company like Granini in fruit juice, which relies strongly on the taste and behaviour of the German market, or even the 'Europe' of a Seagram (a Canadian company) with its very strong UK base.

3 Similar challenges in Europe for both US and European companies

Even if differences in perceptions and in strategic challenges can be outlined, as has been partially shown in the previous section, the real forces of change for corporate restructuring in Europe, for US and European corporations alike, are economic and business forces. These forces act as constraints and opportunities common to both US and European companies. Even if European and US firms have many diverse and unique approaches to managing European Single Market complexity, their *objectives* are mostly similar. Moreover the real driver behind their behaviour is less their home business culture than the business constraints which confront them. Increasing the global and European competitiveness of European industries and businesses often depends on two generic interrelated efforts, common across all industries and corporate nationalities: enhancing cost competitiveness and adapting the organizational structure to improve decision-making and cross-border co-ordination where needed.

The European Single Market has been the same impetus to change for all organizations, but the specific reactions of these organizations have been guided by the peculiar effects of this impetus on their unique, individual businesses. For instance, the decision to centralize or decentralize is not a generic corporate-wide decision, but rather is dependent on the specific demands of the Single Market on each corporate function, and sometimes even on each task within a function. These changes are typically not related to corporate nationality (especially European or non-European). In fact, US companies respond to market changes and requirements in the same way as Europeans do rather than in a predetermined US way, focusing on changes in functional centralization and coordination and headquarters reorganization. And like their European competitors, US companies face resistance to change (a major and painful issue) by employees, managers and stakeholders. This view that 'US companies are not so different', documented through two examples, will be completed and altered by elements in the next section showing that although the challenges and overall behaviour are not significantly different, the way that managers implement European solutions in practice show interesting specificities for US companies operating in Europe.

Example 1: Revisiting functional centralization and coordination depending on the specificities of the business environment

The decision to centralize or decentralize operations does not have to be consistent for all business functions. Functional responsibilities related to sales and service (i.e. customer-responsive functions) need to be more highly decentralized while operations, logistics and common support functions (such as finance and R & D) can more easily be centralized and coordinated to take advantage of economies of scale. Similarly the decision to coordinate activities is highly dependent on the balance between the benefits gained from potential synergies or operational consistencies, and the potential costs to be incurred through delayed responsiveness or potential inconsistencies. For example, coordinating pricing in the Single Market is essential to avoid excessive discrepancies that could jeopardize customer or distributor confidence. But companies must be careful not to allow common European pricing to develop into bureaucratic, non-responsive pricing mechanisms which ignore the flexibility required in a highly competitive and still fragmented market.

A comparison of similar business functions between corporations allows for a more focused comparison of different corporate responses to similar Single Market issues. The differences in responses clearly result from different business challenges and different company-specific approaches to their challenges rather than from their nationalities. For example, the four US companies Microsoft, Gillette, Compaq and IBM have taken different approaches to marketing strategy. Microsoft has taken a decentralized approach, as opposed to the centralized, pan-European strategy of Gillette (Mitchell, 1993, p. 17, p. 79; *Marketing*, 18 February 1993). The differences are largely the result of the specific requirements of the market segments that each of these companies targets. Microsoft produces mostly application-specific software to fit specialized customer needs. As opposed to a more traditional approach of a pan-European marketing programme that allows a corporation to break internal national barriers and encourage economies of scale, Microsoft has focused first on establishing a consistent and compelling corporate culture and image that acts as the glue in a European marketing network noted for strong national autonomy. Their focus is on simple federating factors: creating a homogeneous mission, core proposition and corporate identity which allows national management to add value in terms of local marketing and, independently, meeting the specific demands of the rapidly changing and fiercely competitive local computer software markets (Mitchell, 1993, p. 79).

Whereas Microsoft has been willing to give up economies of scale to gain an insider advantage, Gillette has taken the opposite approach. In an often cited example, Gillette has perhaps gone the farthest of many companies attempting to pan-Europeanize their marketing strategies by standardizing product-lines and capitalizing on economies of scale in packaging and advertising. Gillette has embarked on this strategy by recognizing that men, without regard to nationality, essentially look for the same thing in a shaving product. Gillette's pan-European branding, packaging and marketing has allowed them to combine the budgets of several formerly separate national marketing departments to produce a higher quality marketing campaign than any of the individual budgets would have allowed. Marketing and manufacturing are now completely centralized at Gillette's London headquarters, while national and regional managers are expected to concentrate fully on establishing retailer relationships and learning the peculiarities of their own markets, i.e. the next key factors of success after a successful marketing concept. Access to trade can only be performed efficiently with a high degree of decentralization.

Compaq, which markets hardware solutions, has also chosen to pursue a centralized marketing strategy (Mitchell, 1993, p. 30). Their target is large pan-European customers with pan-European account managers. Although they have maintained some local autonomy to respond to some elements of European diversity, their strategic choice to eliminate the redundancies created by what was originally 13 free-standing national subsidiaries in Europe has resulted in the centralization of most activities, including administration, distribution, finance and marketing. Although local sales offices are empowered to handle local tactical sales campaigns Compaq's centre handles pan-European advertising recognizing that, like Gillette, their products have similar characteristics that can be 'mass-marketed' to similar clients.

IBM, although still undergoing significant change, has in its own way identified the highly differing characteristics of its fundamental product lines: mainframes – where economies of scale are essential, and PCs – mass-marketed and highly service-oriented (*Business International*, 5, 1992). In response to this, in December 1991, IBM split into 13 lines of business (LOBs). Nine businesses are responsible for global manufacturing and development, while the other four are responsible for world-wide distribution and support (Hingorani, 1992; *The Economist*, 16 January, 1993). The goal of these organizational changes is to increase the speed of product development and to focus on competitiveness in the high-growth PC market.

IBM was designed, originally, to sell high-margin, high-cost mainframes. Although it has the structure, the support staff, the manufacturing and research staffs to succeed in mainframes, mainframes represent a declining share of all computer purchases. In 1974, when PCs were just taking off, mainframes represented almost 80 per cent of the value of the hardware market. By 1992, mainframes represented only 20 per cent while the share of PCs has risen to more than 60 per cent (Kehoe and Cane, 1993). These significant structural changes in the PC market are forcing IBM to rethink its strategic positioning. In order to succeed in the fast-paced, fast-growing PC and related services industries, IBM has realized that it must become a smaller, more flexible organization, but at the same time not lose its size advantages. Although IBM is facing these challenges on a global level, it is also the fundamental paradox that many large corporations are presently facing in Europe.

Example 2: Reorganizing headquarters and facing the challenge of managing change

With large overcapacities and redundancies, the greatest impact on costs for European businesses, aside from falling input costs, will be the result of corporate reorganizations capitalizing on economies of scale and on the elimination of functions and tasks performed in the centre (and for which the value added by being in the centre is debatable). Corporations are discovering the *subsidiarity* principle, realizing, as the Commission did a few years ago, the malaise associated with overstaffed head offices and overweighted top–down decision-making. As the current recession squeezes profit margins, there is increasing incentive as well as a unique opportunity to eliminate burdensome headquarters costs and to push some coordination responsibilities down to national or product-line managers.

In Europe, IBM has recently pursued the flexibility strategy described above through a complete decentralization into a network of fully autonomous business units which should increase responsiveness and agility of sales and service, particularly in the high-growth PC market. The Chairman of IBM Europe, Renato Riverso, in March 1993 completed a year-long effort to slice the 'Continent' into approximately 200 autonomous business units (Levine, 1993). These actions are empowering local operations to stand on their own, but it has come at a significant cost: by the end of 1993 IBM expects to cut some 10 000 continental European jobs. This strategy of increased accountability for decentralized profit-centres gives IBM the opportunity to respond to local markets and fast changing product innovations. At IBM's UK operations, the most significant personnel cuts will occur in the headquarters staff where only 100 key executives should remain by the end of 1993 compared to 2500 in 1991 (Cane and Summers, 1993; Cane, 1993; Levine, 1993).

Rank Xerox, the European division of Xerox, following significant resistance to change by the established hierarchy in 1990, is planning drastic restructuring of its European headquarters and the reorganization of its European marketing, sales and service (Lorenz, 1993). As announced by Bernard Fournier, Rank Xerox's French-born Managing Director, Rank Xerox will remove the costly traditional freedom of each European subsidiary to develop and operate its own processes and systems. In place of this, seven 'basic processes' are being designed to span all functional departments across Europe. Responsibility for each of these will be handled by the top managers from across Europe within a country-led pan-European coordination framework. Significant resistance is expected as the new 'process owners' begin to operate across the company's traditional structure, still heavily functional. In line with these changes, Rank Xerox is therefore also implementing a variety of behaviour and culture-change initiatives that include a leadership programme, workshops for self-managed work-teams, empowerment, organizational learning, and process re-engineering.

ABB, one of the few European companies to be mentioned here, makes the most advantage of a very slim central headquarters staff. Until October 1993, ABB consisted of 6 operating divisions covering 65 different business areas and over 5000 profit centres as a result of a major multi-year effort on the elimination of corporate overheads (ABB Annual Report, 1991). With corporate staffs kept at a minimum, a total of 250 global managers were leading 210 000 employees (Rapoport, 1992). Between 1989 and 1991, 4000 HQ positions were cut to 150. On 1 October 1993, ABB's CEO, Percy Barner, decided to streamline and strengthen its organization further by reducing the number of operating divisions to four and by creating three strong regions (US, Asia and Europe). This change should allow ABB to capture the economies of scale not yet tapped in the new European environment; to enhance at the same time the consistency of European cross-border initiatives; and to reflect the company's three world zone strategies (Redger, 1993; Studer, 1993).

As one of the pioneers in European organizational change, 3M began their 'Europeanization' in the mid-1970s, following the expansion of the European Community to include the UK, Denmark and Ireland (*Business International*, 1989). A traditionally hierarchical company with an extraordinarily diverse product range, 3M originally operated independent national divisions which had little interaction. Foreseeing the development of a unified Single Market, however, 3M's European management instigated plant rationalizations to take advantage of economies of scale, and by the mid-1980s 24 plants in Europe each produced a single product for all of Europe. This eliminated significant redundancy as 3M shifted from profit centres in each country for each product (12 countries with 46 product groups each) to strict product lines across Europe (46 product groups total). 3M's UK Chairman and Chief Executive explained that this should allow 3M to 'avoid problems to which international companies operating national subsidiaries are susceptible, and which have beset the European Community at large: parochialism, duplication of resources, incompatibility of national goals and unnecessary internal competition' (*Business International*, 1989, p. 36). In this process, 3M established their European headquarters in Brussels in order to coordinate European activities and centralize redundant functions such as finance and marketing. In addition, warehousing and transportation have been centralized at their distribution facility in the Netherlands. Fundamental to the coordination of European operations was the development in the 1980s of a common mission for all EC divisions, stating similar goals and values, the focus of which was to instil a 'European' thought pattern on divisions which were previously highly nationally oriented. This case demonstrates that large companies, with the proper internal impetus, can achieve radical redesign in Europe.

We have observed that corporations tend to respond to market changes in a way that best suits their unique challenges and situations, as well as in ways that the organizations themselves or their CEOs, are most prepared to pursue. Recognizing the need for decentralization of product lines or the relative potential of functional coordination is not difficult, nor is making the decision to change the organizational structure. The much more difficult challenge is to actually implement the change and restructuring. This is particularly true of organizations with traditionally well-entrenched headquarters staff and country division managers.

Todd Martin, Vice-President of marketing and business development at Kraft, set up in 1992 eight core groups covering Kraft's principal product categories (de Jonquières, 1993). These teams identify issues of common concern, but leave the ultimate decision-making to national managers who decide cooperatively. The objective is a consistent European strategy which can be tailored to local markets. Kraft, in a search for strategic coherence, has set out on this effort in order to make the group's eight European core groups responsible for initiating and implementing cross-border collaboration. While 10 years ago Kraft failed in its attempt to impose uniform product and marketing strategies across Europe, their new business environment may now allow the company to implement a change that otherwise faced too much resistance.

The difficulty of making significant, successful organizational changes (like the kind required to become more effectively European) in a large, bureaucratic organization has been well documented in cases such as IBM and Philips Electronics. IBM has initiated several restructurings since its peak performance years in the mid-1980s, and European restructurings have appeared to be an incessant theme for the past few years, even though Europe represents the fastest growing and largest information technology market at $150 billion (Cane, 1993). In a move which has increased the complexity of European operations, IBM in 1991 shifted product-line responsibilities to their managers in their four largest country markets: France, Germany, Italy and the UK. The original restructuring of activities appeared largely arbitrary and after six months IBM redistributed the product-lines in a manner that was more consistent with local strengths. For IBM, these assignments apparently were not intended to be permanent, but to be flexible in order to meet changing European demands.

Presently IBM is further restructuring its European operations. Although IBM's European operations had earlier (in 1992) been restructured into eight general product divisions, these divisions will be further decentralized into individual profit-centres in order to improve accountability. For example, its UK sales operation is to be divided into no less than 30 separate businesses, each with responsibility for determining its own prices and costs and answerable to the head office for its performance (Cane and Summers, 1993). In a move which is fairly typical of US companies, IBM 'businesses' which do not meet agreed targets face closure.

The IBM case illustrates well two forces that are mercilessly at work in Europe: the Single Market and the faltering economic environment. The Single Market promises radically to restructure European businesses with the short-term cost of thousands of jobs. Furthermore, the recession has put considerable pressure on consumer spending and business profits forcing further corporate adjustments. All told, at the time of writing, IBM's UK operation's staff will have been cut by 40 per cent by the end of the 1993 summer from a peak of 18 600 in 1985 to just over 11 000.

After more than ten years of restructurings, Philips NV is still struggling to establish a successful pan-European operating structure (Hagerty, 1990, *Business International*, 1989, p. 40). The Dutch electronics firm appears to face considerable difficulties in overcoming a bureaucratic and change-resistant organization. In a process which has been labelled as 'controlled decentralization', old national divisions with high autonomy are being forced to surrender responsibility to product divisions which span national borders. The objective is to become a streamlined company with a global marketing and manufacturing strategy while forcing responsibility for implementation, decision-making, and profitability down to product-lines and independent business units, to ultimately increase responsiveness to local needs.

It has been proven difficult to wrest power away from national hierarchies and, in parallel, the corporate centre appears unprepared for the reactions to significant change from a well-established bureaucracy. Layers of committees and management still exist. The particularly relevant practical point here is that in order to implement change in a large organization with deeply rooted bureaucratic power structures, it is necessary to have the backing and the willingness of top-level management to make the extraordinary effort and commitment to change. For Philips, as well as many other monolithic enterprises, this appears to be a perpetual challenge.

In restructuring operations it is difficult not only to choose new location and management teams for new product-line divisions, but also to overcome the complexities that remain when some of the original national management structures have to be left in place. The resulting structure is dual responsibility to top managers (product-line and region), which increases the complexity of interaction between managers. This new organization tends to lack hierarchy and clear chains of command, which in a traditionally bureaucratic organization can be difficult for entrenched old-style managers to accept. Both US and European managers will have to contend with this issue as Europe becomes increasingly integrated.

In none of these examples is what could be called a US specificity apparent. The drivers of change for all examples have been deteriorating economics, the need for a competitive positioning, or operating opportunities presented by the Single Market. The behaviours of US companies, at this point, are relatively heterogeneous and do not appear to differ significantly from those of European companies. However, the level of the above approach was broad, considering only the outcomes in terms of the decisions made and the directions taken. It is now worth pursuing this apparent similarity further by looking at the ways in which the adjustments were envisaged and at the practicalities of the moves.

4 US specificities in the 'ways' adjustments are made

US and European companies tend to face the European challenge from similar economic and business perspectives. However, a deeper analysis shows that shareholders and managers' perspectives are often drastically different for US and European companies, which results in differing practical implications of the way they manage change in Europe. These differences between US and European firms can be characterized as resulting from differing *stakeholder* interests. As discussed earlier, for a US firm shareholder value is the single criterion by which success is determined, accordingly, corporate decisions are focused on maximizing earnings, returns or some other measure of value. European firms, on the other hand, are forced to consider a myriad of other factors along with stakeholder or constituent interests, which can inhibit the maximization of profit, at least in the short run.

In addition to stakeholder interests, and naturally related to it, European corporate decision-makers are considered to have a different time perspective than their US counterparts, which often leads to significant differences in the required timing for both strategic decision-making and implementation. European firms, with a longer time perspective, can more easily pursue growth and market-share strategies as opposed to the less flexible and shorter time frame that regularly constrains US companies, forcing them to focus on yearly or quarterly profits. On account of this the levers or means by which a corporation achieves change can be very different for US and European companies. In a sense US companies enjoy a larger degree of freedom (being accountable only to shareholders), but in another they face more constraints (being responsible for immediate returns) than their European counterparts. In their competition struggles, US companies will need to go through a series of learning curves adapting to European peculiarities while their European counterparts will need to learn to leverage their 'local insider' advantages in the most competitive way.

US companies: more degrees of strategic freedom

A lower susceptibility to government and other stakeholder demands and a stronger shareholder role, by which US corporate decision-making is influenced, give US corporations more degrees of freedom to undergo some change. The greatest of these freedoms is their ability to lead change in restructurings and increased efficiencies in a way that their European counterparts cannot easily, if at all, enjoy.

For European companies, the greater number and deeper involvement of stakeholders, as well as the resulting complexity, make it difficult to instigate change which could be to the detriment of one or more constituent stakeholders. US companies do not face these restrictions (or if they do, they are on a much smaller scale and are much less of a decision-making factor). Therefore US companies are better positioned to be leaders in 'experimental' change in the restructuring of European business. In Europe, decision-making resembles a black-box system with considerable pressure from a whole range of stakeholders, including trade and labour unions, local, national and supranational government authorities, industry groups, workers and managers, and equity and debt holders including banks, insurance companies, governments and shareholders. In this sense it is much more difficult for European managers to make decisions which negatively affect the well-being of one or more mostly local constituencies. Because US companies have fewer ties to European 'local' or 'home' territories, they are freer to transplant or shut down production and operations without suffering severe repercussions of home-based stakeholders. Not only do US shareholders appear to care less, in general, about constituents like local workers and communities, but they are in addition far from Europe and are consequently less inclined to take into consideration these local European interests. As a significant part of European Single Market strategy is dependent on restructuring, including rationalization and integration, it is almost impossible for a European company with significant ties to local home-base operations and markets, *vis-à-vis* stakeholders, successfully to implement truly integrated pan-European strategies like a US company could. Only European companies that have generated successful multi-local, or multi home-based, operations (but do they really exist?) or US companies with no perceived European home-base operations can fully play the Single Market restructuring game. It will always be easier for a Hoover or an IBM to close a plant in France in favour of a plant, for example, in Spain, than for a large French group. Putting the two names Hoover and IBM close to each other also clearly shows the very wide gaps existing between US groups operating in Europe and the care to be taken when generalizing any point of view or data. IBM is known for having developed sophisticated 'insiderism' and 'good citizenship' strategies for many years, while the Maytag group, to which Hoover belongs, had only very limited European experience when it purchased Hoover in 1988. This lack of experience was even considered by some as a cause of what they considered to be management errors made by Hoover in Europe in 1992 (see *Le Monde*, 18–19 July 1993, p. 18).

Because Europe is not the home operating country for US companies, it also seems that they are more prepared to go as far as abandoning operations in Europe if they become unacceptably unprofitable. This is clearly an option that European companies do not have, as it is usually thought impossible for a company to leave its home operating base. A Volvo or a Renault cannot stop producing and selling automobiles in Europe while Federal Express and Tandy are two examples of US companies having chosen to abandon European operations. Tandy, facing unsatisfactory results, decided in 1993 to close completely its European operations in order to concentrate its resources on its home market – the US (Vanesse, 1993).

Likewise Federal Express, expecting the Single Market to allow for improved logistical operations and to create an expanded market for cross-border courier services, has abandoned intra-European deliveries (Mitchell, 1993). Having begun their European build-up in the late 1980s with purchases of several small British services and the major air cargo carrier Tiger International, Fed-Ex encountered three problems. First, substantially shorter distances in Europe, compared to the US, increased costs and complexity per kilometre; second, a plethora of local practices, attitudes, and national prejudices inhibited successful integration of operations at the European level; and third, Europeans had not yet developed a taste for overnight courier services and the significant boom anticipated by Fed-Ex never developed. In contrast to the 'want-it-yesterday' attitude of Americans, European customers are unwilling to pay the substantial price premium for overnight service while cheap, regular mail service exists with often less than three-day delivery. These two examples of Tandy and Federal Express, however, do not imply that many US companies would lightly abandon Europe. In fact, many US companies, as will be discussed later, have made strong efforts to improve their European positioning despite poor financial performance.

A further implication for US companies of not having alliances to stakeholder groups in Europe and not having Europe as their home-base country, is that American managers are able to give less consideration to the immediate social costs of their corporate decisions and actions. The single objective of profit allows, or forces, US managers to make investment and operation decisions which can adversely affect large regions or populations. The case of Hoover managing its plant restructuring between France and the UK is an example of this behaviour. However, it also shows the limit to the degrees of freedom outlined here, since with the increasing unemployment levels in Europe, it is probable that some US companies could harm their image and possibly their long-term potential if they behave in an overly unconcerned, uncaring manner. In this context it is worth noting the comments of the TUAC (Trade Union Advisory Committee to the OECD) on the Hoover plant relocation case:

> The TUAC wishes to point out that relocations can and do take place with the cooperation of Trade Unions. Recent examples at both Nestlé and BSN show that the failure of Hoover was in the way the relocation was done. With BSN the union's experience is that there is full and early discussion which includes consideration of alternatives which may save jobs. With Nestlé's relocation of biscuit production from Glasgow, an announcement was made well in advance without threats or demands for concessions from the workers and with full information disclosure to unions.

This implies that, relative to European companies, Hoover, as well as other US companies, could improve their way of working with labour and other local constituents.

US companies: less degrees of strategic freedom

The sharp focus of US companies on profit, particularly short-term through stockholder pressures and management evaluation practices, gives US managers significantly fewer degrees of freedom for some corporate decisions. American corporations appear to be regularly unwilling to pursue market-building strategies, particularly in foreign markets, which have substantial short-term costs and potentially high risks, while European companies tend to perceive these short-term costs as long-term investments. Entry into newly opened, or not yet fully developed markets, can therefore be a difficult strategic direction for a US company to pursue.

The overall 'late-comer' behaviour of US companies in Eastern European markets illustrates this point. (Informal observations of corporations active in Eastern Europe suggests that European companies are leading in penetration and development.) US companies and stockholders, relying considerably more on strict quantitative financial analysis for decision-making, tend to discount heavily the future cash flows of business ventures or corporate investments in new markets. This heavy discounting tends to discourage critical investments that would otherwise be necessary for US companies to maintain or develop a presence or competitive advantage in new products or markets. Additionally, most US managers are evaluated internally on yearly (or even quarterly) performances and objectives. Thus, there is little incentive for US managers to spend other than marginal efforts on developing longer-term market share and new products or markets. It must be said that this is presented as a stereotypical view: all US companies do not consider investments from this narrow perspective. On the other hand, US companies tend to exhibit these characteristics far more and to a greater degree than can be observed of their European counterparts.

To make this point clearer, let's assume that, in a simplistic way, it is possible to distinguish two routes for profitability growth in a slowly integrating Europe. The choice between the two depends largely on market maturity, sophistication of activities, strategic intent, and external market or internal corporate opportunities. The first route targets efficiency gains, is commonly used in stable markets by established pan-European players, and relies on rationalizations and increased coordination of operations, 'milking' existing product-lines, and concentrating on internal efficiencies. For a US company, such a strategy depends on a) convincing shareholders and executives that synergies, economies of scale, and European integration benefits really exist; b) managing middle managers so they accept change and cooperate internationally; and c) convincing shareholders that this route best protects long-term positions.

The second route focuses on aggressively gaining market share and leveraging existing skills on new markets. It is more typically found in growing markets and used by those players who are not yet sufficiently pan-European, i.e. those having market-share discrepancies between markets. While the change energy of the first route is more internally focused, the second one is more externally focused. It includes getting access to the best local managers and properly managing a team of international managers; becoming 'insiderized' in local business communities; convincing shareholders that this route is the best for long-term profits (i.e. superior to the improvement of existing management); and, in the case in which alliances and acquisitions are used on this route, convincing executives and middle managers that some (acquired's or acquirer's) formulas and skills are superior and transferable.

US companies, as a consequence of their relationship to stockholders, appear to prefer to pursue the efficiency path, focusing on generating quick profits from the opportunities presented by Single Market openings. In some cases, this may be at the cost of longer-term market share potential. In the food industry few US players have been as aggressive in getting access to new markets through expansion or acquisitions as Nestlé or BSN of Europe.

The fact that US companies seem to invest less in long-term market development than European companies could be a competitive disadvantage for US companies. The successful long-term company will be the one that builds successful European operations, investing in developing markets and products as well as building critical networks for capturing future market growth. In this respect European companies have an advantage over US companies. If this seeming unwillingness by US companies to invest in Europe as a developing long-term market is a true representation of their actions, and is confirmed by further analysis, it could be a substantial strategic error. Western Europe (EC and EFTA) boasts more consumers currently than the United States or Japan. Moreover, it has increasingly greater market potential as Central and Eastern Europe become integrated with the West.

US versus European companies, a race after excellent stakeholder management?

Not all US companies neglect the long-term potential of European markets and the complete departure of some of them, like Tandy or Fed-Ex, is not the rule. Neither do all of them neglect the still untapped markets of Europe. However, even in choosing the 'market development' route they are running the risk of making serious strategic and tactical mistakes. Part of the future competitive game between US and European companies will be played between the speed at which US companies can adjust to the changing European environment and the speed at which European companies will be able to build on the superiority of their field knowledge without being hindered by their rigidities.

United Parcel Services (UPS) is an interesting case exhibiting both the common US misjudgement of long-term and short-term issues in the European environment as well as the will to go along a learning curve to compensate for it. In 1992, UPS endured a costly one-month strike by drivers in Spain where they had, in 1990, purchased a package delivery company called Cullado (Taft, 1993). The drivers were frustrated by UPS's 'US style' working conditions, which included no-smoking rules and uniform requirements. UPS failed to realize that European employees, particularly southern Europeans, are less willing than their US counterparts to abandon habits which they consider as personal freedoms rather than elements of service. The critical error for UPS, however, was in failing to recognize the priorities required by the market situation for Spanish overnight delivery services. In this rapidly growing infant market what could have mattered most was capturing market share – not generating internal efficiencies, homogenizing the work-force, and focusing on service and quality. UPS contributed to this error by importing their home-based management model without adjustments. The market situation in Spain was the opposite of that in the US, where UPS behaviour had been successful. In the US, a mature market where high efficiency and service quality make the difference in a highly competitive game, UPS's conduct was highly justified. In Spain, a fast growing market, gaining market share quickly before the market matured, and therefore motivating personnel and developing clients, could be the first priority even at cost of some service quality.

In some circumstances, such as the rapidly expanding Spanish parcel delivery market, US companies must be more willing to accommodate European stakeholder interests, to understand the intricacies of a single but not integrated market, and to ignore their traditional management styles. The failure of overnight delivery services, as well as many other US ventures in Europe, has largely been considered to rest in the mismanagement of local differences, both cultural and corporate. Many analysts following Euro-Disney's failures with its US-formula leisure complex stress the negligence of Disney decision-makers to consider significant stakeholders as a major cause. In particular, French customers were not given proper consideration, although they represent the largest potential group of customers. In addition, European tour operators were not courted enough and employees complained heavily about long hours and poor wages (*International Management*, July–August 1993, p. 26).

The UPS case, however, also exhibits a counter-example to the previous evidence of US companies abandoning unsuccessful markets, and shows that some US companies are ready to go through the painful European learning curve if necessary. After three years of losses in the European overnight delivery market, UPS made the critical decision to change their European strategy from a prototypical pan-European 'all-or-nothing' approach (Taft, 1993). Although the integration of the European market did not result in the increased cross-border delivery demand which UPS and other players had anticipated (and although the penetration of individual markets like Spain proved so painful), UPS did not abandon its operations. Rather, UPS chose to shift their focus to services within individual national European markets as opposed to concentrating on continental services. The chairman of UPS, 'Oz' Nelson, hopes that this focus on domestic operations and local management problems will allow cross-border operations to eventually be 'gravy'.

It is likely that a European company would have avoided most of the early errors of UPS in Spain. Europeans have an advantage in their knowledge of stakeholder management. But unlike US companies, European companies face heavy constraints to pan-Europeanizing with integration strategies. German companies with significant ties to local economies and governments cannot easily move manufacturing operations to Spain. In a way there is a balance of opposing competitive advantages between European and US companies and European companies might be better off playing another game than the US companies – notably building their success on superior stakeholder management and on better understanding of Europeans. This is potentially European's strongest competitive advantage if the demands of the myriad of European stakeholders can be refocused to require their increased cooperation on critical factors for the long-term success of European industry.

This is particularly true for European management of local stakeholders. European companies stand to gain considerable local stakeholder commitments by explicitly committing themselves to the development of the local economy and local skill base. As European citizens and governments realize that they are competing with each other for industry, they will be more willing to adjust to corporate needs. This might, interestingly, imply some shift back towards nationalism but, if not accelerated by government interference, it should result in healthy national competition, not detrimental protectionism.

To summarize this section briefly, although US and European companies all face common Single Market issues, the impact of the differing shareholder and stakeholder structures on their operations significantly affects the specific ways they implement their strategy. Neither group, US nor European, appears to have a significant 'as is' competitive advantage in Europe. Both must recognize their own specific constraints and opportunities and leverage them. In such efforts, facing the same strategic challenge is far from implying that the way to define and implement the strategies will be the same.

5 Conclusion: do future winner/loser models appear?

The previous section has aligned the issue of the relative competitive positioning of US and European companies with specific stakeholder management issues and those of short-term versus long-term focus. The observations of the various cases of US companies in Europe can lead one to think that the issues are deeper than the ones of strategy implementation identified, and that some further issues could be raised on the pertinence of a specific US or a European model to strategic development in Europe. This section's aim is to provoke a debate through a series of 'thought starters', all of which need to be further documented.

Are US companies playing the right game?

It appears that US companies are focusing mostly on developing fully integrated Single Market business strategies in Europe. Fundamental to survival in the European market place, however, is the ability to manage successfully a company's constituent stakeholders. Although this is more true for European companies, US companies must also be conscious of these demands. This then provokes the question whether US companies are going too far in integration strategies at the expense of an awareness of local market intricacies and stakeholder demands.

For many US companies there might not only be an overemphasis on rationalization and integration, but sometimes even a complete ignorance of the stakeholder concept and related issues. Fundamentally, then, for these companies, it is essential first to identify the relevant constituent stakeholders for their specific business. Generically, stakeholders are those individuals, groups, or institutions that influence corporate decision-making. They are heterogeneous and tend to compete with each other for influence. One must understand the influence of stakeholders on the business and the influence of the business on the stakeholders. Significantly for US companies, in any European country the 'insider' status of a company depends on its skills in becoming part of the inner groups which have an influence on the specific business activities in which one is engaged. A relation to a stakeholder can be an asset or a liability. For example, having privileged access to a specially skilled work-force in a given region is an asset giving a competitive advantage but one which could become a liability if employment has to be reduced in the region. In addition, different management perspectives and decisions can turn a potential liability into an asset, or vice versa. For instance, many European acquisitions have been made less for the specific skills of the acquired company than for the insider status and the network of local relations of the acquired company. Coca-Cola in France illustrates this very well (Sellers, 1990). Coca-Cola executives were able to recognize the relevant stakeholders who were critical for their long-term success and, interestingly, also those stakeholders who were jeopardizing their growth potential. Coke bought out the interest of the local bottlers of their product who had a stronger interest in also bottling and selling other products. These bottlers, acting as the intermediary to retailers, were prohibiting the usual merchandising strategies of Coke. After buying back their interests in the bottlers, something they have not done in any other country, Coke was able to go directly to the retailers and begin heavy merchandising campaigns.

Stakeholder management is presently in an evolving state, and difficult to grasp without a strong understanding of what a future European vision should be. Although conceptually there are many potential stakeholders with highly complex interactions and strategic implications, in reality there are relatively few relevant stakeholders for particular businesses and the complexity of these relationships tends to be more operational than strategic.

It is unclear whether US or European companies are best positioned in Europe to play a multiple insider game, but the skills acquired by each European company in its home market could give them an advantage in the identification of and the approach to relevant stakeholders. On the other hand, US companies have been responding rapidly to the opportunities presented by the Single Market and they may be ahead of the competition in pan-Europeanizing their organizations and operations in some industries (e.g. electronics, computers, medical equipment, photographic material). However, success of this strategy depends on the answer to a critical question: 'Will the EC fulfil its ultimate objective of becoming fully integrated?'

US companies tend to pursue strict business-based decisions and aim at building their future business system as close as possible to what is required by the size of the market (economies of scale), making the best possible use of resources across Europe (cheap labour here, excellent engineers there, superior infrastructures elsewhere). European corporations, however, still (consciously?) make suboptimal business-system design decisions to realize insider advantages (e.g. maintaining a plant here is not using the best possible resources but it gives clear access to government procurement) and thus optimize across a broader range of variables.

This sensitivity to insider factors is precisely the skill that US companies still appear to lack and, further, to be failing to develop. If Europe remains highly segmented, this could be a competitive disadvantage for US companies, leaving them with economies of scale but a weak insider base. American companies have taken the approach of an international company in Europe. However, being 'effectively European' is not being an 'international' in Europe; becoming a multiple insider in Europe takes a different magnitude of efforts. As opposed to strictly business-based issues, the issues for 'effectively European' companies are 'identity'-based and sometimes 'soft' stakeholder management-based. Perhaps only time will tell if US companies are able to adapt, and if it is necessary for them to adapt.

Can and should European companies pan-Europeanize in the way that US companies do?

ABB is a European company often recognized as one of the most pan-European *and* local European companies. In this sense, ABB is attempting to combine the best of the US and European approaches to capitalize on the advantages of economies of scale and of advanced insiderism in its markets. ABB's organizational structure is built on the combination of two apparent contradictions: big and small, or global and national (ABB Annual Report, 1991, p. 8). For ABB, global and big refers to an emphasis on world-wide coordination, transfer of technology and know-how across country borders, as well as taking advantage of economies of scale in the specialization and high volume of engineering and production. Small and national refers to ABB's 'multi-domestic' organizational solution, which emphasizes a highly decentralized structure, bringing national companies close to their customers. This structure, as well as CEO Barnevik's pressure, promotes flexibility and entrepreneurship in ABB's highly independent local profit centres.

ABB is the primary example of a company which is considered to have been able to manage a pan-European reorganization, coordinating operations across borders and using the multi-domestic approach of being a local company everywhere with many home countries. This emphasis has apparently allowed ABB to overcome potentially impeding stakeholder interests and claims, although they may still be faced with significant challenges in fully managing their European insiderism and their pan-European coverage. (Their presence in Europe is not homogeneous across countries.) Interestingly enough, ABB is also a relatively neutral case since it is linked mostly to Swedish and Swiss nationalities, both being geographically and culturally in a relatively neutral position in relation to other Western European countries. One could argue that playing the ABB game was easier because ABB was neither French nor German.

Before deciding to pursue the US approach European firms must understand the demands of their particular business and the effects that such a move would have on their stakeholders. American companies, more than an ABB, are in a unique position relative to established European companies. They possess an advantage over most European companies in so far as they are considered as outsiders for whom there is no long-term expectation for the improvement of any national standards of living. European companies, on the other hand, are expected to consider the citizens and employees as vital stakeholders in their businesses. If, then, European companies attempt to follow the US pan-Europeanization pattern, they risk damaging the complex interrelationship with key stakeholders which are vital to their short and long-term operating success. Conversely, European companies are better positioned to leverage these same potential local stakeholder interests for building a European competitive advantage.

Do US companies bring a cultural common denominator that makes them better able to manage European diversity?

An interesting question which follows from the comparison of US and European management challenges and strategy routes in Europe is whether US or European managers are better at managing pan-European operations. The common hypothesis in international management studies has been that European managers are better adapted to managing international and/or cultural diversity than their US counterparts. This hypothesis has been founded on the premise that Europeans, confronted with greater national diversity closer to their own borders, are more often required to manage in a cross-cultural context and therefore are better adapted to its demands.

However, little concrete evidence could be found to support this hypothesis. As an alternative hypothesis perhaps European managers, confronted with greater national diversity closer to their own borders, tend to maintain their cultural identity more strongly, particularly in a European environment that is rapidly homogenizing. Looking at most European multinationals, the issue facing senior management, for example, is more often expressed as: 'How can I find enough of my nationals to manage abroad?' than 'How can I find foreign high quality managers to enrich and diversify my pool of senior quality people?'

US managers of 20 or more years ago, as US companies expanded around the globe, had very little appreciation for cultural diversity and the demands that it placed on management. However, in today's environment more often US managers can be found who, when open-minded and properly trained, are able to manage well potential cultural conflict. Furthermore, US companies and managers can often bring a common cultural denominator that provides other non-local managers from different cultural backgrounds with an accepted means to bridge cultural barriers. Companies like Procter & Gamble and IBM, with world-wide operations, maintain a highly visible and internationally accepted US-style culture and work environment.

This cultural denominator is a significant advantage for US multinational corporations in Europe. Local managers often seem to find less conflict within themselves and with their co-workers when acting under commonly accepted US cultural constraints, which are increasingly becoming accepted business standards, than when they are operating under the company cultural standards of a neighbouring nation. This hypothesis would be worth testing since its implications, if proven valid, are quite substantial from a sociological and cultural perspective. It is easier for an American company to impose a certain management style in France or Germany (or both) than for a French company to impose its style in Germany or vice versa, even if the managerial style in itself is not especially culturally earmarked. One of the most striking examples of this appears in recruitment. US companies may have a recruiting advantage over other non-local European companies because of the cultural common denominator that they bring. Although the limited data of this work does not allow us to consider this point as conclusive, it seems that, confronted with a choice of companies in which to venture for a career, a European national (from nearly any European country) would prefer, in descending order: a national company, an American company, a company from another European country (with again some preferences), and lastly a non-European, non-North American company. As one can see, Japanese and other Asian companies face the greatest difficulties in attracting people and the US actually the least. This is a considerable advantage for US companies in Europe looking to hire excellent local people to help them become insiders in local markets.

Many other issues could be raised on this field of the superiority of some models of management over others in the European environment. This area of research and observation is as open as is the field of experimentation for corporations. The corporate experimentation field, however, is certainly the more treacherous one, heavily mined with the stakes of survival and long-term profitability of European operations, which depends on just how integrated the Single Market becomes.

Single Market integration is a microcosm of global corporate restructuring. In Europe, as well as the world, cost-cutting and productivity improvements are critical to gaining competitive advantages. Markets are opening to all countries as telecommunication technology improves and expands. Consumers are becoming more informed and homogeneous. Products are becoming increasingly harmonized and standardized. Although all of these are critical issues, firms cannot simply take business and financial cost analyses as the single determinant of business strategy. Different regions, different countries, have delicate, specialized needs and requirements dictated by their local stakeholders. Managers, particularly foreign, must become adept at handling these stakeholder constituents and leveraging these potential local constraints to gain competitive advantage. It appears that the future success of European business operations lies in this ability of managers and statesmen to satisfy these delicate stakeholders' needs while simultaneously monitoring the more well-known and understood business–economic decisions.

Notes

1.   The views expressed in this chapter reflect the opinion of the author only. The author would like to thank Joseph Morrow, a MBA student at the University of Chicago and

at the Université Catholique de Louvain, for his help in data gathering, issue identification and editorial work.

2. *Note on methodology*: this work was designed to study an aspect of international management that is not yet well defined. Its main purpose is to raise substantive issues and to generate hypotheses for management consideration. Following this objective, it is more of an essay than a research work, and therefore the methodology was purposely open-ended. As an essay, it does not purport to be scientific or conclusive, nor is it intended to be representative of all US companies operating in Europe.

The initial selection of US companies was based on discussions with several management experts. The list for sample case studies contained 18 firms. Press searches for these companies were conducted on generic 'key words' focused on US firms operating in Europe and general European management and organization. The list of companies included: Coca-Cola, Levi-Strauss, IBM, Goodyear, UPS, Fed-Ex, 3M, Gillette, Procter & Gamble, Colgate-Palmolive, Kraft, Quaker, Rank Xerox, Kodak, NeXT, Microsoft, Compaq and Tandy. Notable exceptions to the sample include financial services and banking companies. This was due to the limited material available on their recent European development and restructuring operations. The data collection work used exclusively information publicly available, including press clippings from a period covering January 1992 to July 1993, annual reports for 1990, 1991 and 1992, and recently published 'management' studies as outlined in the bibliography. This information was analyzed to develop a view of the major strategic issues that have been faced by the individual companies and the decisions that were taken. In general, it was not feasible to assess the results, financial and non-financial, of these decisions due to our choice to rely only on publicly available documents.

The reader should be aware that this methodology presents many caveats and particularly makes the work biased towards those companies that have been considered sufficiently successful or unsuccessful in the European environment to warrant mention in the press.

3. Again a sort of fractal framework: certainly, a deeper analysis of the US economy shows that the country is not perfectly integrated, although the US is well integrated in terms of elements such as monetary policy and language. Disparities like banking regulations, case law, taxation levels, transportation infrastructures, environmental regulation exist between states.

References

Bartlett, C. A. and S. Ghoshal (1987), 'Managing across borders: new strategic requirements', *Sloan Management Review*, Summer, pp. 7–18.

Bartlett, C. A. and S. Ghoshal (1988), 'Organizing for worldwide effectiveness: the transnational solution', *California Management Review*, Fall, pp. 54–74.

Bartlett, C. A. and S. Ghoshal (1989), *Managing Across Borders: The Transnational Solution*, Boston, Mass.: Harvard Business School Press.

Cane, A. and D. Summers (1993), 'IBM may force job cuts on European staff', *Financial Times*, 30 June.

Cane, A. (1993), 'Europe cut down to size', *Financial Times*, 5 May.

de Jonquières, G. (1993), 'Cross border Kraftsmen', *Financial Times*, 17 June.

Douglas, S. P. and Y. Wind (1987), 'The Myth of Globalization', *Columbia Journal of World Business*, Winter, pp. 9–30.

Doz, Y. L. and C. K. Prahalad (1981), 'Headquarter influence and strategic control in multinational companies', *Sloan Management Review*, 23 (1), pp. 15–29.

Doz, Y. L. (1978), 'Managing manufacturing rationalization with multinational companies', *Columbia Journal of World Business*, Fall, pp. 82–94.

Doz, Y. L. (1980), 'Strategic management in multinational companies', *Sloan Management Review,*, 21 (2), pp 27–46.

Editors, *Business International* (1988), 'The BI 50: case studies in management success', London.

Editors, *Business International* (1989), 'The 1993 company: corporate strategies for Europe's Single Market', London.

Editors, *Business International* (1992), 'Management Europe: how companies are dealing with critical management issues', London.

Editors, *Business Wire* (1992), 'HP and IISI Help Levi-Strauss to expand electronic retail services', 12 February.

Editors, *Business Wire* (1992), 'Next appoints Bernhard Woebker VP Europe, completing European reorganization', 29 June.

Editors, *Business Wire* (1993), 'Goodyear restructures European organization', 4 June.

Editors, *Computing* (1992), 'IBM reorganizes European management structure', 17 September.

Editors, *DJ News* (1991), 'Quaker Oats restructures its European organization', 21 March.

Editors, *International Management* (1993), 'Disney's jungle book', July–August.

Editors, *L'Echo* (1993), 'Tandy: fermeture de 92 magasins belges', 17 May.

Editors, *Marketing* (1993), 'Microsoft adds local colour – adapting to local markets', 18 February.

Editors, *The Economist* (1992), 'The elusive Euro-Manager', 7 November.

Editors, *The Economist* (1993), 'To save Big Blue', 16 January.

Friedman, A. (1992), 'The ascent of Everest', *Financial Times*, 16 January.

Ghoshal, S. (1987), 'Global strategy: an organization framework', *Strategic Management Journal*, vol. 8, 5, pp. 425–440.

Ghoshal, S. and D. E. Westney (eds.) (1993), *Organization Theory and the Multinational Corporation*, New York: St. Martin's Press.

Groupe ESC Lyon Report for the ERT (1993), *The Characteristics of Management in Europe: Paths for the development of managers*, Brussels and Lyons, January.

Hagerty, B. (1990), 'Electrical storm: a reorganizing Philips plans 10,000 layoffs expects $1 billion loss', *Wall Street Journal*, 3 July.

Hagerty, B. (1990), 'A beleaguered Philips hastens to rethink the way it does business', *Wall Street Journal*, 18 December.

Hamel, G. and C. K. Prahalad (1985), 'Do you really have a global strategy?', *Harvard Business Review*, July–August, pp. 139–48.

Hingorani, S. G. (1992), 'IBM Corporation – company report', *Nomura Research Institute Europe Ltd*, 27 August.

Kehoe, L. and A. Cane (1993), 'A separation of powers', *Financial Times*, 19 January.

Levine, J. (1992), 'IBM's PC comeback could begin in Europe', *Business Week*, 19 October.

Levine, J. (1993), 'For IBM Europe, this is the year of truth', *Business Week*, 19 April.

Lorenz, C. (1993), 'Time to get serious', *Financial Times*, 25 June.

Mitchell, D. (1993), 'Reorganizing For Europe: effective low cost approaches', London: The Economist Intelligence Unit Ltd.

Prahalad, C. K. and Y. Doz (1981), 'An approach to strategic control in multinational companies', *Sloan Management Review*, 22 (4), pp. 5–13.

Prahalad, C. K. and Y. Doz (1987), *The Multinational Mission*, New York: The Free Press.

Quelch, J. A., R. D. Buzzell and E. R. Salma (1991), *The Marketing Challenge of Europe 1992*, Reading, Mass.: Addison Wesley.

Rapoport, C. (1992), 'How Barnekiv makes ABB work', *Fortune International*, 29 June.

Redger, I. (1993), 'ABB managers strip for action', and 'ABB restructures to strengthen competitiveness', *Financial Times*, 29 August.

Sellers, P. (1990), 'Coke's brash new European strategy', *Fortune*, 13 August.

Studer, M. (1993), 'ICI chief introduces firm's new strategy', *Wall Street Journal*, 8 July.

Studer, M. (1993), 'ABB plans major overhaul of management structure', *Wall Street Journal*, 25 August.

Subramanian, D. (1991), 'Colgate shift to Brussels aids profits in Europe', *International Herald Tribune*, 17 October.

Taft, N. (1993), 'UPS rethinks its deliveries of red ink from Europe', *Financial Times*, 15 June.

Taylor, W. (1991), 'The logic of global business: an interview with ABB's Percy Barnevik', *Harvard Business Review*, March–April, pp. 91–105.

Vanesse, M. (1993), 'Tandy Belgique tire sa révérence', *Le Soir*, 16 May.

Wortzel, H. L. (1989), 'Global strategies: standardization versus flexibility', *1989 International Business Strategy Resource Book*.

CHAPTER 5
Japanese subsidiaries: strengths and weaknesses

Etsuo Yoneyama

The high growth of Japanese direct investment in Europe in the 1980s has been considered both as a threat and as an opportunity – a threat of more direct competition in the European market, and an opportunity for job creation in the regions where Japanese production units were settled. The main concern of European policy-makers is the dominant logic and long-term behaviour of Japanese firms on the European scene: will they behave like insiders or just take positions inside 'Fortress Europe'? There is no simple answer to such a question: it depends on the industry and on the firm, and varies by country in the EC.

The case of the automobile industry serves as a good example here. The car manufacturing industry has significant induced effects on other sectors and on employment: it is estimated to represent around 4 million jobs and 7 per cent of the GNP of the EC. Thus Japanese entry to the industry in Europe is a major economic, social and political challenge. American manufacturers in Europe, such as Ford Europe and GM Europe (Vauxhall and Opel), are considered as insiders to such an extent that they participate in the European association of car manufacturers (ACEA), lobbying in Brussels for a limitation of Japanese sales in the EC! Under pressure from France and Italy an agreement was reached at the end of 1991 freezing Japanese car exports to the EC and monitoring the development of Japanese transplants in Europe so that their production would not exceed 1.2 million vehicles at the end of 1999. The diverging policies of the United Kingdom, with its openness to Japanese transplants, and France and Italy certainly was a source of tension within the EC.

Whether responding to constraints or pursuing a global strategy, Japanese firms dramatically increased their direct investments in Europe starting from 1985. This chapter first briefly analyzes Japanese direct investments across sectors and countries in Europe, the motivations behind these choices, and the management practices in Japanese subsidiaries, based on studies conducted by the Japanese External Trade Organization (JETRO). Then the main part of the chapter is built upon interviews with Japanese executives working in Europe in six firms representing diverse businesses (trade, financial services, electronics, mechanics, telecommunications and clothing). The interviews, conducted in 1992, aimed to uncover the problems

112

Japanese managers face on the European scene (cf. Group ESC Lyon study for the ERT).

1 Japanese direct investments in Europe

Japanese direct investments in Europe grew from US$1,982 million in the period 1982–4, to $7,876 million in the period 1985–7, and $26,566 million in the period 1988–90. After that peak, the decrease in 1991 was seen as momentary (JETRO, 1992a). Comparison with the level of US direct investments in Europe – $35,848 million (in the period 1988–90) – shows the relative importance of Japanese investments for the European Community. However, comparison with the amount of Japanese direct investments in the United States, $65,791 million in the period 1988–90 shows that North America still represented the main target for Japanese firms.

In Europe, the UK and the Netherlands attracted respectively 40 per cent and 23 per cent of the total of Japanese direct investments. Table 5.1 gives a more complete picture in terms of number of units (1991), total investments, subtotal of manufactured goods, and manpower employed (1991). Banks, finance, insurance and real estate represent two-thirds of total investments. As far as manufacturing is concerned, electric and electronic appliances represent 32.6 per cent and transportation equipment 16.7 per cent of the total.

Periodically the Japanese External Trade Organization conducts a study of the motivations of Japanese firms opening units in Europe. Among ten possible motivations, the 1992 study ranked the following as the first three:

1. Replace exportations by local production in order to profit from growing demand (Single European Market and Eastern Europe); score: 331;
2. Avoid trade restrictions and anti-dumping regulations which may increase with European integration; score: 251;
3. Improve adaptation to local customers' demands, including specific design; score: 166.

It was also found that, on average, 67 per cent of the sales of European Japanese subsidiaries are made in the country where it is established, and 29 per cent are made in other European countries. This leaves only 4 per cent as exports to other trade zones. Such figures and the results of the above study tend to demonstrate that the dominant logic of Japanese firms is to *gain market share* from within the attractive European market when it cannot be done from Japan.

Japanese investors in Europe seem to prefer to have 100 per cent control of their operations, and they achieved this in about 50 per cent of the cases studied, with the percentage growing since the 1980s. A higher level of financial control is found in the UK and in the Benelux, where for years governments have been favourable

Table 5.1 Japanese direct investments by country in Europe

	Number of units	Direct investments (cumulated 1951–91, $US million) Total	Manufactured goods	Manpower
United Kingdom	195	26,186	5,184	64,397
Netherlands	44	14,776	3,223	4,345
Germany	111	5,802	1,725	23,417
France	128	4,973	1,576	20,737
Spain	67	2,245	1,336	18,228
Belgium	39	1,941	609	9,986
Italy	47	1,222	472	4,620
Ireland	30	716	206 ⎫	
Portugal	14	192	119 ⎬	11,615
Luxembourg	3	5,873	105 ⎭	
Total	678	63,926	14,447	157,345

Sources: JETRO 1992b, Japanese Ministry of Finance, MITI (adapted by F. Sachwald, 1993).

to Japanese investments. However, joint ventures and cooperation agreements between major European and Japanese competitors developed in some capital and/or technology intensive sectors such as electronics, car manufacturing, pharmaceuticals and, more recently, aeronautics.

Bartlett and Ghoshal (1989) define the organization of Japanese companies world-wide as a 'centralized hub'. They compared Kao to Unilever and Procter & Gamble (in the cosmetics industry), NEC to ITT and Ericsson (in the telecommunications sector), and Matsushita to Philips and GE (in electronics). The 'centralized hub' appears to be typical of the Japanese administrative heritage. It is characterized by a centralization of assets, resources and responsibility; subsidiaries have less freedom to create new products or strategies. Bartlett and Ghoshal argue that with centralized decision-making and control, Japanese companies could retain their culturally dependent management system based on group-oriented behaviour.

Of course there are exceptions to this general rule. A more dynamic perspective shows that Japanese, American and European multinationals tend to converge slowly towards a form of 'integrated network' (Bartlett and Ghoshal, 1989); however, the respective administrative heritages have not been rubbed off yet.

Both the preferred strategy and the dominant organizational form adopted by Japanese companies contribute to giving them an image of 'outsiders'. Kenichi Ohmae (1990) vigorously criticized the 'headquarters mentality' and the 'non-equidistant' view of many globalizing companies. Getting rid of these certainly is a major challenge for Japanese multinationals in Europe. They may not be 'worse' than their American counterparts in this respect, but their strategic moves are more recent and as such more visible.

Cultural differences and language barriers may also contribute to form the image of Japanese companies as outsiders in many European countries. Cultural differences and language barriers may also make Japanese executives *feel* like outsiders. Simple things like 'the possibility of employing English speaking managers', of being 'in a relatively favourable cultural environment' (no anti-Japanese atmosphere) seem to be important in companies' choices of the host country, and partly explain the preference for the United Kingdom (see Dunning, 1986, and JETRO, 1991). Indeed, the steep cultural differences between Japanese management and management in Europe (discussed in Chapter 1) have led Japanese firms to limit the transfer of their home management practices to their European subsidiaries. Table 5.2 gives some results of a study conducted by the JETRO in 1992, which confirms the cultural dilemma for Japanese executives.

Among Japanese multinationals, Sony is considered one of the most advanced towards having a form of 'integrated network', in which global integration and local responsiveness are reconciled. Sony Europe is based in Germany (Kerne); television sets are manufactured in the UK, and the French subsidiary manufactures hi-fi, video and cassettes. A closer look at the organization of Sony France (1992) shows that the President was French and the Chief Executive was Japanese – the only Japanese on the board of directors. Among the 450 employees of Sony France, 7 Japanese had been sent by headquarters. The heads of the three production plants were French. Only 12 per cent of the 2000 employees were Japanese (mainly technicians). In an interview given to *France Japon Eco* (no. 45), Mr Watasaki, Chief Executive of Sony France, stated:

> For everything that has to do with France, we believe that it is better to rely on the French, who take the responsibility for their decisions. Of course the headquarters in Japan gives strategic guidelines and defines the objectives concerning products. The policy of the company is to ask

Table 5.2 The transfer of Japanese management practices in Japanese wholly owned subsidiaries in Europe.

Percentage of Japanese wholly owned subsidiaries in which the management practice is implemented	
Just in time	10.9
Lifelong employment	14.9
Promotion by seniority	4.6
Bonus	33.3
On-the-job training	69.9
Firm union	15.5
Quality circles	39.1
Daily general meeting	36.2
Morning physical exercise	5.2
Common cafeteria	68.4
Open ofifices	71.8
Evening events	79.3
Work uniforms	56.9

Source: JETRO, 1992a.

the Japanese to adapt themselves to the foreign context *and* to keep their Nippon concepts. However, decisions (wherever they come from: the headquarters or the subsidiary) are often interpreted differently. It takes a lot of time to regulate different interpretations between the headquarters and the French unit; it requires a constant dialogue.

We tried to integrate some of the positive aspects of each of the two cultures, such as the French egalitarian style in interpersonal relationships and the Japanese open offices... managers have the same working conditions as other employees.

As a French firm, we now re-invest our profits in France, whereas in the past they went to Japan. We want to contribute to the increase of the sales of good products in the world. We also want to create more jobs in France. We feel it is necessary to inform the public about the Japanese in general.

Some Japanese firms like Sony progressively move from an 'outsider' approach towards an 'insider' approach. However, some ambiguities still remain, and some difficulties related to the encounter between two different business cultures still have to be overcome. Indeed the loosely structured interviews we had with Japanese executives working in Europe confirmed that managing people is the key issue.

2 Japanese management in Europe: strengths and weaknesses

The European subsidiaries of Japanese companies are still trying to solve the dilemma of reconciling the Japanese and the European management styles. Most of their European operations are relatively recent, and their adaptation to local ways has not been achieved. In general the key managerial positions are taken by Japanese expatriates who do not have full mastery of the local language and the subtleties of the local culture. Nevertheless, they have to manage the local personnel of the subsidiaries. Cultural differences increase the complexity of their tasks.

Then why do they not recruit top, senior, and middle managers in the country where the company settles? The Japanese top managers we interviewed gave two reasons:

1. The Japanese headquarters themselves are not international.
2. It is hard to find European top managers who can fulfil this role.

Most of the Japanese senior managers in the Japanese headquarters do not speak fluent English and do not have significant international experience. They believe that recruiting European top managers for their subsidiaries could improve the effectiveness of the subsidiary (and would also cost less). But they are reluctant to do so because they fear that the communication between the subsidiary and the headquarters would be too difficult and that they would lose control. They say it is difficult to find European *senior* managers who speak fluent Japanese and deeply understand the Japanese style.

This looks like a vicious circle. The problem may be related to the newness of the situation. European universities and business schools only began teaching Japanese in the 1980s. More and more young graduates now can speak Japanese fluently, but they do not have enough experience yet to take senior management positions. The reverse is also true for young Japanese graduates.

As the Japanese promotion system works by seniority, it could take even more time before we find foreign managers in Japanese company headquarters. However, the internationalization of the headquarters in Japan seems to be a necessary condition for developing truly global companies (in the sense given by Ohmae, 1990). A first step in this direction would be to name European managers at the top of European subsidiaries, and then attract the best back to Japan. But again we are back to the vicious circle. It seems that it will take a long time before this issue is solved, unless trust replaces control.

The second issue is related to the transfer of Japanese management methods. The management of Japanese subsidiaries in Europe is the result of a stressful adaptation. The media have sometimes publicized the fact that the performance of Japanese transplants in Europe is superior to the performance of their European counterparts, and even in some cases superior to the performance of the plants in Japan. Such results show that in the domains of manufacturing – in both organization and quality – the transfer of Japanese practices in Europe has been achieved and proved successful. However, in the field of human resources management, Japanese firms only grafted some of their practices; they were forced to adapt to local practices. Japanese management in Europe is now mixed: half Japanese and half European. The challenge now is to become more effective in managing people and dealing with cultural differences.

Japanese expatriates in Europe

Europe is a patchwork of different countries with different languages and cultures. It looks quite complex to the Japanese expatriates. By contrast Japan is an isolated island populated by a single race. It was never invaded and ethnic groups or races never mixed with the locals. Such a high ethnic and cultural homogeneity helped Japan to maintain its traditions, but it did not prepare the Japanese to coexist happily with foreigners or to live in a different cultural context. The Japanese expatriates have to deal with language and cultural obstacles in Europe. Even if they speak English well, they have to adapt to several other languages and business cultures across the continent. It seems much easier for them in the vast North American market and also in Asia, which is geographically, racially and culturally close to Japan.

Because of its history, Japan was in close contact with the United States for about 50 years after World War II. Trade flows and cultural flows developed earlier than with Europe. The American way of life and typical American products pervaded Japan and were welcomed by a majority of Japanese in search of a modern culture and style. By comparison, during the first 30 years after the war Japan did not exchange much with Europe. Trade flows and direct investments from Japan started to increase in the mid-1980s. Now about 60 000 Japanese expatriates work in Europe. The increase in numbers has been steep and recent – too quick and too new to be handled properly.

Four factors stand out:

First, there is a lack of competent Japanese personnel who could take positions in Europe; a lack of experience of European markets, because of limited trade flows; a small number of students of European languages (except English); and few young Japanese graduates or managers come to study in Europe (for instance for MBAs). Japanese exports towards Europe represent 18 per cent of total Japanese exports, and imports from Europe represent only 13 per cent. Japanese newspapers and TVs do not pay much attention to Europe. Students start to study French, German, or Spanish only when they are at the university.

Some firms send young Japanese managers to Europe for about two years: the first year to study the language and the second year to study management. When they return to Japan, they may be transferred to the headquarters, which lack knowledge of European markets. They may also be transferred to any department in order to continue their long-term integration in the company through job rotation.

Second, the process of expatriation is often hurried and, as a consequence, the preparation is insufficient. Some of the Japanese managers we interviewed felt personally that they were not prepared enough to do their first job abroad in Europe. Their English was not fluent enough, and they did not have time to improve it before they began their job. Many Japanese firms do not organize any significant training prior to expatriation. Some even believe that technical knowledge is enough to succeed abroad. In the Japanese tradition, training is achieved on the job. Exceptions to this rule can be found in some sectors, such as electronics, banking and trade (Sogo-Shosha), where the international network is strong enough to provide opportunities of stays abroad and skills for specific training. In short, it appears that Japanese firms do not have a well-organized international management of human resources, especially if they have to act under limited time constraints.

Third, the term of the expatriation creates a dilemma. Generally the expatriation period is supposed to last from three to six years. The first three years are seen as stressful: the expatriates try to adapt themselves to the host country, improve their language skills, but are not fully effective yet. They work abroad but think about their return to the Japanese headquarters. The Japanese as a whole are very concerned with the education of their children, especially when they are getting close to the age for highly selective exams. As a consequence, many Japanese managers prefer to move abroad alone for a three-year period. On the other hand, the managers who agree to stay for six years start to like their lives in the foreign country and want to stay longer. The wives adapt themselves well and start working in the host country. Then the couple enjoy a higher standard of living than they could have in Japan and they do not want to return any more. In order to avoid such a scenario, a few companies give a salary to the wife so that she stays at home.

Japanese expatriates also worry about their career and the reintegration when they come back to Japan, particularly as human relationships are crucial in a Japanese firm. The expatriate may become a foreigner in his own firm, and fail to reintegrate in the group. On top of these problems, the United States and Europe may not be perceived by Japanese managers as that attractive any more. As the standard of living has risen in Japan, intercontinental holidays fulfil the dreams to discover occidental countries.

Fourth, and most of all, expatriates face problems of adaptation related to the cultural gap between Japan and Europe. Due to their insulation for 2000 years, the Japanese shaped a very original character which can be roughly described in the following way:

- Group spirit.
- Introversion.
- Sentimental.
- A respect for elders.
- Consensus.
- Meticulousness.

Such characteristics are opposed to many European characteristics:

- Individualism.
- Extroversion.
- Logical.
- Equality between generations.
- Acceptance of the diversity of opinions.
- Approximation.

The Japanese expatriates have to live with such differences; in particular, they have to tolerate individualism and learn how to argue. One Japanese in three has serious adaptation problems. The main source of the problems is their introvert character. When a Japanese meets difficulties in work, he interiorizes the tension, becoming stressed, frustrated and depressed. His work relations suffer from the frustration and his effectiveness decreases. In turn, unsatisfactory results will increase the stress, particularly as Japanese have a high sense of responsibility towards their company. As a consequence, the Japanese manager may have to give up his mission. Indeed in such cases the company should (and generally does) repatriate him quickly.

Such problems could be minimized if Japanese companies would select candidates for expatriation according to their personality and not only according to their skills. In particular, they should select managers who are more extrovert, open to the diversity of opinions, and ready to argue in their work relationships.

Cultural conflicts

Japanese managers are surprised by the top–down mode of management in European firms.

Top–down decision-making

European managers are seen as excessively authoritarian in giving orders to subordinates. The heads of small and medium-sized businesses are perceived as the 'locomotive' of the firm, often directly involved in commercial negotiations. Such a top–down approach contrasts with the bottom–up approach in most Japanese companies.

In the Japanese firm, the locus of decisions is at the level of middle managers ('Kachô') the heads of departments, who are between 35 and 45 years old. The middle managers are the locomotives of the firm, and it is they who initiate and develop projects. First, they consult the heads of several services and lower levels in the hierarchy in order to test the idea and improve the project before making it public; this is the 'Nemawashi' process in order to build consensus. Then the middle managers consult the senior managers to whom they report, using an official form: the 'Ringisho'. This form circulates among all the managers concerned with the project in order to get their approval. It then goes to the top manager. After agreement and signature by the top manager, the 'Ringisho' is returned to the middle manager who initiated the project. Implementation may then begin, but if anyone disagrees, the project must be amended and the revised 'Ringisho' must circulate again.

In Europe as well there is sometimes a process similar to the 'Nemawashi'. However, circulation is confined, a smaller number of people are involved in the process and it seldom includes workers; the view of senior management dominates. The Japanese decision-making process certainly takes more time, but it prevents mistakes and eases implementation. Japanese managers in Europe feel sorry for European middle managers and supervisors 'who are always watching out for signs from the boss'. In Japanese firms the boss is highly respected but seldom feared. He takes care of external relations with stakeholders and leaves middle managers free to develop their talents. As a consequence, Japanese managers in Europe find it difficult to play the role expected by their personnel and to cope with their responsibilities.

Heavy responsibilities

Japanese managers are surprised by the heavy responsibilities put on European managers; top managers are under pressure from the company's shareholders, who can dismiss them if profits decrease. Japanese top managers are less dependent on shareholders. For instance, in the Keiretsus, share swaps make shareholders interdependent, thus giving executives more freedom and time.

European managers are also seen as powerful, making decisions and communicating them to their subordinates. Japanese managers find it difficult to explain their strategies and decisions to local European managers. First, because the Japanese educational system stresses teamwork and neglects individual communication skills, and second because the language barrier makes communication even more difficult. They also have problems with the speed of decision-making: being accustomed to the 'Nemawashi' and 'Ringi' processes, they seldom give a quick answer to an issue raised by local managers. They consult headquarters in Japan before making a decision. Their European colleagues sometimes interpret this behaviour as a lack of power and assertiveness, and show signs of what Japanese bosses see to be contempt.

Vertical organizations

The Japanese are also challenged by the vertical organization they find in the European firms they have taken over. Each department is seen as relatively autonomous, and depends on its boss according to a well-determined hierarchical order. No one from outside a department may intervene in it without getting the agreement of the department head, which is seen as a major rigidity.

In Japan communication between units is much more direct. Information is shared – it is a common intangible asset – whereas in Europe information is an asset owned by each service (which derives some of its power from it). The Japanese work in large open offices where it is easier to get information from others. Europeans consider individual offices as a normal privilege for managers who should not be disturbed by neighbours. The Japanese, however, are convinced that working in open offices is much more effective for the following reasons:

- It creates a family atmosphere.
- It stimulates team spirit.
- It improves vertical and horizontal reciprocal information.
- It helps the observation of subordinates.

Some Japanese managers in Europe do not mind changing to individual offices, some of them even like it. However, many suffer from feelings of isolation when they move.

Contracts

Europe is seen as a society based on contracts, whereas Japanese society is based on trust. Japanese expatriates are astonished to find contracts necessary for hiring employees and dealing with suppliers and clients. They think writing contracts is a waste of time. In Japan there is no contract when hiring someone. When there is a dispute, very few people engage in a lawsuit. In business relationships contracts are considered to be a mere matter of form and much less important than the atmosphere of the relationship. Japanese business people take great care in strengthening human links; they spend a lot of time meeting their suppliers, their clients and their peers. Adaptation to European practices is not easy, but the Japanese do protect themselves against breach of trust. When in Europe, they start using contracts and they hire lawyers.

Class differences within the firm

One of the Japanese managers we interviewed told us that he started his career in Europe as a deputy director of a plant. He did not know anything about the French tradition of class differences within the firm. A couple of weeks after his arrival he went to visit the plant and wore overalls. The French workers looked at him with such open surprise and suspicion that he felt embarrassed for the whole day, and since then has never worn overalls when visiting the plant.

European engineers seldom visit workshops, whereas Japanese engineers visit them frequently as they are more concerned with quality all along the production chain. There are exceptions in Europe, but in many countries the Japanese perceive deep status differences between white-collar and blue-collar workers, in spite of the fact that individuals from the two categories talk to each other in a quite egalitarian manner. In Japan status and salary differences are both narrower.

The vertical organization of European firms raises barriers between the categories of personnel. According to the Japanese system of promotion by seniority, young graduates start their careers at the lowest level. They work in the plant or in the yards for several months or several years before being promoted. Engineers are qualified after several years of work, not just after their graduation from university. Such differences are sources of misunderstandings. At the very least they require a delay for the adaptation of individuals to their new context.

The Japanese are also surprised by many other aspects of business life in Europe: the specific claims of women at work, the length of meals, the reluctance of employees to work overtime, the haughty attitude of powerful suppliers... all these cultural differences require individuals with the capacity to adapt themselves, and that adaptation can take a long time. It is recommended that experienced expatriates should work alongside newcomers. Experienced expatriates in the subsidiary can also help other Japanese expatriates who come for shorter periods.

Problems in managing human resources

According to the Japanese managers we interviewed, the management of human resources is crucial to the success of the Japanese subsidiary in Europe.

The Japanese HR style has to be adapted

The Japanese style of managing human resources is considered a major factor in the success of Japanese firms after the war. But the management of people certainly is the hardest thing to transfer across countries and cultures. Japanese practices in this domain focus on six factors:

1. Recruiting young people just after they finish their studies.
2. In-house training.
3. Internal job rotation.
4. Promotion by seniority.
5. Lifelong employment.
6. Company unions.

Several constraints impede their transfer to Europe and the six factors are only applied to Japanese expatriates in European subsidiaries. Other personnel are managed according to a different set of practices, which is closer to that of the host country. Understanding the constraints explains the duality.

Recruiting young graduates

In Japan, firms prefer to recruit young graduates because they are still 'manageable': they will be integrated more easily into the community and trained in-house according to the specific needs of the company. The recruitment is considered as a very long-term investment. Several constraints impede the transfer of this practice:

- The links between European schools and universities and Japanese companies are not strong enough.
- Many of the subsidiaries are too small to generate a regular flow of recruitment.
- There is no necessity to adopt lifelong employment.
- The system of promotion by seniority does not work.
- The mobility of European personnel is relatively high.

In-house training

In-house training is highly developed in Japanese companies. Human resources are considered as *the* key factor of success and lifelong employment with proven very low mobility justifies high intangible long-term investments in training.

Since the mobility of personnel is much higher in Europe, Japanese subsidiaries are reluctant to invest in training their European staff. After having been trained, Europeans are often tempted to look for another job quickly, seeking a promotion in another firm, so why invest in them?

Job rotation

In Japanese firms job rotation is widely used in order to help recruits to get to know a variety of jobs, and to create a large network of interpersonal relationships throughout the firm. Such networks are essential to succeed in a managerial position: companies require managers to have experienced at least three functions in different departments before they are promoted. By comparison, in many European countries diplomas are often specialized and people prefer to follow the specialization which corresponds to their training and experience. It is also difficult to convince managers to go against the usual European entry and promotion route.

Promotion by seniority

In Japan the differences between salaries are narrow at the beginning of a career. Promotion by seniority is fully consistent with a step-by-step approach and a group orientation (as opposed to an individual orientation). Most of the European educational systems produce a hierarchy of diplomas and a career is based on the diploma and the effectiveness of the individuals. At least in the private sector, it would be inconsistent to transfer management by seniority to Europe.

Lifelong employment

Lifelong employment fits perfectly with the other components of the Japanese management system. But do Europeans want lifelong employment in a Japanese firm? Also, are they ready to accept the other elements of the system? The answer is unclear. Many European managers and technicians in Japanese subsidiaries leave the firm after three years and sell their skills to competitors. For the Japanese three years is the necessary time frame for training! The relatively high turnover of their European managers and skilled work-force is seen as a major problem by the senior managers we interviewed.

Company unions

Finally, Japanese subsidiaries can sometimes ignore the labour union tradition of the host country, but they cannot go against it. Under such constraints, as far as management of the European personnel is concerned, Japanese subsidiaries generally tend to adopt the system of the host country, so as to avoid inconsistencies and cultural clashes.

The slow Europeanization of top management teams

The picture differs from one firm to another, and from one sector to another. For instance, in trade subsidiaries (Sogo-Shosha) the percentage of Japanese in key positions is higher than in the manufacturing sectors. Moreover, the percentage of Japanese managers in key positions is much higher in wholly owned subsidiaries founded by Japanese than in firms which have been taken over.

We have already discussed some of the reasons why Japanese expatriates still take most of the key positions in European subsidiaries:

1. The Japanese headquarters lack international experience and are reluctant to communicate in a foreign language,
2. There are few Europeans who speak fluent Japanese, fully understand the subtleties of Japanese management, and are experienced enough to take senior management positions.

As a consequence, in order to guarantee good communication between the headquarters and the subsidiary, senior management positions are given to Japanese expatriates. It will take time before the vicious circle is broken, as the Japanese promotion system is based on seniority. Two additional reasons should be noted:

1. The temptation for Japanese firms to use expatriation for 'on-the-job training', giving Japanese managers the chance to start their international career by taking senior management positions in a foreign subsidiary.
2. The conservatism and lack of trust of some top managers in the headquarters.

The expectations of Japanese headquarters concerning the senior management of their European subsidiaries may also tend to discourage European candidates. First, the Japanese do not tolerate approximations and errors: they will look for the origin of an error until they find it, even if it is of no importance – just for the sake of it. A European would easily forget or overlook a small error and would get annoyed if someone forced him or her to correct it. Second, the word 'responsibility' is not understood with the same intensity by a Japanese and by a European. A Japanese manager would sacrifice his private life to fulfil his responsibility for the subsidiary. The Japanese believe that most Europeans would hesitate to do so. They may be right.

The slow Europeanization of top management teams frustrates many European managers in Japanese subsidiaries. The frustration partly explains the relatively high mobility of European managers. Chief executives give the following explanations:

● The young European managers think that their careers are blocked by the Japanese senior managers above them.

- Important decisions are made by the Japanese in contact with their headquarters.
- Most of the research and development is carried out in Japan.
- In the end, European managers have little responsibility, or their responsibilities remain ambiguous.

Frustrated by any of the four reasons mentioned above, European managers may resign. On the other hand, European workers seem to value the Japanese management style and they demonstrate much higher loyalty. The Japanese priority given to the workshop and the egalitarian view of white- and blue-collar workers, 'cadres' and 'non-cadres' is very well accepted. Workers feel that they are important for and to the company: they participate in product quality improvements and productivity gains through the 'Teian' system of idea generation and the 'Kaizen' system of incremental improvements.

As far as management is concerned, the general trend is towards more Europeans in the top and senior management positions, especially at the heads of the sales force and the personnel department, which are in most contact with local populations. But the evolution is slow.

The transfer of business policies

The previous section showed that the Japanese still have to learn how to manage international managers effectively. However, most of the typical Japanese business policies and techniques have been successfully transferred to their European subsidiaries. These include long-term thinking, customer service, top quality, priority to manufacturing, and horizontal integration.

Long-term perspective

Japanese top managers are less constrained by short-term profitability objectives than managers in the West; they generally manage by long-term strategic intent. They also take a long-term perspective when they head European subsidiaries. Japanese firms generally start their business in Europe with a small investment. As they become more familiar with the market they establish a network of relationships with suppliers and clients and in the following stage they widen the network. While Europeans would tend to write a business plan when launching a business abroad (at least to please their bankers), the Japanese are happy without a business plan. They have a concrete and pragmatic approach: they try to adapt to the opportunities and to problems when they arise. They refuse to rigidify the development of the subsidiary from the beginning.

Japanese subsidiaries in Europe have flexible objectives which are in line with the strategic intent and are considered as incentives. They do not give up on these easily: when the financial results are not good, they try harder. The dominant goal is to grow and gain market share. This philosophy seems to fit well with their

European subsidiaries: European managers and business partners appreciate it. Indeed, many European companies which are not too dependent on their shareholders are also managed with a long-term perspective, and tend to loosen their planning procedures.

Service to clients

The business strategies of the Japanese give a priority to clients in terms of the quality of their products and services. They take great care of the quality of their contacts with customers, delivery times, packaging and merchandising, and after-sales services. The Groupe ESC Lyon study for the European Round Table has shown that engineers tend to dominate marketers in many European countries (cf. Chapter 2); European firms still lag behind as far as service is concerned. Although more and more European managers are convinced that improving service is a powerful competitive weapon, they may have problems in *implementing* service strategies. Japanese companies in Europe apply their skills in this domain without facing much resistance: customers certainly appreciate superior service (as long as the price differential is not too high), and employees try to do their best (as long as they are trained). For instance, in the automobile industry Japanese firms in Europe were the first to offer a three-year guarantee and free repair to customers. Other competitors followed.

Top quality

Japanese customers have the reputation for being the most demanding in the world in terms of product quality (level of performance *and* no defect). Japanese business strategies are based on product quality, both in the home market and the foreign markets they target. They also developed superior skills in *implementing* quality, as customer surveys and studies by the Massachusetts Institute of Technology prove in the automobile industry. When the Japanese import foreign products, they meticulously check every single detail. They may repaint a whole car because there is a small scratch. Sophisticated European customers are certainly also attracted by quality. European managers are convinced that product quality (no defect) is crucial, and European workers have nothing against good work. In such a favourable context, Japanese subsidiaries in Europe did not have much difficulty in implementing their quality strategies.

Priority to manufacturing and to the workshops

Quality originates in the workshops. That is why Japanese managers often visit them. Many managers have a technical background, and many started their career as a workshop technician. With the exception of Germany, in European firms, manufacturing is often less prestigious than marketing, R & D or finance. Therefore

European technicians and blue-collar workers in Japanese subsidiaries welcomed the attention paid to their function, and Japanese skills in this area were easily transferred to Europe.

Horizontal integration and group work

In their wholly owned European subsidiaries, the Japanese organized horizontal coordination through project groups in order to achieve integration between marketing, sales, research and development and manufacturing. Implementation of horizontal organization is made more complex when geographical distances increase and when the European subsidiary has been taken over, but in general Japanese senior managers consider that the transfer to Europe was successful.

Group work and team spirit are the bases of Japanese management. Group work requires team spirit in order to be effective. In Japan, the head of a service, workshop or branch brings people together, he or she does not 'manage' in the Western style. In their European subsidiaries the Japanese try to transfer group work but team spirit is sometimes missing. European individualism is often stronger, especially among managers. Nevertheless, managers are encouraged to socialize with employees, visit workshops, talk and listen to their subordinates. Open offices are generally preferred and at least accepted. Evening events and weekend excursions are also organized, but they seem to have limited success.

Networking

The 'Keiretsu' is the ultimate form of multiple cooperation with suppliers and clients. Even when they do not belong to a Keiretsu, Japanese firms tend to form a network with their partners in the value chain. They also cooperate with their competitors in joint projects and in powerful industry associations which negotiate with the MITI (Ministry of International Trade and Industry). Networking is a typical Japanese strategy. How do they apply it in Europe? The subsidiary naturally belongs to the network of the mother company, but does it develop its own network in the host countries?

Relationships with European suppliers are not the same as in Japan. During the last eight years Japanese firms invested heavily in Europe in order to gain access to an attractive market. They now manufacture their products in local 'transplants'. In order to get a manufacturing label they *must* buy at least 60 per cent locally manufactured components which forces Japanese companies to strengthen their relationships with European suppliers.

Japanese managers perceive a deep difference between the links they have with suppliers in Japan and the links they have with suppliers in Europe. The size of many European suppliers is bigger, making it difficult to secure exclusive relationships (as often exist in the Japanese Keiretsu). In Japan, manufacturers collaborate with their suppliers on the development of components, and the suppliers draw up the industrial plan (a system called 'design in'). Suppliers are also responsible for the components they produce until the manufacturing of the product or system is achieved. On the other hand European suppliers prefer to remain independent from their clients and cooperative relationships are harder to establish.

Japanese suppliers do their best to maintain low production costs and low prices, whereas European suppliers often raise their prices without consulting their clients beforehand. European suppliers are less reliable than their Japanese counterparts as far as delivery times are concerned. They treat their clients as equals whereas the Japanese suppliers show more humility. In brief the Japanese find it difficult to work with European suppliers. The biggest Japanese manufacturers in Europe react by training their European suppliers to improve their technical performance and by creating a cooperative atmosphere and more stable effective partnerships.

Relationships with European clients are not considered satisfactory either. Japanese managers in Europe are puzzled when their European clients do not pay in time. They have to fight to get paid, and have to manage the tensions and sometimes the antagonisms.

In Japan, supplier–client relationships are viewed as a harmonious positive-sum game between partners. Mutual trust is the basis of long-term relationships. As suppliers feel responsible for their products, their clients do not have to control them. The 'Kanban' system (just-in-time) only became possible in a context of mutual trust and long-term partnerships. European clients, on the other hand, often change suppliers in order to get better prices. Japanese expatriates feel they do not have the necessary skills to manage relationships with their European clients. They feel they cannot manage the tensions successfully and have difficulties in adapting themselves to the European mentality. The language barrier is another reason why Japanese subsidiaries prefer to hire local sales managers and local sales people.

Relationships with public authorities. Japanese subsidiaries in Europe mainly cooperate with European public authorities in preparing and implementing the layouts of their factories. Given the problem of unemployment, European regions compete with each other to attract investments, including those by the Japanese. In this area government policies differ across Europe, for instance in the protection of national firms and the level of local content imposed on the Japanese transplant. There can be inconsistencies between national policies and local regional policies, which show local authorities as more favourable to Japanese investments. And generally Japanese companies tend to focus on the relationships with local/regional authorities. However, these companies seem to involve themselves much less in networking with public authorities than they do in Japan.

Relationships with competitors vary between extremes. When cooperation with a European competitor is at the basis of the creation of a Japanese subsidiary in Europe, by definition the cooperation is strong and selective. In all other cases Japanese subsidiaries do not involve themselves much in the industry network of competitors. In this respect their attitude is different from the attitude of the mother company at home. In Japan, there is stiff competition between firms in the same industry, but at the industry level professional association is generally very active. Japanese managers tend to think that the reverse is true in Europe. Moreover, they feel that they are not welcome in the industry networks and that locals firms perceive them as invaders. As a result the Japanese subsidiaries in Europe belong to the network of the mother company more than to the local network.

This leads to a broader conclusion on the practice of networking by Japanese subsidiaries in Europe: they seem to have difficulties in developing their strategies in the European environment, get discouraged, and mainly rely upon the Japanese network. One of the top managers we interviewed commented: 'It takes decades to become an insider.'

3 Some conclusions

The interviews we had with top managers of Japanese subsidiaries in Europe showed that the transfer of Japanese business policies and techniques was successful: long-term strategic intent, service to clients, top quality, priority to the workshop and horizontal integration all fitted the European context and culture and were sources of superior competitiveness. Group work was not as easy to transfer given European individualism. Developing partnerships with suppliers and clients proved to be difficult in the European context, where the supplier–client relationship is often viewed as a zero-sum game. As a consequence Japanese subsidiaries in Europe feel more comfortable in the network of the mother company at home.

Japanese subsidiaries had to adapt the management of their human resources to Europe. The Japanese system for managing human resources is a consistent whole: 'You cannot adopt one practice and leave out the others.' Given the deep differences between the two business cultures, particularly in terms of mobility of staff, the Japanese tend to manage Europeans in the European way. European technical and blue-collar workers are quite happy with the Japanese style, which values their contribution. On the other hand European managers are suspicious of the slow Europeanization of top management teams. Indeed, the gaps between the two business cultures and language differences are sources of frustration for both the Japanese expatriates and the European managers.

Managing managers has become the crucial challenge for Japanese subsidiaries in Europe. Several guidelines may be suggested:

● Improve the selection of Japanese expatriates, choosing them according to personality profiles and not only professional competence.
● Improve the preparation of Japanese expatriates.
● Improve the conditions of their reintegration to the headquarters back in Japan.

- Create good career plans for both Japanese and European managers.
- Manage by tandem (teaming a Japanese and a European) and intensify language training for both during a transitory period.
- Speed up the promotion process in the international subsidiaries, naming Europeans at the head of European subsidiaries.
- Internationalize the headquarters by having Japanese staff with international experience and employing foreigners.

All of this sounds like good sense. However, the four last points may go against the tendency to control from the centre which exists in many Japanese corporations. Ultimately, the whole transformation of European subsidiaries of Japanese companies is dependent on the personalities and philosophy of the top management team at the Japanese headquarters.

References

Bartlett, C. A. and S. Ghoshal (1989), *Managing Across Borders: The Transnational Solution*, Boston, Mass.: Harvard Business School Press.
Dunning, J. H. (1986), *Japanese Participation in British Industry*, London: Routledge.
Japanese External Trade Organization (1991), *Current Management Situation of Japanese Manufacturing Enterprises in Europe*, 6th Survey Report, Tokyo: JETRO.
Japanese External Trade Organization (1992a), *White Paper on Foreign Direct Investment 1992*, Tokyo: JETRO.
Japanese External Trade Organization (1992b), *8th Survey of European Operations of Japanese Companies in the Manufacturing Sector*, Tokyo: JETRO.
Ohmae, K. (1990), *The Borderless World, Power and Strategy in the Interlinked Economy*, London: HarperCollins.
Sachwald, F. (ed.) (1993), *Les Entreprises Japonaises en Europe, motivations et stratégies*, Travaux et Recherches de l'IFRI, Paris: Masson.

Complementary bibliography

Callies, A. (1986), *France–Japon, confrontation culturelle dans les entreprises mixtes*, Paris: Librairie des Méridiens.
Hayashi, K. (1990), *Global Kigyo No Kaigai Genchika Senryaku*, Toyko: PHP Kenkyujo (translation: The strategies of local adaptation in global companies).
Ikawa, T. (1987), *Kokusaika Jidai No Kaigai Chyuzaiin*, Tokyo: Yuhikaku Business (translation: Japanese expatriates in the internationalization process).
Macklon, C. (1991), *Nihonjin No Boss*, Tokyo: Soshishya (translation: Japanese boss: English worker).

Yoshihara, H. (1989), *Genchijin Shyatyo To Uchinaru Kokusaika*, Tokyo: Tokyo Keizai (translation: Local presidents and the internationalization of headquarters).

Yoshihara, H., K. Hayashi and K. Yasumuro (1990), *Nihon Kigyo No Global Keiei*, Tokyo: Toyo Keizai Shinposhya (translation: Global management in Japanese companies).

CHAPTER 6

German management: at the interface between Eastern and Western Europe

Peter Lawrence

The two German states that were reunified in 1990 were the product of World War II. Both their political and economic format were the result of Germany's defeat in 1945 and of developments in the early post-war period.

The areas that became the two German states, in popular parlance East Germany and West Germany, had begun to diverge even before the end of the war in May 1945. West Germany was conquered by the Americans and the British, with a spirited contribution from the French in the south. East Germany was primarily conquered by the Russians, although both the British and Americans originally occupied parts of what were to become the Russian Zone and later East Germany. By the time the Russian and American armies met at Torgau on the Upper Elbe in April 1945 it was clear that there would be neither harmony nor unity in post-war Germany.

The pattern of conquest indicated above was both confirmed and rationalized by the victorious Allies meeting in the Cecilienhof hunting lodge in Potsdam, southwest of Berlin. The three Western occupation zones – American, British and French – were at least united in that the three countries were all committed to parliamentary democracy and free enterprise capitalism, and especially in the case of Britain and the United States, had a sustained record of working with each other. Even the French, whose occupation zone policy was the most idiosyncratic (Willis, 1962) eventually came into line (as a result of American pressure and funding) and first common economic policies and then a new common currency (the Deutschmark) were adopted for the Western zones.

Russia, however, was neither democratic nor capitalist, and was committed to an economic system and political ideology that were anathemas to the West. For most of the period after 1917 when the communists came to power Russia, or more properly the USSR, had been isolated, economically and culturally. Even from 1941 onwards when the three countries – Britain, Russia, and the USA – all found themselves on the same side fighting against Nazi Germany, the Russians always kept their distance. The plaque by the side of the Elbe bridge at Torgau is in Russian (and in German as a reminder to the defeated); there is no English inscription, and the Americans get a less than fulsome mention!

Four years after the war ended Russia and the former Western Allies created their rival German states: in September 1949 the three Western occupation zones became the Federal Republic of Germany (FRG) while in October 1949 the Russians turned their zone into the German Democratic Republic (GDR). The former was largely independent, speedily integrated into the Western economic system, and eventually into NATO – the West's military alliance. The GDR on the other hand was far from independent, but was of course integrated into the communist economic system of COMECON and into the Warsaw Pact alliance.

And so it remained until the heady events in the summer of 1989. Two states, divided by economic system and ideology, as well as by one of the most awesome land frontiers the world has ever seen. Yet there are other more subtle differences. While East Germany eventually achieved some economic pre-eminence within the Eastern bloc it was always outshone by West Germany. East Germany became the doctrinaire and unloved client state of the USSR, West Germany became the successful exemplar of free enterprise capitalism. East Germany was semi-invisible to the West, especially after the building of the Berlin Wall in 1961; only a few East European specialists knew much about the GDR, either as economy or society. West Germany on the other hand was unavoidably high profile. Early on it became clear that it had recovered economically from war and defeat; shortly after the Korean War (1950–2) the FGR achieved a positive trade balance – and kept it up for decades. In the 1970s the easy period of world economic expansion that the French call 'les trentes glorieuses' started to falter, and has never been resumed in an unbroken way. Again this development served to cast West Germany even more into the role of 'economic hero' country. The world might go into a recession, inflation rates might rise dramatically, but whatever happened elsewhere it never seemed to be as bad in West Germany. Unemployment rates in the FGR never rose to the extent they did elsewhere! Whatever happened, it seemed, West Germany's low inflation rates and enormous trade surpluses would continue for ever.

From the mid-1970s at least, until the late 1980s, West Germany was a country people were interested in, wanted to look at. People wanted to know what was different about West Germany, how had they achieved the original economic miracle, and how had they sustained their economic performance? We will make these questions our focus for the next few pages.

1 The rise of West Germany

In the early months of 1945 a joke circulated in Germany: 'Enjoy the war while you can, the peace will be awful when it comes!' And so it was to be. In the 'peacetime' period of 1945–8 ordinary Germans suffered as they had never done during the war itself. The problems in and after 1945 were severe.

'Die stunde null'

First there was the question of the physical destruction of Germany, primarily the result of Allied bombing. American secret service reports dating from 1945 put the destruction of the centres of the larger towns at 75 per cent plus (Borsdorf and Niethammer, 1977): heaps of rubble, impassable indeed unrecognizable streets, water available only from standpipes, no gas or electricity, no public transport, no street lighting. Thousands of recently liberated foreign workers, the slave-labourers of the Third Reich, roamed the desolate streets in search of loot and alcohol; people stealing from damaged homes, people trundling their possessions in prams and wheelbarrows, people waiting, people queuing – for food, for goods, for travel permits from the occupation authorities, for news of missing family members. This is what it was like.

Second, homelessness, exacerbated by overcrowding, was an intractable problem. In the first few months of peace most Germans in big city urban areas lived in cellars, in remains of their, or someone else's, former homes. In a small way the problem was made worse by the endless requisitioning of buildings and accommodation by the occupation authorities, measures that produced acute resentment. And in a big way the solution in the Western Zones was made very much worse by the influx of people from elsewhere. There were four streams of people coming into the Western Zones:

1. People from the east fleeing before the Red Army in 1944–5.
2. Refugees from the Russian Zone and later from the GDR itself, a phenomenon that only really ceased with the building of the Berlin Wall in 1961.
3. Returning prisoners of war; prisoners of war from the USSR were still returning/being released, in their thousands, well into the 1950s.
4. The expellees or 'Heimatsvertriebenen' (people driven out of their homeland) as a result of territorial changes at the end of the War, namely: East Prussia being divided between Poland and the USSR; Poland moving its border westwards up to the line of the Oder-Neisse rivers; Czechoslovakia expelling the Sudeten Germans and expanding its territory up to the natural frontiers.

The last of these four sources of refugees is the more important. Something like 2.4 million Sudeten Germans were expelled, and the territorial changes involving Poland saw the expulsion of another 5 million. Not all of these made for the Western occupation zones, but most did.

Third was the breakdown of normal economic activity at the end of the war. The Nazi government had simply printed a lot of money to pay for the war. This did not matter too much so long as there was substantial production and output together with rent, wage and price controls. But with the end of the war the most productive activity ceased, at least temporarily, and the provision of services was also conspicuous by its absence. This, crossed with an overabundant money supply naturally led to inflation. In the former great inflation of the early 1920s prices had risen astronomically but the currency was still legal, albeit in very large denominations. In the inflation at the end of World War II, however, ordinary people very largely abandoned the use of the discredited Reichsmark and resorted either to barter or to the use of cigarettes as alternative currency units.

Fourth, within a few months of the end of the war the food shortage was serious. Throughout the late 1940s undernourishment and malnutrition were widespread, and so were all the illnesses associated with them. The TB rate rose dramatically; there was an upsurge of all the bowel and stomach infections – typhoid, typhus, cholera; the death rate climbed, the marriage rate sank (except that marriage to members of the occupying forces was seen as very attractive); and the infant mortality rate rose.

These in outline were the problems that beset Germany in the post-war period. Yet by the mid-1950s in West Germany all these problems save the housing shortage had been solved. The currency was stable, manufacturing industry was booming, and there was a substantial trade surplus. This suggests two related questions. First, what happened; how was this epic of reconstruction achieved? And second, did the Germans do it themselves, or did someone else do it for them?

Helping the Germans

To start with a paradoxical consideration, some of the material destruction and expropriation inflicted on the Western Zones by the victorious Allies led to a measure of plant and technology renewal which was to West Germany's later advantage and contributed to that country's industrial success.

Towards the end of the war US Secretary Henry Morgenthau promulgated what he termed the pastoralization policy for Germany; the country was to be forcibly deindustralized and obliged to revert to being largely a farming society. To this end ambitious lists of industries and companies that were candidates for dismantling were compiled. In the event, these lists were successively revised downwards and ultimately the grand total of factories dismantled in the three Western Zones was a modest 668, representing according to the leading authority on the Occupation Period (Piettre, 1952), a reduction in total industrial capacity of 8 per cent (the figure for the Russian Zone is much higher).

If we add to this 8 per cent the loss of industrial capacity that resulted from the cumulative effect of Allied bombing, some 15 to 20 per cent for Germany as a whole (and an estimated 25 per cent for the Ruhr) then we can see that the Western Zones lost something approaching a quarter of their industrial capacity. This destroyed or dismantled capacity was for the most part eventually replaced with plant and machinery that was newer and better than the Allies themselves typically possessed. This consideration has often been exaggerated by those who would detract from the German economic miracle; clearly it is not a sufficient or necessary condition but it does have some importance.

The next point we would urge is in no way paradoxical. The material suffering and food shortages referred to in the previous section were recognized by the Western Allies, and in 1946 the Americans and British introduced a relief scheme known as GARIOA (Government and Relief in Occupied Areas). Under GARIOA food, seed corn, fertilizers and heating fuel were delivered free to the Western Zones. This scheme was supplanted in June 1948 by Marshall Aid, or more properly the American funded European Recovery Programme (ERP). The Russians refused to allow their zone to accept Marshall Aid, so that it benefited only the Western Zones, the future West Germany.

It is sometimes objected that Marshall Aid was received by most of the (non-communist) countries in Europe and therefore cannot be cited to explain the rise of West Germany in particular. Indeed the prime beneficiary was Britain; France was in second place, and Germany in third! If, however, one adds West Germany's receipts under GARIOA to those under the ERP then Germany indeed received more help than any other country. While the GARIOA scheme was oriented to relief, ERP was oriented to reconstruction: it helped the Western Zones/West Germany to achieve currency stability, to avoid a trade deficit in the early years, and contributed significantly to the renewal of that country's industrial infrastructure.

There is another consideration, open to different interpretation, that on balance was probably 'a good thing' for the economic future of West Germany. It is a matter of demographics. It is estimated that some 5 500 000 to 5 700 000 Germans lost their lives due to World War II. Yet in October 1946 when the first census was carried out in the three Western Zones it emerged that the population had gone up by 5 million! This, of course, was the result of the various waves of refugees referred to earlier.

In the short term this influx placed further demands on food supplies, and certainly produced overcrowding and made the shortage of living accommodation much worse. We would like to suggest, however, that there were a number of benefits:

- The refugees made good what would otherwise have been a major population deficit resulting from the war.
- The demographic mix of the refugees was favourable to economic activity, i.e. an overrepresentation of men in the 14–45 age group.
- The refugees for the most part constituted a *mobile* work-force, the majority of them having no attachment to any particular locality in the Western Zones/West Germany.
- Particularly as regards refugees from the Russian Zone/East Germany there was an overrepresentation of both skilled workers and professionally qualified people.

Yet perhaps the greatest gain from the various waves of refugees is in fact something intangible. These refugees had lost everything (or left everything they owned behind them). They arrived in the West with an overriding desire to rebuild their lives and fortunes economically, to achieve a level of material well-being as fast as possible. In this they were prototypical of the population as a whole, they espoused the same desires, but more intensely. Within 10 years of the end of the war in West Germany it was already noticeable that former refugees were over-represented among the ranks of the economically successful, and indeed the overachieving refugee was a taken for granted social phenomenon.

The start of the Deutschmark

The currency reform of June 1948 was reckoned a huge success by contemporaries. The old Reichsmark (RM) was abolished and replaced by the new Deutschmark (DM). Everyone was given DM60, in two stages, to cover their immediate needs. All other currency holdings – savings, bank deposits, etc. – were reduced on a 15:1 basis (i.e. RM100 = DM6.5), while debts were cancelled on a 10:1 basis (i.e. you owed DM100 before, now you owe DM10).

Now clearly there is a element of rough justice about these measures. Debtors, farmers and the owners of real estate benefited, while creditors and savers were somewhat disadvantaged. But what struck contemporaries was the fact that the achievement of a stable currency was a great spur to the production of goods (the currency reform was accompanied by the loosening of various price and production controls). Germans old enough to remember these events invariably tell you that 'overnight goods appeared again in the shops'. Indeed industrial output increased by a magnificent 60 per cent in the Western Zones in the 12 months following the currency reform. What is more the currency reform was immediately followed by the introduction of Marshall Aid, with the benefits already indicated. These two developments ended the immediate post-war period, the worst was over, and within two years the Korean War had begun. By this time the Western Zones had become the German Federal Republic (September 1949) and the new state enjoyed a privileged position as supplier to the Americans while being a neutral country.

Trade unions, politics and economic policy

There are some other factors or conditions that contributed not only to the economic 'take off' presaged in the previous section, but even more to the sustained economic achievement of West Germany over the next several decades.

The first of these factors is government policy in the sense of what was called the 'soziale Marktwirtschaft' or social market economy. The essence of this doctrine/policy was quite simply to allow free market capitalism. This simple formulation may not sound very dramatic, but it should be remembered that free enterprise and the absence of government controls was not only in sharp contrast to what was happening in East Germany at this time, it was also in contrast to the economic policy of the Third Reich with its battery of controls and government interventions. In a sense the new economic freedoms seemed to parallel the political freedom that was betokened by the demise of fascism and the establishment of a democratic federal state. The 'social' bit of the social market economy indicated a concern that market forces would not be allowed to operate in an unfettered way such as to severely disadvantage lower income groups. While there was much outcry in the 1950s concerning the economic inequalities of the new state, particularly the gap between the poor and the new rich, West Germany did in the middle term develop a decent system and high level of social welfare benefits. The government also introduced a whole series of measures to encourage saving, i.e. capital accumulation.

The second consideration concerns trade unions and the quality of industrial relations in West Germany. In the occupation period German union leaders with explicit encouragement from the British Authorities (Britain had a Labour government with a big majority in the 1945–50 period) set up a system of industrial trade unions (as opposed to craft, general, enterprise-based or managerial–professional unions such as are to be found in other countries). The essence of an *industrial* union is that all employees in a given industry who wish to join a union join *the same* trade union, notwithstanding differences in skill levels and job content. It makes for industry-based solidarity and simplicity of representation, and it renders demarcation disputes technically impossible. There were only 16 of these industrial unions, plus two white-collar ones, and the whole system was well-regulated from the centre by the Deutsche Gewerkschaftsbund (DGB). While in the mid-1980s the DGB, or more properly its subsidiary mortgage and building society Neue Heimat has been the object of criticism and scandal, for most of the post-war period the DGB has been regarded as a well-resourced, well-organized and disciplined coordinator of trade union representation in West Germany, and has often been held up as a model for other countries.

To this should be added a note on the structure of wage bargaining as it developed in West Germany. Typically, wage deals are struck as a result of bargaining between a trade union and the relevant employers' association, on an industry-wide basis, the operation being conducted on a Land (federal state) by Land basis. We have said 'typically' because there are exceptions: at the top very large companies such as Siemens will negotiate directly with the trade unions (not via the appropriate employers' association), while at a lower level smaller firms may not be verbandspflichtig, bound, that is to say, by the employers' association, but will 'go it alone' in the sense of making a deal direct with their own individual work-force. But the trade union × employers' association system outlined at the beginning of the paragraph does represent the arrangement for both the majority of companies and the employees.

The key features of the bargaining process are:

- Its structural simplicity (only two partners; on the rare occasions where the work-force in a given industry belong to more than one trade union the dominant trade union takes over – negotiates for both).
- Its predictability; the whole system runs according to a well-understood timetable, including a sequence of industries and a sequence of Länder (federal states).

- Its stability; the wage bargains have the force of law (and West Germany is a country with a high respect for the law); if there are any strikes these will invariably occur in 'the bargaining season' and are therefore quite predictable.

In more general terms labour relations in West Germany differ from those in the Anglo-Saxon countries by being legally regulated to a higher degree. In Germany the law covers a wider range of issues, there is a system of Labour Courts for the settlement of disputes, and the respect for the majesty of law is more deeply felt than in Anglo-Saxon countries. A consequence of this orientation is that the personnel manager's job in West Germany is conceived much more in legal terms (and in terms of implementation rather than of initiation). The traditional qualification of the German personnel manager is that of Dr Jura – the equivalent of a first degree followed by a doctor's degree in law. German personnel managers endlessly ask themselves: what is the law, have I applied the law, and above all 'what would it look like in Court? (if my actions were ever challenged)'.

One phenomenon that is legally enshrined *par excellence* is the codetermination or industrial democracy system. Employee participation in Germany operates at three levels:

1. Worker representatives on the Aufsichtsrat (or supervisory board),
2. An Arbeitsdirektor or labour director on the Vorstand (or executive committee),
3. Elected employee representatives on the Betriebsrat or works council.

The whole system is legally based, on a series of laws from (principally) 1950 to 1976 spelling out the particular arrangements, and the rights and powers of various bodies within the system (the system is more complicated and differentiated than is suggested by our summary here, with different rules and arrangements applying to different types and sizes of company).

The points to emphasize are first that at least the origins of the system have been in place for a long time; the early legislation dates from the 1950s and represents an expression of post-war democratic idealism. Second, and related to the first point is the fact that the industrial democracy arrangements are very widely, 'indeed matter of factly' accepted by employers. It is not uncommon to hear the works councils, like the trade unions, referred to as an Ordnungsfaktor, a dimension of the public order. Third, in the view of the present writer, the works councils are by far the most important part of the system. They have existed since 1952, they are widespread in the sense that the law requires that any place of work with more than five employees must have a works council, and legislation subsequent to 1952 has refined and elaborated their rights and duties. The case for the importance of the works council would be that:

- They are widespread and of long standing.
- They have induced a measure of cooperation between employers and employees.

- There is a committee of the works council called the Wirtschaftsausschuss (economics committee) that is empowered to receive information on the company's economic position – sales, orders, profits, prospects – and to treat this in confidence; this arrangement has traditionally induced an element of well-informed and economically responsible realism into the consciousness of employees and their representatives,
- The works council has the legally enshrined power to decide on a lot of practical issues, such as: working hours (not how long but when), holiday arrangements, break times, canteen prices, appointments, transfers between jobs, and so on; the fact that the works council has the right to decide such issues means that they cannot become the source of conflict between management and the workforce – there cannot, for example, be a British-style wildcat strike over tea-breaks because the works council itself will have set the arrangements for tea-breaks.

If we take collectively the issues raised in the last few pages – the nature of the trade unions, the wage-bargaining system, the legalistic (and law abiding) nature of German labour relations, as well as the worker democracy system – then one has identified not only a nexus of considerations that facilitated the economic rise of Germany out of the dark days of the early occupation period, but also a range of factors which have underpinned the economic success of West Germany for several decades. Labour relations in Germany have not been perfect, there have been some severe strikes and some bitterness, but on the whole the system has worked well throughout most of the post-war period.

Finally in this section attention should be drawn to the consequences of political stability in the post-war period. In 1945 no one would have believed that Germany would make a success of democracy. All evidence was against this. Germany had achieved national unity late – in 1871, about a thousand years later than Britain and France – and one school of thought inclined to the view that this made the new state insecure and inclined to end acts of self-justification and of self-aggrandisement; the 'verspätete Nation' (belated nation) theory of Leopold von Ranke. Germany's only experiment with democracy, the Weimar Republic of 1919–33, was anything but encouraging: a regime born from the defeat of World War I (1914–18) beset by challenges from the extreme right and left, and marked by weak central leadership and ministerial instability, was finally swept away by the Nazis in 1933–4. The 12 years of the Thousand Year Reich are best understood as a study in dynamic nihilism, the abnegation of both democracy and equality. In the view of the civilized world in 1945, Germany was never likely to 'make it' as a parliamentary democracy.

Yet with the benefit of hindsight it may well be that the newly funded German Federal Republic (1949) was 'doomed to success'. After all, democracies that fail are usually:

- overthrown by the extreme right (e.g. the Weimar Republic; Spain in 1936);
- or by the extreme left (e.g. reformist Russia under Karensky in 1917);
- or undermined by economic failure.

In the Western Zones of Germany in and after 1945 a challenge from the extreme right was unthinkable given the recent experience of fascism; and a challenge from the extreme left was equally unlikely given the widespread fear and hatred of the USSR – the state responsible for the oppression of fellow Germans in the Russian Zone and for the division of Germany into two politically separate states. And as we know from subsequent developments the economic performance of West Germany was a major source of strength and legitimation for that state.

We have emphasized the issue of political stability because it is an important condition for economic success, and especially for international trade. In the early post-war period such political stability was anything but taken for granted, yet it was not until the 1990s, and the post-unification tension, that there has been any cause to doubt it.

In the last few pages we have considered a whole range of issues – trade union organization, collective bargaining, government economic policy, industrial democracy, political stability – all of which facilitated not only the rise of West Germany out of the economic and other miseries of the post-war period, but also contributed to the sustained economic performance of West Germany up to the time of the challenges and burden of reunification (1990). The one key feature that has been missing from the account so far is the contribution of management in West Germany to that state's economic performance. This is the issue to which we now turn.

2 Management in West Germany

What is management in (what used to be) West Germany like? The question can be answered in a number of different ways. Let us start with a non-German's view.

A formal style

If there is one characteristic that managers from other countries like to attribute to the Germans it is that of formality. The German style, one is told, is very formal. It is probably fair to say that this is true, but not especially significant. It is true in the sense that German managers, unlike say their American counterparts, will not normally dress in a casual way, will not adopt postures just because they are comfortable, do not chew gum, do not use Christian names, do use some formal titles in addressing each other – particularly the doctor title (a lot of German managers have a PhD), do not joke around very much, and do take the practice and objectives of their work seriously.

The formal system

There is another dimension to this formality which should be explored. The organizational behaviour (OB) literature distinguishes between the formal system and the informal system. The formal system is made up of what is formally ordained: the task and authority relations depicted in the organization chart, the formal work roles perhaps supported by job descriptions, rules and procedures, formal specifications of actions and purposes. At the same time it is recognized that there will be departures from this: people who are formally equal 'in the sight of the organization chart' may in fact enjoy different levels of informal status and real power, people may get things done by breaking the rules, the corporate culture may legitimize cheating ('bringing customers and resources together more quickly than the system allows'). Or again individual purposes may exist side by side with organizational ones, sometimes the two may be entwined:

'Why did you speed up production on your section?'
'Because it is an important order, and I wanted to discredit that blackguard in quality control!'

Or again employees may develop informal work group norms about what is a reasonable day's work, what orders are acceptable, how one should relate to supervision, whether or not it is OK to steal the company's property. Thus the informal system represents a bundle of practices of the kind hinted at above, the totality so to say, of deviations from, or adaptions to, the formal system.

So far we have described conventional OB wisdom. The additional consideration that should be urged is that this formal vs. informal system distinction is primarily an Anglo-Saxon phenomenon. It has been propounded by OB writers from Britain and more particularly the United States, and fuelled by empirical studies in those countries. This is not to say it has no reference to the rest of the world, but rather that its application should not be taken for granted. In particular the strength, presence or absence, of the informal system is variable as between different national cultures.

Germany is a case in point where by Anglo-Saxon standards the informal system is rather weak and somewhat less important. In German companies what is formally ordained tends to be the real agenda not a backdrop to creative adjustment. In Germany the official version is much more likely to be what is actually happening!

One can probe this phenomenon with German managers by asking them questions about 'how things really get done' or how decisions are made 'in the grey areas'. The interesting thing about this approach is that it is totally unrewarding, and evokes replies along the lines of:

'We have a committee that decides'
'It has never happened'
'This contingency is covered by paragraph 2004 of the Works Council Act'

The Works Council Act has a more substantial ontic status than the informal system.

Formalism and associate values

Notwithstanding the case we have made to the effect that German interactive style is formal, and that the informal system seems to us to be relatively weak in German companies, we would like to argue against 'bundling' other thought-to-be-associated features. In the popular view, that is, the formalism is sometimes linked to a putative love of bureaucracy, massive concern for authority, and with a penchant for ritualistic behaviour in the organizational setting.

Now there is little evidence for any of this in any of the surveys or studies of the last quarter of a century. The famous LEST (Laboratoire d'Economie et de Sociologie du Travail) study compared the organizational structure and adminis-trative arrangements of matched French and West German firms (Brossard, 1974) and found that the French companies had longer hierarchies, smaller spans of control, more rules, more clerical and administrative workers, fewer women in non-routine posts and more compartmentalization than the Germans. A subsequent study of companies in Britain using the same methodology and sampling frame (Sorge and Warner, 1978) found Britain to be in an intermediate position between France and Germany. That is to say, the companies in West Germany were the least bureaucratic of the three countries studied.

As another instance, André Laurent has sampled the attitude and values of cohorts of managers attending courses at INSEAD (Laurent, 1985). In this survey it is managers from Italy and France who show the strongest concern with hierarchy and authority, and who are also the most negatively oriented to conflict. A further piece of evidence is offered by Hofstede (1980). One of Hofstede's four dimensions is what he calls power distance, or the willingness of people in different cultures to accept differences in power. Again Germany has a quite modest score on this dimension, the same in fact as for Britain (so much for the war films!). It has also been argued by the present author elsewhere (Hutton and Lawrence, 1979; Lawrence, 1980) on the basis of a series of observational case studies at German companies that there is in fact in that country a marked lack of deference between people at different hierarchical levels. These case studies showed staff variously criticizing their superiors (and each other) for breaking rules, dereliction of duty, getting things wrong, expressing silly ideas, not taking precautions, not looking ahead, and not spending enough on the plant and equipment.

Education and training

In 1973 the West German Wirtschaftsministerium (Economics Ministry) decided that it would like to have an objective (non-German) appraisal of the quality of

German management and commissioned the Düsseldorf branch of the American consultancy organization Booz, Allen and Hamilton to undertake this. The ensuing report (Booz, Allen and Hamilton, 1973) was severely critical of management in West Germany, and we will take up its overall critique shortly. One particular point made in the report, however, is of immediate concern, and this may be expressed as a paradox, namely, that German managers are well-educated but not well trained.

The first part of this proposition is undoubtedly true. There was a flood of surveys of the background and qualifications of German managers in the quarter of a century after the war (the flood has now ceased) and this material has been neatly summarized by May (1974). The main findings from these various studies are:

- Higher management in West Germany is virtually a graduate occupation.
- The possession of a doctor's degree is common.
- Those managers who are not university graduates are typically qualified at the next level down, that of the 'Fachhochschule', broadly a three-year full-time course beginning at the age of 18.
- Managers in Germany are qualified in law, economics and engineering.
- More of them are qualified in engineering than in anything else.

Comparisons with other Western industrial countries have also cast a favourable light on the educational qualifications of German managers; see, for example, Glover's comparison of managers in Britain, France, Germany and Sweden (Glover, 1978).

What, then, is the purport of the Booz, Allen and Hamilton judgement that West German managers are poorly trained? The essence of it is that they are not trained in management *per se*, and certainly not to the extent of their American counterparts. There is not an exact equivalent in Germany of the undergraduate degree in business administration so common in the United States; there is the degree in 'Betriebswirtschaftshehre' or business economics which overlaps in content with a business administration degree, but is not exactly the same and is 'coming from' somewhere else. Or again until the late 1980s there were no MBA degrees in Germany, and this qualification is still not commonly available in the way that it is in, say, Britain. It was also noted by Booz, Allen and Hamilton that German managers were underrepresented at international management training institutions such as INSEAD in France, IMEDE in Switzerland, or at the Harvard Business School.

To complete the picture it should be added that there is considerable management training activity in Germany but it is in-company training to a much higher degree than in, for example Britain or the US. This, of course, makes it relatively invisible, and it is not so easy to generalize about it. But it would be fair to say that in-company management training in Germany is:

- more specific, that is to say more oriented to particular jobs and functions,
- more technical,

- less concerned with the more general processes of communication, coordination, decision-making and control, i.e. with expressly managerial elements.

Serious but not professional?

The main burden of the Booz, Allen and Hamilton report, however, is not about education but about professionalism. While crediting managers in West Germany with seriousness of purpose it criticizes German management as lacking in professionalism especially when compared with American management. More particularly the charge levelled is that German management is relatively unsophisticated or tends by American comparison to neglect:

- planning and control,
- analysis especially quantitative analysis, and
- marketing and business strategy,

together with all the systems and techniques that support them.

Now this judgement was delivered in the 1970s. Clearly there will have been changes since then, and no doubt German management does more in these areas than was the case 20 years ago. Yet no one writing about German management has ever contradicted the Booz, Allen and Hamilton judgements; there is no rival view that asserts that in fact marketing, for instance, is a German strength; German industrialists in their rather rare public utterances tend not to lead on any of these. In other words there is a certain consistency and continuity about this judgement. But what is it telling us? The broad answer is that German management does differ in interesting ways from the Anglo-Saxon mainstream, and is not necessarily disadvantaged thereby. Consider some of the positive features.

'Technik.' Thanks to the Audi advertisement the German word 'Technik' has passed into everyday speech in the English-speaking world. 'Technik' connotes the engineering knowledge and craft skill that goes into making things and producing three-dimensional artefacts. German companies 'lead on products' in the sense of identifying with them, valorizing them, and treating the products as the corporate *raison d'être* – a message that is very clear, for instance, in a popular book from the early 1990s (Head, 1992). Representatives of German companies when asked open-ended questions about corporate achievements and sources of pride tend to give product-related answers (Lawrence, 1980) rather than economic performance answers. More German managers are qualified in engineering than in anything else. Comparative survey evidence suggests that German engineers have high standing in society (Hutton and Lawrence, 1978) and higher than in Britain. Comparative salary evidence suggests the same thing (Fores, 1972).

While there is substantial evidence in, for example, Britain to suggest that the production function is underresourced and has relatively low status (Hutton and Lawrence, 1978) the reverse seems to be the case in Germany. Indeed all the technical functions including production appear to have higher standing in Germany than in Britain (Lawrence, 1984). Studies of German production managers show them to emphasize the technical rather than managerial aspects of their work (Hutton and Lawrence, 1979). The most recent work on German management (Randlesome, 1993) suggests that there are currently some 500 occupations in Germany for which a formal apprenticeship exists. Getting on for 60 per cent of the age group in (West) Germany do an apprenticeship (it is less than 20 per cent in say Britain). So accepted is the idea of the effort put by German companies into the design and production of goods that Colin Randlesome (1990) in an earlier book refers to 'the over-engineering' of products as a possible weakness!

Specialism versus generalism

It is possible to conceive of management in generalist terms, as an activity having its own dynamic, which can be taken apart and discussed in general terms, and made the subject of generalizable exhortations. Cultures committed to this conception will recruit managers with regard to general qualities and capabilities. The French, for example, conceive of management in general terms and recruit in terms of formal educated cleverness; the British have a generalist conception too and recruit in terms of leadership and character and social skills; American generalism again emphasizes professional competences that can be applied in any situation – company, industry, function – together with energy.

The German conception of management is not like this. In the German scheme of things management is not so much a job, separate and distinct, but an element in most jobs. And these jobs will in turn be conceived primarily in particular terms – with reference, that is, to the particular skills and knowledge and experience that is needed, in a particular function (design, manufacturing, personnel, sales or whatever) in a specified industry. It is always revealing to ask German personnel managers how they recruit, for example, graduate trainees: the answers are typically more precise with regard to content of education and specificity of knowledge, in contradistinction to the Anglo-Saxon emphasis on character or management virtuosity.

Here we have a clue to the German de-emphasis on the dynamics of professional management that so appalled the writers of the Booz, Allen and Hamilton report. For the Germans it is all about particular products in a particular industry, and this implies specialism not generalism, and technical specialism above all.

Stocktaking

In the last few pages we have offered a characterization of management in West Germany suggesting that:

● The interactive style is formal.
● The informal system is relatively weak.

- But that German management is neither bureaucratic nor authoritarian.
- Subject-based education predominates management training.
- There is a relative neglect of American-style managerialism.
- This is related to a specialist rather than generalist understanding of management work.
- And that in turn emphasizes 'Technik' as both means and end.

Clearly this formula has some limitations. German management has been relatively insular and self-sufficient (and a little bit self-satisfied as well). American managerialism is a powerful way of mobilizing resources and raising the likelihood of desirable outcomes. Nothing is gained by neglecting its potential. German management is found by some to be a little outmoded in its implicit formula of:

design plus manufacture plus reliability

and all of this driven by wilful individuals rather than by system builders.

Yet withal this German model has an engaging simplicity in its conviction that well-made products will be eagerly bought. Its strengths – 'Technik'-specialism-particularist education-design and manufacturing emphasis – are also consistent in the sense of mutually reinforcing. It is difficult to resist the conclusion that this single-minded brand of management is one of the key factors in the success of post-war reconstruction as well as in the sustained economic performance of West Germany up to the time of reunification.

3 East Germany

We began the discussion of West Germany with a review of conditions in the Western Occupation Zones after the war and of developments in this period and after which shaped management and manufacturing. There is an historical research literature on the Western Zones, and it is all in English and German and occasionally French. No one writing about these Zones had any particular reason to distort, cover-up, or rewrite history. None of this holds for the Russian Occupation Zone which became the German Democratic Republic (GDR) in October 1949.

Nonetheless a few generalizations about life and events in the Russian Zone and later GDR are possible. First, going back to the last few months of World War II it is clear that the Russians were feared by the German civilian population in a way that the British and Americans were not. As the Red Army moved west in 1944–5 so did hordes of German refugees. On the night of 7–8 May 1945, just before the armistice negotiated by Hitler's successor Doenitz came into effect, just about every German who could walk, ride a bicycle, or push a perambulator attempted to get out of what was about to become the Russian Zone and into the British Zone. Second, with the arrival of the Russians on German soil it was clear that these fears were justified. Not only was the régime harsher, but the soldiers seem to have been less restrained, more drunken, more bent on loot and above all on the rape of German women than were their opposite members in the Western Zones. Third, the Russians were concerned not to restore democracy but to impose a system. This was made immediately clear by property confiscation and the summary execution of landowners. Fourth, the USSR had reparations in kind as an official policy. Or to put this point more colloquially they looted on a grand scale. Interestingly their looting went further down the scale than would have seemed credible in the West. Whereas, for example, the French felt it was both legitimate and worthwhile to hunt down and take back railway rolling stock that the Nazis had sequestrated during the war, the Russians went down to the level of taking light bulbs and waste-paper baskets. The effects were more obvious in the City of Berlin which had surrendered to the Russians on 2 May 1945; the Russians were left in sole control of Berlin for some eight weeks until the Western Allies were allowed in to take over their sectors of the City: in this period the Russians stripped Berlin bare. In an earlier section we cited the leading authority on the Occupation period (Piettre, 1952) to the effect that official dismantling of plant and equipment in the Western Zones had reduced their industrial capacity by 8 per cent: the same source gives the corresponding figure for the Russian Zone as 45 per cent.

But the all-encompassing difference, the overriding consideration which shaped the GDR throughout its lifetime, was the fact that the Russians sought the total integration of the GDR into the USSR-dominated Eastern Bloc, not only politically and militarily, but ideologically and economically. And in the East ideology and economics are indissolubly linked. The result is that while the West's knowledge of early events in the Russian Zone and later GDR may be a bit sketchy, we do have a clear picture of the economic system that emerged and of the way in which productive organizations were structured.

The command economy

Although everybody 'sort of knows' what a communist command economy was like it will do no harm to 'spell it out' in terms of the formal tenets and linkages within the system. It is after all very different from anything that Western readers have experienced. And from this macroeconomic outline we can move on to look at the nature and *modus operandi* of manufacturing units on the eve of the downfall of communism in East Germany.

Macroeconomic level. The GDR was a monolith based on Marxist-Leninist ideology. This ideology was embodied in the ruling Socialist Unity Party or SED to give it its German initials. The GDR differed from Western states in that it was Party-driven rather than government-driven; that is to say the Party, not a Western-style government of the day, controlled 'the legitimate means of force'. It also controlled education and the media.

The East German trade union, the FDGB, was also naturally controlled by the party (SED); indeed it was East German orthodoxy to refer to the FDGB as 'the transmission belt of the Party'. The FDGB counted some 95 per cent of the East German work-force as members. The Party also sported a youth organization, the Free German Youth or FDJ to give it its German initials. Something like 70 per cent of East Germany's 14–17 year olds were members of the FDJ. Clearly it took a bit of courage not to join it; it also pushed the non-joiner in the direction of social isolation, since much more recreative activity in the GDR was organized, driven by the Party and its organs, than is the case in the West.

As an economy the GDR was distinguished from the West by a high level of state ownership of the means of production, and by incorporating the principle of economic planning. According to Barratt Brown (1984) the central planning model which became the key feature of the GDR is characterized by four non-market principles:

1. Plans for a range of production facilities will be articulated and coordinated.
2. Economic policies will be socially directed, i.e. concerned with the good of society rather than the optimization of the economy.
3. Long-term strategy will rule, not considerations of short-term profitability.
4. Pecuniary motivation will be replaced by social-ideological commitment.

For anyone writing after the event there is clearly a danger of giving an ahistoric account of the economic system of the GDR, of writing as though the whole system in elaborated form was in existence from day one until the night the Berlin Wall was opened. Of course there was development within the system, and change over time. The nationalization proceeded in phases, though it was largely complete by the mid-1950s. The GDR also experimented with degrees of centralization vs. decentralization. It is also clear that the output of the GDR's economic system varied over time. It 'got away to a slow start' by the standards of West Germany; but then it had begun to catch up, to narrow the gap with the West. For a time in the 1970s the GDR ranked as the world's ninth largest economy; it even sported *GNP per capita* figures higher than those of Britain (even though this tells us nothing about relative consumption levels). These erstwhile successes of the GDR were reflected in the age composition of those who took part in the demonstrations of 1989 that helped to overthrow the Honecker régime. For the most part these anti-Honecker demonstrations were the work of GDR citizens in their 30s and 40s: younger people were too brainwashed by the Party, and interestingly older people took a more favourable view of the régime recognizing what it had achieved by comparison with the early post-war years. Then again in the 1980s the gap widened, the international borrowings of the GDR increased, and economic decline foreshadowed political demise.

With these qualifications about change during the course of the régime it should be urged that the system of production organization, largely in place by the late 1970s, had the following features:

●   Individual manufacturing sites, nationalized of course, were known as VEBs (people's own companies).

- VEBs with the same or similar products were grouped into/reported to Combines (Kombinate).
- R & D (research and development) was typically 'bulked' at the Combine level; the Combines were also expected to maximize economies of scale.
- Groups of Combines in turn reported to industry ministries (not a single Ministry of Industry, but a number of ministries, each for a different branch of industry).
- The ministries in turn reported to the Plan Commission, which was responsible for long-term, middle-term, and short-term one-year plans.
- While there was some iterative element in the origination of the plan, that is inputs upwards from the lower echelons, the Plan, 'the one year very tangible output plan' in its final form would come down, via the industry ministries to the Combines, at which point it would be broken down again and production quotas passed on to the individual VEBs.

Finally, the education system was also 'harmonized' with the presumptive needs of the economy. What in the West would be called 'work experience' was an integral part of the education process at both school and higher educational level. People would not in the Western sense choose what to study at university: entry for university was handled on a subject quota basis and graduates were allocated to jobs by the state, for example, sent to work in particular VEBs, or whatever. It will be clear from this account that a former East German VEB was radically different from a Western company – and so were the demands upon the managers who worked in them.

The GDR: plant level

The plants, or VEBs (*supra*) in the former GDR, were production sites *par excellence*. They were judged on output, the output required by the Plan. And the Plan would not be easy to fulfil, it would not be 'a pushover'. What in the parlance of the day confronted the VEBs of the communist régime was 'ein anspruchsvoller Plan', a demanding plan, one that would make claims on the energy and resourcefulness of those working for, and especially managing, the typical VEBs. But who managed a typical VEB?

People who made management their career in the former GDR would normally be SED party members. And there were right and wrong times to join the Party: midway through university was ideal. Joining when one was too young might appear calculative, joining at 35 might be interpreted as a 'mariage de convenance'. Being a party member was usual rather than essential, but it was essential to be politically clean, a state defined in terms of negative rectitude – no acts of teenage rebellion, no refusing to join the FDJ (communist youth organization), nothing known against one, no discrediting contacts with the West.

This is not to say that managers in the GDR were simply party hacks. All the normal criteria of qualifications, personal qualities and relevant experience would be required, as in the West. Indeed the demands of managing in the GDR were such that the GDR manager required rather more in the way of resourcefulness, manipulative skills and sheer nerve than is normal in the West.

The party-dominated nature of the former GDR outlined in the previous account of the system at macro level, was also very much in evidence at plant level. The nearest approach to a Western managing director or chief executive in the VEBs was the 'Betriebsdirektor' (works director), but he (and in our experience they always were men in manufacturing industry) would not enjoy the same managerial prerogative as would opposite numbers in companies in the West.

First, as made clear in the previous section, the 'Betriebsdirektor' would be 'executively diminished' by his place in the GDR system of vertical integration running from ministry to Combine to VEB. Second, he would to a significant extent be confronted by the Plan. Third, he was in any case no more than *primus inter pares* on the Betriebsführung, a collegial decision-making body also representing the SED Party and the FDGB trade union. And fourth, these equal power centres on the Betriebsführung – executive, party, trade union – further eventuated in parallel hierarchies running down the organization.

A number of things follow from all this:

- The VEB was more of a production site than an independent Western-style company.
- The 'Betriebsdirektor' was more circumscribed and less powerful than his Western equivalent.
- Decision-making in the VEB tended to be slow and compromise-driven; the result of the collegial Betriebsführung and the parallel hierarchies.
- Management in the VEB was much more about implementation than about initiation.

If the *raison d'être* of the VEB was production, it is only fair to raise the question, was this easy to achieve? After the VEB *was* freed from a lot of the constraints of the Western company – it did not have to devise strategy, seek markets, construct distribution systems, or make profits; indeed it did not even have to worry much about quality, new product development, or not damaging the environment.

Notwithstanding this litany of advantages it has to be said that there were all sorts of difficulties in the way of timely and simple production.

First, the Plan itself was often too demanding and too inflexible. Second, and this is by far and away the most important consideration, the VEBs would frequently lack the raw materials and/or bought out parts they needed; again this was due to the inflexibility of the system, the lack of competition among suppliers, the dependence on other companies in the GDR or at the very least in the Eastern Bloc, and on the fact that all the supplier companies suffered from the same shortcomings and problems as the VEBs to which they delivered. Third, equipment and machinery tended to be older and more prone to breakdown than is normal in the West; this could only be overcome by spending hard currency (severely limited) and buying superior technology from the West. The problem was compounded by the fact that the two countries that the former GDR most disliked on ideological grounds – West Germany and the USA – are major equipment suppliers. Furthermore when GDR companies did apply for permission to spend hard currency to buy equipment from the West, to keep the cost down, and to enhance the chance of approval from the authorities, it was normal not to buy spares or replacement parts. So that even when VEBs acquired decent Western equipment it was still more prone to stoppages, and spare parts would be cannibalized or fabricated 'in house' (and a side effect was to encourage 'spare parts smuggling', especially in Berlin).

To these problems should be added various work-force considerations. To put it bluntly, work-force discipline was poor. Coming late, going early, taking prolonged breaks, were all common. Absenteeism rates were high. It was possible to fire people, but if a VEB did this the Arbeitsamt (labour exchange) would be likely to send as replacements people fired by other plants – alcoholics, drug addicts, malingerers, and social inadequates. On the whole it seemed better to keep the alcoholics you knew.

One should also add a side-effect of life in communist countries that impacted on employee behaviour. This quite simply is that everyday life was hard in the former GDR. The range of goods was limited, the provision of services poor; there were shortages of all kinds, one queued for everything. The prevailing ethos was one of bureaucratic inefficiency. The rule seemed to be: whatever it is you want you can't have it! At least not without form-filling, waiting and a lot of hassle. Life was particularly hard for working women responsible for running households. More of the travel to and from work was by public transport rather than by private car; labour saving devices in the home were few and far between by Western standards. Domestic heating was more likely to be by lignite (brown coal) burning stoves that had to be lit, and tended, and cleaned out – and maybe the coal would have to be humped up a few flights of stairs to the apartment in the first place. Shopping was more demanding than in the West. While basic food items were readily available and very cheap, there were standing shortages of other goods, for example, fresh fruit and vegetables. In the former GDR one did not do household shopping once a week, by car, at a supermarket. One shopped daily, on foot, and carried away the purchases in a nice old-fashioned shopping bag (one result of reunification is the demise of the shopping bag!). Given these rigours of everyday life, where better to go for a bit of a rest, to wind down, and build up your strength for the next bout of queuing and shopping but to one's place of work.

4 Change in the East

In the previous sections we have outlined the macroeconomic system of the former GDR, and attempted to give some sense of what management and manufacturing were like. This in broad terms is a portrait of the GDR as it was up to the autumn of 1989. What has changed since then?

Privatization

The first key development is that the VEBs no longer exist. They have either been sold, or are candidates for privatization. In between the opening of the Berlin Wall in November 1989 and reunification in October 1990 the de Meziere government set up the Treuhand, an organization charged with privatizing the 8000-odd VEBs. By the summer of 1993 by no means all of them have been sold. Among the companies that have found buyers a few have been bought by foreign (non-German) companies, but the majority have been acquired by West German concerns. It is probably fair to say that there has been more interest by potential buyers in service sector organizations in the former GDR than in manufacturing companies. And it has been the heavy industry VEBs – steel, chemicals, ship building, traditional mechanical and electrical engineering companies – that have been most difficult to sell. This is in part because it is in these areas that the quality and productivity differential with the West is greatest, and partly because in many of these sectors there is world overcapacity anyway – and of course these two factors interact. Unsold VEBs that are still on the books of the Treuhand are frequently supported by that organization, that is to say, get loans/investment money and sometimes working capital from it.

Take-over not merger

The reunification of the two German states was not a merger, but a take-over of East Germany by West Germany. In consequence West German forms and institutional arrangements quickly replaced East German ones, so that much of the paraphernalia of the former GDR simply disappeared, including:

- The concept of the state-owned company.
- The VEB; former VEBs were converted into the West German company format, usually the AG; this typically preceded privatization.
- The Betriebsführung, the collegial body at the head of the old VEBs went; VEBs transformed into AGs now have the West German two-tier board system with a non-executive supervisory board (Aufsichtsrat) and an executive committee (Vorstand).
- The SED party has disappeared and no political party is represented at the workplace anyway.
- The former FDGB trade union has been abolished and replaced by the West German FDGB and industrial trade union system described in the first half of the chapter.

- The former FDJ youth organization has been abolished, likewise the former BDSF (league of German–Russian friendship); both these organizations were formerly represented in the industrial workplace – this kind of social-political activity at work has ceased.

Furthermore the former VEBs often had a variety of care and welfare-providing institutions, including crèches and kindergartens, holiday homes for employees and the Ambulatorium. The last was a work-based medical centre providing a range of treatment for employees and often serving as a medical facility for the wider community in which the plant was based. Facilities of this kind in the former VEBs have variously been closed down, sold off, privatized. The West German system of codetermination or industrial democracy has also been extended to the former GDR. The most evident consequence is the appearance in the former VEBs of the elected Works Council (Betriebsrat) described in the first half of this chapter. The present writer has had the opportunity to interview a number of these newly established Works Council members and found them very positive. This is so firstly in the obvious sense that they feel it to be a significant role, there is plenty for them to do, critical issues especially work-force reduction do concern them. Second, these East German Works Councillors also tend to be positive about the institution, training and more general support they have received from the West German trade unions.

Currency union

For the former VEBs the decisive event was neither the opening of the Berlin Wall nor the subsequent reunification of the two German states: it was the currency union of July 1990. Currency union means quite simply the replacing of the GDR's Ostmark with West Germany's Deutschmark, with the exchange being on a 1-to-1 basis. Now it is important here to distinguish between the response to this measure of the East German general public on the one hand and the consequences for East German companies on the other.

The currency union was for the most part welcomed by the general public in the former GDR. They were thrilled to receive a DM handout, the exchange at parity was generous, and it gave people the instant wherewithal to acquire some coveted West German goods. It also opened up a nice little swindle for any East German who already had some DM. In the run up to the currency union one had the paradoxical spectacle of people with DM changing them into Ostmark at 4 or 5 Ostmark to 1DM, then at the time of the union changing them back to DM at 1 to 1. Neither should we forget that the currency union followed by reunification gave rise to a nice little boom in 1990–1 for some West German industries, who acquired at the taxpayers' expense a new market of some 16 million people in the former GDR, all thirsting for West German goods and with DM in their pockets to pay for them. In some cases West German companies were selling into an untouched market: to give just one example there were no vending machines in the former GDR.

Side by side with this popular consumerist effect, however, the consequences of currency union followed by reunification for East German companies was quite awful. They were exposed to West German competition, which for the most part they could not match, while at the same time their own products were designated in hard currency so that they became inaccessible to the GDR's former trading partners, the other communist countries of Eastern Europe that made up COMECON until this organization was disbanded in 1991. Consider the market possibilities for East German companies after currency union/reunification.

Post-unification markets for East German companies

The post-unification situation was extremely disadvantageous to most East German companies. There were three critical factors.

First, East German companies lost their protected domestic market. They lost it principally to West German companies whom they could not match in terms of quality, reputation, or cost efficiency. The impact of West German competition naturally varied from industry to industry. But it was, and is, a serious overall threat; and the West German advantage was most marked in consumer goods where East Germans simply perceived them as being more desirable – as symbolizing Western affluence. Furthermore the West German advantage was probably at its strongest at the start of 1990. Thereafter there has been some 'drifting back' by East Germans to products made by former GDR companies. One particular piece of purchasing patriotism that has come to light is the preference of at least the present generation of East German doctors for drugs made by their own pharmaceutical companies.

The second factor was the loss of former East European/COMECON markets. It should be underlined here that the former GDR had enjoyed considerable standing in the Eastern Bloc as *the* supplier of industrial goods and equipment, especially to the former USSR. With the fall of communism throughout Eastern Europe and the collapse of COMECON, together with the hard currency problem alluded to earlier, East German companies to a large extent lost their Eastern Bloc markets, at any rate for the time being.

It should be added that this is not a black and white judgement. There has been some piecemeal continuation of trade with the former USSR by barter, and in the summer of 1993 it was even reported that Russia had bought some East German companies from the Treuhand, paying with wood, coal and oil. The German government also recognized the importance of the former USSR as a market for East German companies and in May 1991 introduced the Möllermann Plan (named after the German economic minister of the day) which offered a kind of export credit guarantee to former GDR companies wanting to export to the East. This scheme was decisive for the fortunes of some East German companies. But it was not a comprehensive solution. The credit offered, known as Hermes Krediten, was not enough for all would-be takers; there was a process of application, and waiting, and uncertainty that was damaging for production planning. The scheme also required a responsible authority in the receiving country to guarantee eventual repayment. Given the political instability in the new CIS it was often difficult actually to identify a 'responsible authority' with whom to do business. The extensive collapse of the Eastern Bloc markets is a great shame, and one that has denied East German companies a competitive advantage. After all they did not know how to sell to the United States but they certainly knew how to sell to the former USSR. This brings us to the third consideration.

This is that the apparent advantage being conferred upon East German companies by currency union and reunification is in practice vitiated by the inability of most East German companies to respond – at any rate in the early years of a unified Germany. The apparent advantage is access to the West German market, a mature affluent market of 62 million people, together with automatic membership of the EEC. The problem in practice is that the majority of East German companies simply could not take advantage of their market earnings. Their labour costs may be lower, but this is usually offset by poorer productivity; and for the most part these companies do not have the quality or image needed to sell in the West. In some cases there are also legal or technical impediments such as the need to meet environmental standards, or the obligation of say the East German pharmaceutical industry to conform to Western GMP (Good Manufacturing Practice) standards.

Given the problems indicated so far it is not surprising, however tragic in human terms, that many former GDR companies have gone bankrupt; and many others are (at time of writing in the summer of 1993) limping along, on short-term working, propped up by Treuhand money.

From overmanning to slimming

Turning now away from macroeconomic considerations to what has happened inside East German companies, one of the most dramatic changes has been the reduction in work-force size. And reference here is not to 5 per cent or 10 per cent reductions, but to reductions of 50, 60, 70 per cent and sometimes more among surviving East German companies. To appreciate why this was both necessary and possible one has to know that by Western standards the former VEBs were hugely overmanned, and one needs to know why. In fact there were a range of interlocking reasons.

First of all there was no reason not to take on additional employees in the GDR, it was in line with socialist ideology and the ethic of full employment. Second, it was, as we have seen, difficult to fire people. Third, a larger workforce could compensate for undercapitalization. Fourth, it could also compensate for poor work-force discipline and high absenteeism. Fifth, and this is the most important consideration, because of stockouts and breakdowns the former VEBs simply could not produce a lot of the time, but an enlarged work-force gave them the opportunity to catch up with wild bursts of activity at times when everything was working and all the parts and materials were to hand. In the same spirit it was common to transfer clerical and maintenance workers to production when these catch-up drives were underway.

And there is another, more diffuse reason. During the GDR a kind of bureaucratic inefficiency ruled, captured in phrases of the period such as 'sozialistische Schlamperei' (socialist cock-up) and 'alles hat seinen sozialistischen Gang' (everything has its socialist path, i.e. will be slow and ineffective). This sense of being surrounded by shortages and inefficiency led companies in the GDR to engage in what was called 'Autarkiestreben' or striving for self-sufficiency. This of course impacts upon recruitment. Maybe a precision engineering company has the chance to hire a few construction workers: fine, it would seize the opportunity – they can mend the roof. Maybe next week you get a chance to hire someone who can repair watches: wonderful, take them on, put them in the Purchasing Department (there are so many people there that no one will notice) and we can do a lot of favours by repairing watches for people.

With German reunification all these factors were eliminated, and most important of all there was for the first time competition among companies, East and West German, to supply your company. The need for vast stocks of parts and reserves of manpower was replaced by a drive for cost efficiency and higher productivity. And as the numbers went down, so output went up. Absenteeism declined, worker discipline improved greatly, and at least in these respects the former VEBs began to resemble Western factories.

Functional relativities

Another marked consequence of reunification is that the relative importance of the various functions (design, production, sales, and so on) changed sharply. In the GDR, as we have emphasized, production was the most important function. Fulfilling the Plan was all, output was what counted, management careers were made in and through the organization of production. And if production was important and where most people worked, purchasing was the most critical function, the *sine qua non* for the output task of the VEB. And purchasing departments were also massively staffed by Western standards.

With reunification these functional relativities have changed. Production, as we have seen, has been slimmed; and the emphasis has in any case shifted from pure volume to quality, reliability and differentiation. Purchasing has also slimmed, the procurement operation is now much easier to manage – and is incidentally facilitated by having West German rather than East German computers.

On the other hand there is now a need for sales, which scarcely existed before. In particular East German companies that aspire to sell in West Germany are busy building up and deploying a field sales-force there. East German companies have also used, often for the first time, sales reps in East Germany itself in an effort to retain East German customers or to win back the disloyal from West German suppliers.

Not only is sales very largely a new phenomenon in East German companies, but so is marketing: one can see in the early 1990s former VEBs taking their first steps towards marketing – they have an engaging conviction that it is all about collecting information, but are not always sure what information and why! Again on this theme East German companies are now having to think about distribution – often for the first time. In the GDR a company often just 'delivered' to the state or the appropriate authority who in turn passed the produce on to users. So that a lot of VEBs at the time of reunification simply had no distribution system.

Again some functions are changing their nature. During the GDR the personnel function was not really concerned with recruitment, given the allocative system noted earlier. Nor was executive remuneration or the remuneration package an issue during the communist period. But these and comparable issues are on the agenda now for Personnel, and this function is now coming to approximate its Western equivalent.

R & D (research and development) is also changing. In the GDR there was little emphasis on new product development or upon the need to compete via product differentiation. Thus a good deal of R & D effort was directed to easing the transition to manufacturing, and was research on manufacturing processes rather than on product origination. Or again in some industries, and pharmaceuticals is one example, a lot of R & D effort was directed to taking apart Western products and figuring out how to copy them – after all US patents were not enforceable in the GDR.

The personnel of management

Most managers in East German companies now are not only East Germans but they are the same managers who ran these companies during the communist period. It is important to underline this simple fact because most Westerners do not realize it, and also because it tends to reinforce our earlier contention that the managers of the GDR were not mere political hacks *even if* political acceptability was a criterion for advancement. In many cases the present top manager is the 'Betriebsdirektor' of the GDR time; in others the top layer of management from the GDR period has been forced out and the new top manager is a former manager within the company, sometimes from a relatively junior post, who has been pushed up by popular acclaim. Where West Germans have been hired it is for particular reasons – to head up a newly created marketing function, to staff a field sales-force in West Germany, or say to run a newly sophisticated procurement operation. Even companies that have been sold by the Treuhand to West German companies have in our experience been sparing in their appointment of West German nationals – just appointing West Germans to the few top posts or to carry out a particular assignment.

Status and motivation of management

For managers in East German companies that have survived there have been tremendous changes. First, they are better paid than they were, both absolutely and relatively. In the GDR pay differentials between managers and other staff were small; expanded differentials are new and rather exciting for managers in East German companies – it helps to make them feel like real Western managers! Second, East German managers now have greater freedom to take decisions. In the old days there was a tendency for the manager to try to keep out of trouble – so he would tend to ask for instructions rather than act on his own initiative, get confirmation of orders, check it all out with higher authority, and so on. Now one speaks of the 'Ende der Regression', the end of the buck-passing. Third, managers now exert more control downwards, especially in the production function. They are more likely, that is, to get compliance from subordinates, more likely to be able to control outcomes, less likely to be frustrated by circumstances beyond their control. Fourth, the formal and informal systems have come more into focus than during the GDR. In the old days there were so many rules and so much interference from trade union and party that it was difficult to get things done; the resourceful manager would find himself trying to 'beat the system' to get the job done, a phenomenon caught in an often repeated phrase 'der Betriebsdirektor steht immer mit einem Fuss im Gefängnis' (the managing director always has one foot in jail!).

Finally, managers will normally work harder now, under greater pressure. The emphasis has shifted from being in the right to getting it right. The pressure that some of these managers are experiencing, running struggling companies not yet sold by the Treuhand, is unbelievable. They are among the unrecognized heroes of the 1990s.

The work-force

It has all changed as well for ordinary employees. They have lost the job security that was universally enjoyed during the GDR. They have experienced rises in pay as they come into line with their West German colleagues by stages, and probably most of those who are in work are better off in the sense of greater purchasing power (as well as more to buy) than they were in 1989. At the same time they have not made the gains that their management superiors have made, nor are they having the excitement and freedom (as well as the pressure) that is being experienced by the managers. Indeed a common manager testimony these days, in spite of the pressure, is 'mehr Freude an Arbeit' (more fun at work). Again for the workers the factory has become less of a sanctuary than in the GDR, and more a place where one is supervised and subject to demands.

Ethos

We have suggested at several points in the last few pages that not only did reunification change the organizational structure and management roles, there were also changes in the culture and ambience of the industrial workplace. These latter changes include:

- The new emphasis on efficiency rather than on bureaucracy.
- A single rational ethic in the organization of manufacturing.
- Higher work-force discipline.
- An unsentimental approach to employees.
- A dismantling of the apparatus of socialist paternalism.
- A new management consciousness, and a stronger differentiation of the managers from the managed.

There are, however, perhaps two things that might be added. In the old days the VEB had some of the quality of a sanctuary for employees. In an oppressive totalitarian state one was relatively safe at work, at least manual workers were. In the factory one was unlikely to come to the unfavourable attention of 'the authorities', would skive a bit and joke around. Blue-collar workers are conscious not only that they need their sanctuary less, but also that the workplace has lost this character.

The second consideration is related. West Germans or Wessis in the former GDR are of course rather visible and the subject of characterizing comment from the East Germans (Ossis). The Wessis are credited with energy and efficiency and powers of organization. But they are held to be too openly ambitious, to subordinate human interaction to efficient organization. In the old days, say the Ossis, we had time to listen, the quality of human contact was higher. Within a few months of reunification the present author was hearing regretful testimonies of this kind from East German managers. It is all part of the reality of change.

Company behaviour in East Germany

Finally, we would like to raise the question of what, broadly, the former VEBs have been doing since reunification. The present writer has visited a number of former VEBs starting shortly after reunification, and there do seem to be some patterns.

As suggested earlier all these companies have slimmed on a massive scale. There has also been a measure of decentralization, in the sense that the quasi-vertical integration of Plan Commission–Industry Ministry–Combine–VEB was ended with the fall of communism. Furthermore the former VEBs have tended to decentralize by empowering their managers, debureaucratizing, having R & D devolved to plant level, and sometimes by breaking up central functions such as personnel and finance and assigning them in subunit form to different production entities or even profit centres. These organizational changes have in our experience often been accompanied by critical reviews of the product range, typically followed by simplification or innovation. To give a strong example of this phenomenon, one of the companies we visited had made tanks for the GDR Defence Ministry. After reunification it put its energies into fabricating containers for oil companies.

The companies we have visited have also behaved like 'good Germans': that is to say, they have invested in new plant and equipment, whether from retained earnings, Treuhand subventions, or the capital supplied by new West German owners. The former VEBs have also tended to engage in what in German is called a 'Verschönerungsaktion', a 'tarting up' or beautifying operation: that is to say they have improved the appearance of their sites, put in proper reception areas, car parks, employee facilities, better computers and workable telephones. The result of this investment and technology renewal is in many cases improved quality and productivity.

The ultimate challenge

The effect of the various changes and investments outlined above is to render a lot of the former VEBs competitive in terms of cost efficiency and quality reliability. The irony is that many of them still have little in the way of orders or customers.

This is a tragic paradox for the managers and employees in these companies who have striven and sacrificed, and in fact done a range of sensible things. Yet it is not difficult to explain the paradox if we take the viewpoint of the potential customer. Why should anyone buy from an East German company? These companies have no track record in the West, they cannot publicly demonstrate in a sales-effective way the investments and improvements they have made. No one can be sure of their quality, or reliability. And will these companies still be there in say two years time? And who will own them, and will they still be in the same business? Why take a chance, there is world overcapacity in many of these industries anyway.

We have deliberately formulated this impasse in rather stark terms to push the point home. So what can East German companies do except hope to be bought and somehow integrated into the operations of more substantial West German companies? They cannot enter markets as low-cost producers. Any cost advantage will be purely temporary while trade union initiative pushes East German wage rates up to the level of West German rates; and in any case countries such as Poland, Czechoslovakia and Hungary are much better placed to be middle-term, low-cost producers.

The answer of course is that East German companies can only break in to Western markets by a policy of successful differentiation. But differentiation is notoriously difficult to achieve, even for companies whose managers have read the corporate strategy books, and who have been competing in the arena of free enterprise capitalism for a long time. If companies from the former GDR can attain this objective of differentiation, they will be more than survivors. They will be exemplars of free enterprise achievement.

References

Barratt Brown, M. (1984), *Models in Political Economy*, Harmondsworth: Penguin.

Booz, Allen and Hamilton (1973), Report, 'English translation in German management', *International Studies of Management and Organisation*, Arts and Science Press, Spring/Summer.

Borsdorf, U. and L. Niethammer (1977), *Zwischen Befreiung und Besatzung*, Wuppertal: Peter Hammer Verlag.

Brossard, M. and M. Maurice (1974), 'Existe-t-il un modèle universel des structures d'organisation', *Sociologie du Travail*, vol. XVI, no. 4.

Fores, M. (1972), 'Engineering and the British economic problem', *Quest*, no. 22 (Autumn).

Glover, I. A. (1978), 'Executive career patterns: Britain, France, Germany and Sweden' in Fores, M. and I. Glover, (eds), *Manufacturing and Management*, London: HMSO.

Head, D. (1992), *Made in Germany*, London: Hodder & Stoughton.

Hofstede, G. (1980), *Culture's Consequences*, Beverly Hills & London: Sage.

Hutton, S. P. and P. A. Lawrence (1978), *Production Managers in Britain and Germany*, London: Report to the Department of Industry.

Hutton, S. P. and P. A. Lawrence (1979), *The Work of Production Managers: Case Studies at Manufacturing Companies in West Germany*, London: Report to the Department of Industry.

Laurent, A. (1985), *The Cultural Diversity of Western Conceptions of Management*, in Joynt, P. and M. Warner (eds), *Managing in Different Cultures*, Oslo: Universitetsforlaget.

Lawrence, P. (1980), *Managers and Management in West Germany*, London: Croom Helm.

Lawrence, P. (1984), *Management in Action*, London: Routledge and Kogan Paul.

May, B. (1974), *Social, Educational and Professional Background of German Management*, London: Department of Industry.

Piettre, A. (1952), *L'Economie Allemande Contemporaine (Allemagne Occidentale) 1945–52*, Paris: Librairie de Medicis.

Randlesome, C. (ed.) (1990), *Business Cultures in Europe*, Oxford: Butterworth Heinemann.

Randlesome, C. (1993), *The Business Culture in Germany*, Oxford: Butterworth Heinemann.

Sorge, A. and M. Warner (1978), *Manufacturing Organisation and Work Roles in Great Britain and West Germany*, Discussion paper of the International Institute of Management, Berlin.

Willis, F. R. (1962), *The French in Germany, 1945–9*, Stanford, Calif.: Stanford University Press.

Part III

Integration: people and organizations

[The traveller to Wonderland] will meet strange beings, customs, ways of organizing or disorganizing and theories that are clearly stupid, old fashioned or even immoral – yet they may work, or at least they may not fail more frequently than corresponding theories do at home. Then, after the first culture shock, the traveller to Wonderland will feel enlightened, and may be able to take his or her experiences home and use them advantageously. All great ideas in science, politics and management have travelled from one country to another, and been enriched by foreign influence.

Geert Hofstede, 'Cultural constraints in management theories', *The Executive*, vol. 7, no. 1, 1993, p. 93

The meaning of the word integration should be clear from the start. According to the 'Petit Robert' French dictionary, integration is defined as follows:

Philosophy: creating a tighter interdependence between the parts of a living body or between the members of a society

Psychology: incorporation of new elements in a system (mental integration)

Physiology: coordination of the activities of several organs, necessary to harmonious functioning

Common sense: the way an individual or a group becomes part of a larger group

Integration appears to be the main challenge for European managers and European companies. In Chapter 3 the directors interviewed in the Groupe ESC Lyon study for the European Round Table agreed on the crucial importance of 'involving people in the firm' and 'reciprocal learning' between functions, countries and cultures, as two aspects of the integration effort necessary to improve effectiveness and the quality of working life. In this final part of the book we address some of the key issues involved in integrating people and organizations.

Chapter 7 by Michel Petit, Evalde Mutabazi and Philippe Poirson discusses the process of cultural integration between European countries, first by taking a societal perspective, and then by analyzing some aspects of the international management of human resources in European firms.

In Chapter 8, Tugrul Atamer, Pancho Nunes and Michel Berthelier discuss the integration processes implemented in six major European companies. They highlight two interrelated dimensions: developing a sense of unity throughout an international group and stimulating transverse networks (formal and informal), in order to improve knowledge flows world-wide.

Chapter 9 by Bruno Dufour shows how management education and development can contribute to meeting the integration challenge. Four directions are suggested by the top managers who participated in the Groupe ESC Lyon study for the European Round Table: developing skills in managing people, transnational skills, broad learning, and strengthening cooperation between schools and firms. The requested improvements will require great effort and cooperative strategies from educational institutions: qualification, new products, new organization and partnerships. Thus major changes can be expected in the 1990s.

The importance of management education and development is not surprising. European firms and countries are looking towards more integration. While integration through structures and systems is necessary, it is certainly not sufficient. The stronger source of competitive advantage is integration through people, and this requires adequate management education and development. It is hard to accomplish, it takes time; much has been done already since the 1950s, but much remains to be done. Europeans have no viable alternative: they must improve both their competitiveness and the harmony of their working life.

CHAPTER 7
European cultural integration

Michel Petit, Evalde Mutabazi and Philippe Poirson

On the road that has taken us from the European Coal and Steel Community created in 1951, to the Treaty of European Union, signed in 1992 and ratified in 1994, the prime mover of integration was economic, then strongly relayed by the judicial. Moreover, the hypothesis was made that the economic dynamics would evolve into a political project, naturally bringing about the adhesion of the citizens. The year 1992 showed the limits of this logic. The initial 'no' of the Danish (2 June 1992) concerning the treaty of Maastricht was followed by an extremely close positive result in France where the referendum concerning the treaty ratification barely passed (20 September 1992). Although the Danish electors agreed in the end to Maastricht, under the condition that certain concessions would be made, the warning is very clear. Numerous Europeans question the validity of this integration project. The Cecchini report had promised supplementary growth and creation of numerous jobs due to the realization of a single European market. Now, in 1993, recession is raging and there are 17 million unemployed in the Community. What a deception!

Beyond the economic dimension, the identity of the European Union is being questioned. How is it possible to be European and, at the same time a citizen of a member state? What is European identity in comparison to national or regional identity? The problem is now being phrased in cultural terms, and there should be nothing surprising about this. A process of integration as ambitious as European Union inevitably touches the very foundations of the national communities which are being called upon to live together. Didn't Jean Monnet say, in the wisdom of his old age, that if everything could be done over again, he would start by culture? We are all concerned by this debate, and the present chapter hopes to contribute to it.

We shall proceed in four steps. First, Michel Petit will define a model of integration which can be applied to Europe (section 1). Using this background, he will describe a developing European 'interculture' which preserves the existing national and regional cultural identities (section 2). He will then show how this will have some consequences at the concrete level of daily behaviour (section 3). In section 4, Evalde Mutabazi and Philippe Poirson will analyze the challenge of integration across countries in the domain of human resources management.

1 The dialectics: diversity–unity–integration

Is there a European specificity in the cultural and intercultural realms? After defining the terms culture and interculture, we shall attempt to demonstrate the fundamental character of the diversity–unity–integration dialectics concerning the European interculture.

Culture(s) and interculture(s)

For us, culture is a system in movement. It can be defined by referring to ethnology, for example to Tylor (1913): 'Culture is a complex ensemble which includes the knowledge, beliefs, art, law, morals, customs, and all of the other capacities and habits acquired by man as a member of a society.' By saying 'system in movement', we wish to emphasize the dynamic aspect of the process, rather than its outcome – which is artificially fused at a given time. Cultures evolve in time, in the rhythm of the development of human communities and, in particular, under the influence of other cultures.

The particular situations in which two or several cultures are in contact over a long period of time produce interferences. For example, the interferences between cultures stemming from distinct national identities, as between France and Belgium, France and Germany, Germany and Austria, etc., is designated by the term *interculture*.

The term dialectics is to be understood as the following: 'According to Hegel, a way of thinking which acknowledges the inseparability of contradictions (thesis and antithesis), that one can unite into a higher category (synthesis)' (Petit Robert Dictionary, 1984). In other words, contradiction stimulates a deeper understanding. From the negation of a given term, it is possible to go beyond an irreducible dualism and assent to a more elaborate level of reflection. This is what we shall attempt to do regarding the European interculture.

Diversities

The mind is immediately struck by the amazing diversity of the European continent (Duroselle, 1990, p. 15):

> One can travel three thousand kilometers in the great plains of the
> United States, in the Russian forest, in the plains and steppes of
> Ukraine, in the vast frontier regions of the Amazon and of the Zairian
> equatorial forest, in the great subtropical deserts, in the mountains of
> Central Asia and the Andes without a noticeable change in the
> countryside. On the contrary, in Occidental Europe, it is difficult to

travel more than one hundred kilometers without the countryside changing with an extreme distinctness.

The scenery is planted. All that is left is to put in the diversity of climates, languages, ways and customs, work methods, relationships between men and women in order to gather all of the ingredients necessary for this famous 'culture shock' that affects expatriates some time after the beginning of a stay in a foreign country.

Diversity is also found in some statistics which show the heterogeneity of the conditions of life inside the Community. Between Portugal and Luxembourg, the GNP per capita is in a 1 to 5 ratio. This means that in terms of GNP per capita, Portugal is 30 years behind in development in comparison to the 'Grand Duchy'. We can also compare the annual working hours in ex-West Germany (1697 hours) with those in Portugal (2025 hours). The difference represents around six working weeks of 40 hours each. To top it all off, the German blue-collar worker (ex-West Germany) earns about four times more than the Portuguese blue-collar worker (see *Globus Kartendienst*, 5 March 1990).

European diversities therefore take many forms, and are not evenly distributed across countries. Nevertheless, European diversities literally leap to the eye (Mermet, 1991). They blind the observer, who winds up thinking that these differences largely prevail over any common points and that the process of European integration, therefore, rests on a fragile base. In fact, this is not the case if one considers the underlying unity which is the antithesis of the diversities immediately perceptible.

Unity

Hartmut Kaelble, a professor of economics and social history at the University of Berlin, has collected a great number of statistics concerning the social aspects of Western Europe and North America. He has meticulously studied the data while asking himself the following question: is there any specificity in the social history of Europe? The following is a summary of the conclusions that he reached (Kaelble, 1988).

At the social level, Western European societies can clearly be distinguished from North American ones, and in particular, those of the United States. For instance, the social role of the Welfare State is conceived of as very different on each side of the Atlantic. Indeed, Western European societies have an extensive social coverage at their disposal. They demand from the state that it organizes social solidarity, in particular in relation to health costs. Certainly, there are differences of degree, in particular between the northern European countries, where the state intervenes heavily in the social sector, and those of southern Europe, where this type of intervention is lighter. Nevertheless, the principle of the Welfare State remains the rule of thumb in Europe.

Another major difference between the United States and Europe lies in the lesser mobility of Europeans on the geographic as well as the social level. Then again, there are more cleavages between the social classes in Europe than in the United States, even though there exist very noticeable differences within Western Europe.

Another important dissimilarity lies in the inequality of revenues. Kaelble compares the average wage gain for the fifth and the twentieth percentile of the least well paid in both Europe and the United States. He concludes: 'It is clearly seen that the relative differences are distinctly greater in the United States than in Great Britain and Federal Germany. In 1969, the relative difference between these two groups was even two times higher in the United States' (Kaelble, 1988, p. 41). The author also highlights the different role that the family plays, in particular the importance of solicitude between parents and children, which is, according to him, more pronounced in Europe than in the United States. Finally, he underlines the importance of average-sized towns (between 20 000 and 100 000 inhabitants) in the European landscape and their crucial role throughout the history of this continent.

To the question: 'Is there a specificity in the social history of Europe?', Kaelble globally responds positively: 'As a consequence, there exists, this is at least the thesis I support, a social integration of Western Europe, integration which is simultaneously obvious, continuous, and already greatly evolved; a specifically European path which was and remains often very different from those followed by North America, Japan, Australia or the USSR' (Kaelble, 1988, p. 153). Kaelble's approach is rigorous and innovative. It rests upon a tight analysis of statistics and demonstrates that a little known European identity has been formed over a long period of time and has now become an unconscious European collective.

This European heritage and the needs of the population deserve the attention of all of our political and business leaders, as was emphasized in a report by the European Round Table (Monod *et al.*, 1991, p. 18):

> Europe's principal long-term resource lies in its people, as it always has done. Their skills, attitudes and efforts are the factors which will decide our future. They must be at the centre of any policy agenda.
>
> We have good reason to be confident in this 'human dimension' because of a paradox which we can all see in modern Europe. It is the ordinary people who are coming together in practical terms and integrating the patterns of their daily lives, while the formal institutions, largely established on national lines, have difficulty in adjusting. The events in Eastern Europe have proved this beyond all doubt.

Integration

How can we reconcile the two antagonistic terms: the obvious diversities and the underlying unity?

It must be recognized that until very recently, the diversities of our continent were seen as divisions. For centuries, European history was marked by the aggressivity of feudal systems, kingdoms, empires, and finally nation-states which were set up against one another or grouped together in ephemeral alliances. The diversities were thus a source of spatial fragmentation and exacerbated the most endogenous aspects of each culture. They generated many hatreds, exclusions and European civil wars. World War II tragically completed Europe's auto-destruction. Jean Monnet had the idea of reciprocal control in order to reduce distrust. That idea, taken up by Robert Schuman, gave birth to the European Coal and Steel Community which coordinated the production and sale of coal, steel and iron products in six states of Europe. The process of European integration was launched.

Integration should be understood as a voluntary and conscious dynamic, fundamentally different from the long, profound and unconscious trends that we term 'convergence'. The logic of European integration does not lead to uniformity by erasing diversities. The integration process is pluralistic, in the sense that it accepts particularities and differences. The hand which remained held out in Denmark's direction after its rejection of the Maastricht Treaty is but one example of this. The reconciliatory strategy towards the United Kingdom is another. On the other hand, regional differences find their place in the general process of European integration. To take all of this into account, a subtle game of negotiation has developed, which includes some creativity in the search for compromise. For more than 40 years new behaviours have emerged. As soon as one goes beyond the EC borders the process of integration is less evident. In Eastern Europe, for instance it is more of a disintegration process that is at work for the moment. For these reasons, the EC should play a role as an organizing pole for the European continent.

The dialectics of diversity–unity–integration is our daily reality in Europe. Europeans do not use it consciously and systematically enough. This goes for the European authorities as well as for the European citizen. We should learn to take advantage of diversities while avoiding their becoming incompatibilities. We should also learn to rely on the existing unity, making ourselves more conscious of it and using it to improve communication. Indeed the European interculture is based on integration.

2 European identity and European interculture

The mythological image of Europe – daughter of the king of Phoenicia, taken to Crete by Zeus who was metamorphosed into a bull – does not help us much in tracing the identity of the continent of Europe.

European identity

Denis de Rougemont (1990) suggests a kaleidoscope of definitions. For instance, from the writer Paul Valery (p. 335): 'Every race and every territory that has been successively Romanized, Christianized, and subjected in its spirit to Greek discipline, is absolutely European.' In reading these lines, one can think of a common European heritage as it has been named by Edgard Morin (1987): a 'judeo-christiano-greco-latin culture'. But, everyone does not agree with this concept of heritage, and particularly with its content. According to Uffe Ostergaard (*Courrier International*, 12 March 1992), Europeans are: 'Those who have felt the effects of the French revolution, the British industrial revolution, and German romantism'. Finally, for Jacques Le Goff (*Le Monde*, 4 February 1992): 'The European spiritual unity is a heritage: medieval scholastic thought, humanism, enlightenment, and other artistic and intellectual movements, such as, more recently, surrealism. But from this heritage, something new must be built. Establishing the link between the past and the creation of something new is very exciting.'

These definitions are far from being identical, even though they have points in common. On the other hand, all are validating Europe. One would think that Europe has produced only beautiful and noble things... but our continent also appeared as an aggressive civilization which imposed its models through violence on other populations. Jacques Attali (1991, p. 282) described this visceral tendency of Europeans to colonize the rest of the world:

> Colonization, in the modern sense of the term, began in 1492. After having marked, then labelled the rest of the world, Christian Europe took possession of it. Colonization was actually nothing but a cumbersome preliminary for commerce when it could not establish itself alone. People went around Africa in order to trade in Asia, but they colonized America in so far as this continent had the good taste to have gold and silver lay hidden, and was favourable to cultivating sugar cane.

Europeans became experts in the art of creating 'ideal' societies abroad (for instance perfect Christian states). Within half a century 75 million Americans perished, and in four centuries more than 13 million Africans were deported as slaves in the American continent.

The European cultural heritage is thus quite difficult to define, as it carries a contradiction between humanistic pluralism on the one hand and totalitarian inhumanity on the other. In the future, the scenario of integration can only develop if the pluralistic heritage dominates, in other words if Doctor Jekyll stops metamorphosing himself into Mister Hyde.

A European interculture

The European interculture must avoid the trap of Euro-centrism and the temptation to export national or European fantasies. Within the EC, Europeans should devote themselves to a double opening.

The first opening is within the Community. It exists through the suppression of borders, the expansion of individual and collective spaces, and the play of the four fundamental liberties (free circulation of people, money, goods and services). Economic interactions and cultural cross-fertilization will take place between individuals from the different nationalities through interpersonal contacts, if individuals adapt appropriate behaviour (see section 3). But openness and geographical mobility are hard to learn.

The second opening concerns the rest of Europe and the rest of the world. The European Community is often seen by those exterior to it, as a fortress:

> Let us take the example of 'Fortress Europe'. For the Americans, who are apparently the fathers of this expression, it relates to the fear of an economic, and maybe affective, exclusion. For the Japanese, it is not only a commercial but also a psychological fortress (European egocentrism mixed with some hypocrisy). For the Chinese diaspora, it is the European immigration policy that takes on an allure of a fortress, with the Central European states hidden under cover behind the battlements, ready to turn into economic dragons. For the third or fourth world countries, there is a fortress in the landscape, but Europeans, Americans, and Japanese are side by side within the walls. From one fortress to the other, one slides from reality to fantasy. And so on goes the metaphor. (Petit *et al.*, 1991, p. 286).

One must constantly bear in mind that the perception of the EC is inversed, depending on whether the observer is inside (feeling of openness) or outside (feeling of being closed out) of the Community. It is equally important to understand that any deepening of the Community (in opposition to widening, i.e. the welcoming of new members) is likely to reinforce the feeling of exclusion towards potential membership candidates. (Who also become well aware that the cost of entry is getting higher and higher for them.) As a consequence, the EC *double* opening (internal and external) is a major challenge in the current stage of European integration.

The European interculture must also avoid the trap of simplistic models. Over the centuries, Europe has consumed many models which provided particular conceptions of religion, philosophies or political ideologies. Today many Europeans legitimately react with distrust towards universal solutions which are disguised as models. However, new simplistic models come back through the window.

It has been said that Europe should be organized according to the German economic, monetary and social model. Long live the market social economy, so to speak! Others pretend that we should raise English to the level of the unique European language. Long live the 'Anglo-glotty'! To a certain extent, Europeans should thus turn themselves into English-speaking Germans. This scenario should be opposed with an energetic 'non, merci!' Here are the reasons.

About the 'Rhenan model'

The current German social market economy ('Soziale Marktwirtschaft') rests upon the following principles: free enterprise, free competition, monetary stability, and social redistribution via various actions of the government. The German government limits itself, among other things, to a global orientation of its economic activity ('Globale Steuerung') and is careful not to participate in the collective negotiations ('Tarifverträge') which are the exclusive domain of the employer/ employee representatives (Sozialpartner). Michel Albert (1991) has raised this politico-economical system to the ranks of a model under the name 'Rhenan Capitalism'.

> The main debate opposes two models of capitalism: first, the 'Neo-American' model, based upon individual success and short-term financial profit, which are strongly publicized. Secondly, the 'Rhenan' model, which is practised in Germany, Switzerland, Benelux, Northern Europe, and also in Japan, but with some variants. It encourages collective success, consensus, and long-term solicitude. (Albert, 1991, book jacket).

In the Rhenan model the crossed networks of interests, dominated by the banks, allow enterprises to develop in the long term. The German system of joint management arranges roles for all participants within this network: shareholders, managers, and all other employees.

Our objective here is not to delve into the details of the model, particularly regarding the degree of relevance of a regrouping of German and Japanese systems under the same name. Rather, we shall ask ourselves if this 'model' really has the economic and social superiority that Michel Albert attributes to it, and if it is really applicable to Europe.

First, it is necessary to point out that, in June 1993, both the Neo-American and the Rhenan models were at grips with the recession, and it is impossible at this point to say which of the two will come out of it quicker. Consider the current situation in Germany. As applied to ex-East Germany, the West German 'model' has its work cut out for it. Market forces alone have not been able to rebuild the new Bundesländers. The federal government (Bundesregierung) has been forced to leave its traditional conservative position and intervene more and more energetically, specifically in economic areas. The new Länders are assisted and will be for a long time to come. Here is the first wrench in the model. On the other hand, the salary negotiations, led by the employees' associations, have spread to the Eastern Länders. The catching-up of salaries in the East, without a corresponding increase in the employees' productivity, certainly threatens the very existence of East German enterprises who survived the deindustrialization of ex-East Germany (see *Der Spiegel*, 19 January, 1993, pp. 138–47). But what will happen when prices of consumer goods in the East equal, or even surpass, Western prices? There is a great risk of creating a two-speed society that would burst the 'social peace' of which the Germans are so very proud.

To top it all off, the intra-cultural conflict between Western Germans (Wessis) and Eastern Germans (Ossis) takes on tremendous proportions. The 'Ossis' feel as if they are being colonized by their new Western co-citizens who wanted to apply a model of economic and social organization completely foreign to the local situation without any concessions, or any consideration either. Germany is now coping with an historically unprecedented intra-cultural conflict.

Faced with such a situation, some are thinking that the German social market economy may not be a model, if what is understood by model is a political-economic system or process which produces identical effects independently of the situation in which it is applied. Confronted with problems that are linked to the German unification, the social market economy evolves towards a system in which the state intervenes increasingly and thus has to reconsider its position in respect to market forces and industrial relations.

Should the EC apply the principles of Rhenan capitalism? As far as the British are concerned, this idea seems to be ruled out right away. They do not have the same concept of how companies should be run. The British firm is subjected to the hard laws of financial markets and therefore to the imperative of quick profits. In addition, the British seem to be completely against the German concept of industrial relations. They do not want a 'babysitter' state as far as social matters are concerned. And as far as accepting any kind of leadership from the Bundesbank is concerned, it is really not their cup of tea... In the South, the financial structure of firms, the class differences, the way in which employers' associations and trade unions are organized, and more adversarial industrial relations make the transfer of the German model illusory. France is seduced by some aspects of Rhenan capitalism, but would probably reject many others and prefer to rely on its deep-rooted tendency towards centralization and state intervention. So on the whole, Europeans do not want to adopt the Rhenan model. They may pick up some good ideas there, but that is all.

Should Europeans all become Anglo-glots?

Is it possible to conceive of an integrated Europe without a common European language? If it is not, is there a European language other than English?

For some, one of whom is Alain Minc (1989, p. 225), the answer is obvious:

> There exists a single European esperanto – English – and that language
> is probably the only major contribution brought by Great Britain to
> Europe. Firms have acknowledged it for years, since they have all
> worked with this business lingua franca which is supposed to resemble
> English. And it is often in that way that a Dutch, German, or Italian
> company communicates with its foreign subsidiaries, and not by using
> the mother company's language.

First of all, there is an injustice in Minc's words when he talks about 'the only major contribution' brought by Great Britain to Europe. Let us be reminded that Lord Cockfield, the 'father' of the White Paper on 'the achievement of the European domestic market', is a subject of the United Kingdom. This document has contributed greatly to giving a new impetus to the integration process, starting from 1985. It should also be noted that almost every member state, at some time during the integration process, has been a difficult partner. France certainly has been with its definitive blocking of the Community project concerning a European defence, its empty chair policy, etc. Although we would not wish to start a controversy with Alain Minc over a few words, one can see here a hint of ethnocentrism which leaves a feeling that an intercultural approach is needed when thinking of European matters.

English certainly is the business lingua franca. However, the average level of English is extremely variable within the different European countries. The English that is spoken in many meetings is often very weird. It bewilders the British themselves, and it gives the hives to Anglicists! To say that non-British mother companies use such a lingua franca to communicate with their subsidiaries is a hasty generalization. Some communicate in an excellent English, others systematically resort to their translation departments and communicate in their subsidiary's language. As for the subsidiaries, some have a translation department which is sometimes put to the disposal of the mother company.

The CEO of a subsidiary of a French firm in Germany recently noted: 'In our meetings between the French and Germans, we use English as a working language. Out of eight hours of meetings, we hear eight hours of presentations. Not one question is asked. There is very little interaction.' In this case, the problem being raised goes far beyond choice of languages and differences in levels of language ability. The choice of a working language could sterilize intercultural exchanges and affect the strategic dimension of the relationships between the mother company and the subsidiary.

Testimonies of specialists in international negotiations bring other insights into this debate. One must be very cautious about the interlocutors' level of English and learn to speak, if necessary, an extremely simplified English which is sometimes very difficult for Anglophones. In some cases, it is better to resort to an interpreter, if there is a way of controlling what he or she says and how it is said. Others also say that when one makes a purchase, one is entitled to choose the language to speak; however, when selling something, one is better off speaking the client's language.

Thus the issue of languages in the process of European integration is quite a complex one, and there is no miraculous solution to it. About 40 languages are spoken in various degrees in Europe. They have often been a determining factor of national or cultural unity. Language diversity is perceived as a great cultural wealth by most Europeans. A great deal of attention has been brought to this issue by the European Community. It is the only international institution to have nine official languages.

Without doubt, foreign languages constitute a barrier to communication between people. However, it would be iniquitous to try to solve the problem by imposing a simplistic bilingualism on each European: mother language plus English. The unavoidable consequence would be a dramatic impoverishment of communication and an accumulation of misunderstandings and things left unsaid.

Umberto Ecco pointed out in an interview that he gave to the French newspaper *Le Monde* (29 September 1992):

It could be useful to decide what vehicular language to use: English, Spanish, or an esperanto. It would be a technical problem to solve. However, Europe's problem is to go towards polylinguism; we should

place our hopes in a polyglot Europe. The problem of Europe is to find
a political unity through polyglotism.

Languages are not only used as a vehicle for technical information needed in
everyday life, but also to carry our culture and as real vectors of thought.

Multilinguism is a basis for development of the European interculture, which
is at the heart of European integration. It is important to organize it in an intelligent
and systematic way. For graduate students, a good strategy appears to be the
following: mother language plus first foreign language (other than English to the
level of negotiation skills) plus second foreign language (English to a medium level)
plus third foreign language (understood but neither spoken nor written). When
choosing languages to learn it is advisable to take into account the idea of 'language
of proximity', especially for the third foreign language. For south-western France,
Spanish is self-evident, but why not Catalan? For south-eastern France, Italian
would be more useful. This linguistic networking of Europe should be approached
at a global level (developing a strategy, like the one suggested above) or a regional
level in order to achieve individual *linguistic skills* which are reasonably diverse and
likely to meet the diversity needs of business and other institutions.

Such an approach could seem exaggerated and even utopian. But it is not. Let
us take a little known example, and then finish with an anecdote. Most natives of
Luxembourg speak French and German fluently. They learned English as a third
language. As a mother language, they often use a local dialect. Here is an interesting
example of a small member state that should be borne in mind by those who believe
they are big and who behave with the grace of elephants. Charles Quint, Emperor
of Germany between 1519 and 1556, was a confirmed polyglot. He pretended to
speak Spanish to God, French to his men, Italian to women, and German to his
horses. Should we condemn ourselves to English as a business lingua franca?

The principle of subsidiarity

The insertion of the subsidiarity principle in the Maastricht Treaty opens new
prospects to the Community. Article 3B of the treaty stipulates:

> The Community shall act within the limits of the powers conferred
> upon it by this Treaty and of the objectives assigned to it therein. In
> areas which do not fall within its exclusive competence, the Community
> shall take action, in accordance with the principle of subsidiarity, only
> and in so far as the objectives of the proposed action cannot be
> sufficiently achieved, by reason of the scale or effects of the proposed
> actions, by the Member States and can therefore, be better achieved by
> the Community. (Treaty on European Union)

The intention is commendable. It allows government to take measures while
remaining close to the field. This principle is at the very basis of the sharing of
powers in a federal system. Within the European Union, it should promote new
areas and forms of action at the regional level. According to the Maastricht Treaty,

regions are to be represented at the Community level through a Regional Committee, which will give them the possibility of expressing themselves without going through the intermediary level of member states. In this way, intermediary levels may become more responsible and form a polycentric organization. (This process is similar to the new modes of organization which large firms are trying to implement.)

In reality, applying this subsidiarity principle is quite delicate, since it can lead to two extreme biases: either an indifference from the higher level *vis-à-vis* the problems encountered by lower levels, or a corporatist attitude from lower levels which have become insensitive to common interest. If the Community lost on both counts, we would wind up with a tribal Europe. The European Court of Justice should help avoid such biases in the implementation of the subsidiarity principle. But again, the solution to the problem of European integration lies in the modification of behaviours and in a learning process, both of which go beyond legal frameworks.

The specific role of regions in the future Union should be underlined. Together they can be the melting pots where diversities are integrated in an original way. They can come together on both sides of border zones, or according to their economic or cultural complementarities. Together they can carry out ambitious programmes which otherwise could not be conducted alone (Scardigli *et al.*, 1993). The coordinated action of regions is thus in a position to redefine the economic mapping and the political landscape of the future Europe.

Instead of trying to define a European identity which has been unclear in the past and is not expected in the future, it is more useful to think in terms of a European *interculture*, defined as the integration of national and regional identities. In that matter the principle of subsidiarity will be of great help in defining the relevant subsystems within the whole.

3 The European interculture: a daily experience

As far as interculture is concerned, we often tend to imagine extreme situations, for instance, Touaregs and Laplanders. The first have a dozen words at their disposal which characterize the different tones of beige which are very useful for locating oneself in the desert. The others know about 20 words to designate the different types of snow. Will they be able to understand each other? Do they really have an interest in meeting each other and working together?

In Europe, the intercultural situations are much less extreme. It is more like a realm of little differences (see below). On the other hand, there are national stereotypes which can make you laugh or smile, if they do not make you grit your teeth. How can we handle them and use them for communication (see page 182)? More generally, how must one act and react in an intercultural context (see page 183)? Are there any useful behavioural principles in such situations?

Little differences make big misunderstandings

It is usually thought that the closer the cultures, the more rapid and easy the integration. It is evident that a Frenchman who does not speak any foreign language will be less disoriented going to Torino or Milan than to Saxony or Bavaria. What can we say then of an expatriate in Japan or Southeast Asia! However, cultural proximity tends to make people less vigilant, and vigilance is a very important quality in any intercultural context. The French quickly begin thinking that the Italians are like the French and that the Germans are, in the end, not so different (especially if, in addition, they speak French). Being less on guard leads one to forget the little differences which accumulate and end up by interfering with communication, thus considerably weighing down work relationships. Let us illustrate that by a situation which is partially fiction and probably a little bit exaggerated, but supported by the testimony of numerous foreign students who have come to France to continue their studies.

A Norwegian in Lyon

Our typical student is Norwegian. Her name is Sigurd Christiansen. She started her French studies in Oslo and she came to Lyon for a BA in Modern Literature. She had just moved into a university dormitory on the Fourvière hill. On this first Monday of October, she must go to the Bron-Parilly campus, which is at the other side of the town, in order to register for her courses. While on the pedestrian crossing, which is in front of her dormitory, a speeding car barely misses her. It is clear that the driver saw her because he winked at her while passing. Sigurd thinks that this behaviour is dangerous and astounding.

The bus is jammed full. However, it manages to take in a few more passengers at each stop. It is a 45-minute commute. Sigurd is surprised by how loudly everyone speaks. She is forced to hear the weekend adventures of two students. Our young and pretty Norwegian notices that quite a few men are looking at her. How should she interpret these looks? She is not used to this, and in any case it makes her feel uncomfortable. In Norway, one could interpret this as sexual harassment. How would French women behave in this type of situation? Sigurd will not have the answer today. The bus arrives at Bron, discharging its mass of students who rush towards the department secretaries' offices. The posted information is very difficult to decipher, for a foreigner in any case. Sigurd joins a line only to find out that registration takes place somewhere else. She must wait in line again. There is again this closeness, almost promiscuous; of people who touch you and bump into you without even excusing themselves. Many girls and boys are kissing each other two, three even four times (!) to say hello. Jesus, all of this is so unexpected.

The day goes on without Sigurd being able to finish her registration. Many class groups are closed because they are already full. No one knows if supplementary groups will be opened. 'Come back tomorrow, or the next day'; 'See the teacher in charge'. The clerk in charge is overwhelmed, nervous, impatient and Sigurd's French is too laborious. She is completely worn out so she returns to the dormitory. Unfortunately, her neighbours are listening to rock music. They are going to party until late into the night and the walls are so thin!

And this is just the beginning. Students or teacher-students who have already experienced this know the situation well.

As soon as they arrive at their university, foreign students are literally bombarded with a multitude of visual, auditive, even olfactive stimuli. These stimulate and disorient them, both at the same time. In general, they are not prepared for this because their image of France is rather intellectual and disembodied, coming from books. As far as the university is concerned, the differences are far from being negligible. Sigurd will have to get used to the very magisterial style of French teachers, the students' passivity, the difficulty of group work, making friends, or finding other students on campus during the weekends. It will be a long while before she finds the key elements that will allow her to reconcile the differences between university life in France and Norway.

The accumulation of little differences unite to form the conditions for a 'culture shock'.

As a general rule, such cultural shocks resolve themselves satisfactorily because the students are young and adaptable. The same is not true of working situations where expatriates who are not well prepared for life in a foreign country must make rapid decisions, and hopefully correct ones. They must motivate and direct their collaborators, and cooperate with the firm's hierarchy. It is not necessary to send a French executive as far as Asia in order to expose him to the anguish of a culture shock. Having a job to do in Germany is enough to give him added stress.

No, it is not a question of simply learning German punctuality, but rather of organizing one's time differently, as far as the direction of meetings or management of projects is concerned, while respecting procedures and the delegation of authority. One must equally learn to argue in the German style, more slowly but in a more structured way, while being careful to support each argument. It is also important to avoid interrupting others repeatedly and to respect their turn to speak by paying complete attention to what they say. The Frenchman must also learn to avoid purple language and situations that can lead to verbal duels.

The two examples presented here lead us to the following conclusions:

● Intercultural situations are not as harmless as we think.

- Cultural differences are tolerated, provided that one is able to perceive differences and avoid accumulating the little mistakes that result in misunderstandings.
- It is extremely desirable to prepare actively and seriously for these intercultural experiences. Think of the many expatriations which fail because they have been neither sufficiently anticipated nor sufficiently monitored. Think of all the stress which could be avoided, for instance in Sigurd's situation, by having appropriate information, contacts with veteran exchange students, and a more personalized welcome.

This is already being done in some cases. However, in the EC the rate of student mobility is about 5 per cent. What should we do with the remaining 95 per cent? Intercultural learning is one of the major challenges for the construction of the European Community.

National stereotypes

'Evil be to him who in stereotypes thinks' (Amossy, 1991, p. 11). Ruth Amossy condenses in one sentence what she elsewhere calls 'one of the strongest obsessions of modern times'. Indeed, stereotypes are not well thought of, especially among intellectuals, who devote themselves to tracking them down and fighting against them. Intellectuals even run the risk of replacing stereotypes by 'more serious' notions which will, in turn, be renounced and reduced to the level of new stereotypes. In short, one feels a little bit guilty when raising this subject, especially if one is trying to dedramatize it. Nevertheless, this is what we are going to do now for national stereotypes by exclaiming the motto: stereotypes, one must live with them!

In Europe, national stereotypes abound. Let us enumerate the jumble: the French (French beret and French bread under the arm), the Italian (spaghetti and a mandolin), the Spanish (paëlla and castanets), the English (bowler hat and a certain aloofness), the German (leather knickers and a beer mug). What a parade in front of a debonair Belgian, holding a paper cone of chips, and under the mischievous eye of a native of Luxembourg...

There are less polite stereotypes. For instance, people like to talk about an ideal European who would drive like a Frenchman, have the self-control of an Italian, be as humble as a Spaniard, cook as well as a Brit, have the sense of humour of a German, be as quick-minded as a Belgian, and have the universal reputation of a native Luxembourger! Presented in this way, these preconceived wrong ideas appear quite inoffensive. Nothing is less so though, hence it is useful to take into account the arguments against stereotypes.

We shall consider 'stereotype' in its sociological sense, such as the Encyclopaedia Universalis defines it (1985 edition, volume 17, p. 200): '... opinions and judgements that social groups pass about one another, and indirectly to themselves'.

In the same article, it is shown that judgements passed in this way define unchanging structures and overly simplified 'meanings' which give feelings of security for social groups which then maintain their cohesion. The danger lies less in the stereotype itself, understood as a mistaken concept of classification, than in its use, especially when it turns into a preconceived idea. It is then translated into a mental attitude that is clearly negative towards a representative of a foreign ethnic group. Such an attitude leads directly to discrimination and can gradually lead to reprehensible acts.

Stereotypes are thus far from being trivial. They do exist in the minds of our working partners and in the different European countries with which we are in increasingly closer contact. So it is useless to deny their existence. It is more worthy to recognize them. For instance, for many Germans, a Frenchman is by definition always late and undisciplined. He can easily develop philosophical arguments, but lacks rigour and does not willingly tackle problems in detail. This incisive judgement carries enough weight to offend many of the French. In our opinion, such an excessive judgement, which it is precisely the very nature of a stereotype, does not deserve such a distressed reaction. On the contrary, it might be interesting for the French to use it and to turn it round in their favour. I shall illustrate this idea through an anecdote. When I work with German partners whom I have not met before, it very often occurs to me to say, when the opportunity arises: 'You know, I am French and thus, like all of my compatriots, I am not capable of organizing myself and respecting deadlines...' – 'But you do not believe what you are saying, Herr Petit' reply all of my acquaintances, 'These are nothing but preconceived ideas... By the way, we even know Germans who are completely disorganized.' And, if they try hard enough, they can even find one.

Therefore, long live stereotypes when they allow you to show your foreign colleagues and acquaintances that you have taken a certain distance from your nationality. This capacity to distance oneself from one's ethnic group is particularly useful in intercultural situations.

How to behave in an intercultural situation?

In each intercultural situation, the interlocutors' behaviour is a key factor of success. Here we provide a few guidelines: releasing cultural reflexes (automatisms), refusing assimilation, and metalinguistic communication.

Releasing cultural automatisms

We have been experiencing group life situations since birth. Progressively, we have learned to analyze them, i.e. to interpret words, insinuations, intonations, looks, expressions and gestures, all of which are characteristics of our culture of origin. This complex activity is rarely put into practice in a conscious and reasoned manner. As time passes, we become able to manage a considerable number of ordinary situations with a quasi-automatic reflex. The same process goes on in professional situations, where we have also learned to extract relevant elements, interpret them instantly, and respond with an adequate behavioural answer.

To summarize, we carry out a very selective decoding of the situation (by retaining only relevant elements and barely registering others) and we find in our package of reactions an adequate behavioural answer which we then adjust and modulate according to our interlocutors' reactions and our communication strategy. All of this is fine as long as we stay within our well-known cultural context, where cultural automatisms are effective. But in intercultural situations the game is much more complex and automatic behaviours create problems.

Cultural automatisms operate in social situations, for instance relationships between males and females obey different rules across Europe. Taken separately, these rules are not necessarily very different from one another, but their cumulative effects might well create many misunderstandings. During a party which French and German people are attending, a strange ballet is taking place. As much as the French are stepping forward towards their interlocutors, Germans are stepping back. In extreme cases, the bi-national couples can cross half the length of a room the French moving forward, the Germans moving back. The explanation is simple. The natural interpersonal distance for the French can be gauged as the length of a forearm. For the Germans, the distance is almost twice as far (arm and forearm). Each tries to establish and re-establish the right distance with a quasi-reflex. Other differences such as gestures can also be noticed between French and Germans. In public situations, a German will accompany his words with usual gestures like keeping his elbows next to his body. A Frenchman will be more willing to use his whole arm. Such a large gesture will often be interpreted as being a pure gesticulation, especially by northern Germans, unless they release their cultural automatisms.

Professional examples are also interesting. A German executive who has no experience of France visits a French firm. During the interviews that he carries out with French executives, they are frequently interrupted by the phone, or by different people entering the room murmuring a magic formula like 'Do you have a minute?' If the German executive lets his cultural automatisms play, he has all the reasons in the world to be offended. Numerous interruptions show in Germany a total lack of interest in the visitor. Such is not the case in France. The French are more willing to do several things at the same time and to use the phone in order to communicate information quickly which is not always essential, but could be ...

The conclusion which can be drawn from these situations is quite obvious. In intercultural situations, it is necessary to release one's cultural automatisms. Situations must be decoded in the broad sense by considering as many elements as possible and asking whether they are relevant within the welcoming culture. It is then desirable to develop one's capacities for observation and turn oneself into an amateur ethnologist.

Moreover, the sense of observation should go hand in hand with a sense of reserve which consists of changing one's reactions slightly and avoiding words that are too harsh. The advice works best for natives of Southern Europe. On the other hand Northern Europeans have a natural sense of reserve which could sterilize communication. It might be useful for both to reduce the gap.

Refusing assimilation

During the time it takes to acquire an intercultural sensitivity, it is not unusual to go through a phase where the desire for acculturation becomes exaggerated and even obsessive. One would love to speak the language as well as the natives and be totally immersed in a foreign culture and live in total symbiosis with it. Such an attitude has very positive effects on motivation, thus on the mobilization of energy, and on the capacity for endurance. However, it is also important to know how to stop in time, for this extreme strategy can never end with the desired objective. Indeed, there comes a time in the learning of a language when every supplementary step requires spending very high levels of energy for an uncertain result. This is the case when someone wants to make every sign of a foreign accent disappear. Yet, this very foreign accent may well be an interesting factor of differentiation in comparison to natives.

Where 'foreignism' persists, being 'foreign' has some sort of attractive exoticism. The essential is to attain an optimal communication level in the foreign language, which is often called 'negotiation skill' – a skill in which linguistic and cultural factors are very closely linked. This can be reached without turning one's back on one's culture of origin, under the pretext of becoming even more English than an Englishman or more Germanic than a German, although acculturation always comes with some auto-mutilation of the culture of origin. However, this is not what interculture is about. The creative strength stems from a duality between cultures and their cross-fertilization.

Europeans are right to refuse assimilation to a dominant cultural model, they should develop their 'negotiation skill' in other languages and cultures in order to communicate better and learn *from each other*.

Intercultural communication

We have already broached this subject in the preceding paragraphs. Let us remember the necessity for Europeans to learn not only several foreign languages but also to speak their own mother language as a foreign language when they communicate with foreigners. That is to say, with a reduced vocabulary, by avoiding uncommon words, word plays, and by speaking more slowly without forgetting to reformulate essential information when necessary.

The ability to listen plays a major role in intercultural communication. It should be supported by a talent for asking questions. All types of questions are useful: rhetorical questions, asking for details, etc. The skill for questioning is not developed enough in language studies. There, it is the teacher who often asks the questions and the students who try to reply. It would be a good idea sometimes to reverse the roles.

Generally speaking, communication in a foreign language requires particular care at a metalinguistic level. Metalinguistic activity is not concerned with the technical aspects of the subject in question, but the modalities of the communication in process. It allows the interlocutors to assess if they are on the same wavelength, to check that they understand what is happening in the exchange, and that communication is not being hampered. In a negotiation between a French person and a German, it is important for the interlocutors to understand that they may not have the same way of arguing. The Germans tend to support each of their arguments while the French put much more emphasis on the global architecture of the argument without spending too long on the details. In the same way, the French communicate in a much more implicit way, while the Germans feel it important to explain all elements. When they do not understand such differences, a German and a French person can draw radically different conclusions about how a meeting went. The first may think that no decision was made; the second may be convinced of the contrary.

In summary, it should be emphasized that communication in an intercultural context demands particular qualities: the ability to listen, the capacity for instantaneous lucid analysis, the capacity for changing style and skills in practising a metalinguistic discourse (i.e. discussing the communication problems that the persons involved may have felt). This approach regulates communication and contributes greatly to reducing ambiguity and avoiding misunderstandings. It puts the subject at hand into brackets in order to concentrate on the modalities of communication. As such it is a necessary step in trying to learn about and from foreign cultures.

4 Managing human resources across European countries

The management of human resources in European firms is marked by the same general characteristics which were found to be shared across European countries (cf. Chapter 2): respect for international diversity, people-orientation, negotiation, and balanced positions between the American and Japanese extremes (for instance concerning training, mobility, promotion, and remuneration policies).

The management of human resources world-wide seems to be converging in the following directions (see for instance IBM, 1992):

● Increasingly integrated in strategic decision-making.
● Split between small headquarters staff and decentralized units.
● Integrated in the operational challenges that the firms take up (such as flexible organization or total quality programmes).

However, the differences between European countries or zones in this area still dominate. The annual reports of the Price Waterhouse–Cranfield project, which studies international strategic human resource management across 10 European countries, demonstrate that harmonization is slow. Indeed the management of human resources will probably be one of the last functions (along with sales and advertising) to be homogenized across countries, as it affects individuals' culture and preferences. However, coordination across countries appears to be necessary in a Single Market where the movements of people can now be free. Also the firms which aim at reciprocal learning across borders need to stimulate and organize some forms of communication. Reciprocal learning does not happen by itself or by magic.

According to the 1991 Price Waterhouse–Cranfield project report apparently only 32 per cent of European companies have a human resource (HR) strategy relating to the European Community (Single Market). There are differences here between the north (for instance the Netherlands and Germany) with less than 25 per cent of firms having a European HR strategy, and the south (for instance Italy, France and Spain) with more than 45 per cent. This may be because organizations are still unclear about the effects of the EC Social Charter. In this field, averages and quantitative results to broad questions may be misleading. Most firms which are already established in several countries report facing problems in the domain of international management of their human resources and try various solutions.

Two key issues emerge, particularly in Europe: improving the international mobility of personnel, and improving the effectiveness of intercultural teams. This should not be a surprise: integration through reciprocal learning can only progress if managers move abroad and work with foreign colleagues.

The international mobility of European managers

Managers who move from one company to another one *and* from one country to another at the same time are in a minority. Here we are more interested in the international mobility within a company and the way companies organize it.

Diverse attitudes towards international mobility

There are two types of international managers: those who have chosen a 'truly international career' and who are therefore not particularly preoccupied with their return, and those who are content with a 'temporary posting abroad'. The first category covers mainly engineers specialized in an advanced technique, specialists in a variety of fields and top managers. The second category is much more diverse, taking a temporary post abroad (three to five years) is often recognized as being a career accelerator before taking on an important position at the head office (CESMA, 1990).

Within the first category, 'top level' managers (who use their talents in the highest spheres of the company), generally accumulate international experience as their careers progress. They often work in large European capitals, appreciate the cultural activities which are offered and the size of the community of their compatriots in the host city. These experienced executives are 'Euromanagers' in every sense of the term, mobile from one European capital to another. They are small in number, and there are no significant national or regional disparities in their attitudes.

On the other hand, with middle managers, one can distinguish three groups of countries presenting similar characteristics in terms of international mobility.

1. Scandinavian, Belgian, Dutch and Swiss executives *show a high international mobility*. These countries are small in geographical terms; consequently, their inhabitants are accustomed to travelling outside their borders. The managers from these countries speak several languages (due to travelling, innate qualities and the value placed on languages by their system of education). Some of the natives from these countries may also be attracted to move to regions with a more pleasant climate.

2. French, British, Spanish and Italian executives show a *low international mobility*. International mobility of executives from these countries is still reserved for a certain elite. The French are penalized because of their poor linguistic abilities. The British show relatively high mobility towards other Anglo-Saxon countries or towards the Commonwealth, but they do not seem to be much attracted by the European continent (except for holidays). The economic area of influence covered by Italy and Spain is still insufficient for executives from either of these countries to be able to exercise their talents in other countries. Moreover, intra-country mobility is also low in these four countries (between the capital and the rest of the country, or between the north and the south). However things are changing: taking a temporary post abroad is now being recognized as a career accelerator.

3. German managers show *a highly selective mobility*. They fear finding their living standards abroad reduced, and fear interrupting their career. In addition they are prey to language problems. As Germans are loyal to their company, they will follow the international career which has been designed for them. Sometimes they show preconceived ideas with regard to certain countries with different cultures, and try to avoid these (CESMA, 1990).

This is of course a general picture. Great differences exist within a country.

The level of international mobility depends also on the level of internationalization of the sector and some other structural characteristics. For instance international mobility is high in oil companies (Shell, BP, Total, etc.) as the vertical chain is geographically split world-wide.

Some activities require a world-wide network, like tourism and credit cards, so staff of companies like American Express naturally have a high international mobility. In some sectors, such as electronics, global products and strategies require international staff and expatriations.

Stimulating international mobility

The preliminary condition for a successful expatriation is the mastery of the foreign language.

The family is the prime reason for blocking the mobility of managers. The change implies a considerable upheaval in the family unit. The wife or husband's work is the first reason which dissuades them, followed very closely by the children's schooling. For these reasons, managers are more mobile at the beginning and at the end of their careers. Family reasons appear to be the strongest in Italy, France, West Germany, Spain and Norway. Consequently, companies which aim to develop the international mobility of their managers should:

● find jobs for the *couple*,
● organize the schooling of the children,
● facilitate the whole family moving (preserving the quality of life).

It is hard for firms to solve the issue of schooling alone; regional authorities should participate in the creation of international schools. Every town of sufficient economic importance (not only capitals as it is now) should be equipped with a *truly* international school.

The second reason limiting the international mobility of managers is a double uncertainty related to expected effectiveness in the new position, and to reintegration (and the next steps in the career) after the expatriation. Companies which aim at developing the international mobility of managers should:

● prepare the expatriate and organize a short stay beforehand (three to six months) in order to test the new situation and to reduce anxiety,
● define long-term career plans and clarify the conditions of the reintegration (or the next step) beforehand.

Individuals have preferences concerning the foreign locations where they would prefer or not mind working. The following criteria have been found to influence their attitudes:

● The broad region corresponds to the geographical origins of the individual.
● The cultural attractiveness of the location.
● The quality of living (climate, pollution, taxation, security).
● The degree of Europeanization of the host country.

When the first conditions are fulfilled (language, family and career plans), a company should take preferences into account (at least for the first stay abroad) in order to maintain the motivation. Then if preferences cannot be met financial compensations should be arranged.

Considering the difficulties related to expatriation, more and more firms are trying to organize shorter experiences abroad: periods of one to six months focused on transferring skills, problem-solving or any project where an international perspective is welcome. It is doubtful that short stays develop a real ability to manage abroad, however they are good enough to transfer skills, broaden views and develop reciprocal learning.

International mobility: cases

Creating opportunities for international experiences, contacts and cross-fertilization is not a priority yet for all international firms, but it should become one as the integration of markets progresses. A few firms demonstrate distinctive skills in mixing nationalities in a transnational framework. In the beer industry, for instance, over the past few years Heineken has deliberately been making its top management team more international. At all levels of the hierarchy a priority has been given to *international* training sessions which are the key to knowledge flows between nationalities.

One of the industrial branches of Groupe Rhône Poulenc (chemicals) has industrial units in several European countries: Germany, Switzerland, Italy, France and Spain. Rhône Poulenc instituted a 'transnational' management of human resources. More precisely, from national units of management, it changed to European units *by profession*. For instance, the company identifies engineers who could achieve an international career and manage their careers at the European level. (The same would hold true for sales directors.) The new scheme follows five stages:

1. Identifying professions and specific career paths.
2. Defining the criteria on which to select the individuals with high international potential (and selecting the individuals).
3. Centralizing data.
4. Defining the common rules for the international mobility of operational managers (here the objective is that each national unit promotes the most 'competent' and 'flexible' individuals).
5. Defining rules for international mobility in addition to the traditional system of expatriation.

A 'new agreement' is made between the individual and Groupe Rhône Poulenc. Intra-European mobility becomes a condition of the recruitment of new people (at least when technical and sales managers are hired). Some specific statutory advantages are proposed to the individuals who accept international mobility. However, the tendency is towards narrowing the gap with the ones who stay at home, and reducing salary and social bonuses.

International alliances and mergers, which mushroomed at the end of the 1980s in Europe, also raise issues of international mobility. Here organizational cultural differences are added to national cultural differences, but the high potential for reciprocal learning may stimulate mobility.

When Renault and Volvo concluded their cooperative agreement, both agreed to reach economies of scale and to share knowledge, particularly in three functions: research and development, procurement and marketing. The top managers were personally involved in the success of the alliance, but implementation was not so easy during the transitory period.

At the beginning of 1991, Renault and Volvo started to organize the international mobility of technical staff and managers between the two companies in order to stimulate 'cross-fertilization'. The objective was 'reasonable': 100 Swedish managers coming to France and 100 French 'cadres' moving to Sweden for the next three years. Two and a half years later only 20 'manager swaps' were achieved.

The reasons behind the disappointing implementation are not new: language problems, family, different social security and pension systems. In the case of Renault–Volvo the lingua franca is English, which is not the mother tongue of either the French or the Swedish managers. Also the situation at Volvo was not favourable for welcoming French managers: in 1992 Volvo had to restructure its operations and to dismiss Swedish managers.

Implementing international mobility of personnel costs a great deal (in terms of preparation, training, organization and compensation) and it is risky: early failures create new obstacles for new waves of candidates to international promotions. Indeed firms are often faced with a shortage of appropriate candidates having the competence, the language abilities, and the motivation to succeed abroad. Moreover the contact with foreigners is only the first step. The second step is to be able to communicate effectively in a 'transnational' team.

Transnational teams

Transnational teams prove particularly useful in some situations (which are becoming more and more frequent in European business):

- Mergers, acquisitions and alliances across borders: in order to prepare jointly the merger (or the agreement), and afterwards to implement synergies and transfer knowledge. Asymmetrical power relationships (for instance in acquisitions) are sources of tension, frustration and conflict which add to the difficulty of working together.
- International teams for new product development: here the logic is to put together resources and/or enhance the creative potential through both functional and international diversity. The double diversity can be the source of misunderstandings and conflicts. Professional differences (for instance between marketing and R & D) may be the most difficult to integrate in new product development teams.

- Designing a European strategy with the help of local managers (top managers or product managers).
- Coordinating local actions across countries.
- Transferring knowledge across units and across countries.

The last three situations may not involve different functions. When individuals from different countries share the same profession the complexity of communication is significantly reduced: French and Swedish engineers speak the same engineers' language beyond their differences.

The challenge for transnational teams is to make the positive effects of diversity overweigh the negative effects of misunderstandings and conflicts within the team. Some integration should take place in order to achieve successfully the objectives of the group. As discussed in section 3, the accumulation of details may be at the origin of cultural clashes.

SCS GmbH

At the beginning of the 1980s, Scientific Control Systems GmbH, a German company in the computer services business, was acquired by SD Scicon, a British competitor. Under 'the British reign' the German company did not perform so well. In 1989 SCS was still losing money – a loss of 5.4 million DM with a sales turnover of 105 million DM.

'The British managers saw things through their British insular prism,' recalled one of the German senior managers of SCS. 'We had to work with a team of pleasant gentlemen, talking a lot and writing a lot. But implementation was not so effective and the German mentality cannot accept that' (cf. Roland, 1991, pp. 48–53). Moreover SD Scicon had restructured SCS in line with its 'British style organizational structure' (according to the German managers): that is, with a separation between the technical function and the management function. 'Each subsidiary of SCS was managed by two people: one senior manager for finance and sales and one senior manager (an engineer) for research and development projects.' According to the German managers, this was a double mistake. First, computer engineering is a high technology tailor-made business where interactions with the client and product development are closely linked. Second, this organizational design 'did not correspond to the German mentality in which the scientific culture dominates and in which commercial strategies are determined *according to technical strategies*'.

Cap Gemini Sogeti (the leading group in the French computer services business, with a 1989 sales turnover of 7 billion FF and net profit 0.5 billion FF) has had a subsidiary in Germany since 1975 (Cap Gemini Deutschland). Cap Gemini Sogeti took over SCS in 1990 and created a holding company to control both SCS and Cap Gemini Deutschland and their network of operational subsidiaries (2 in Hamburg, 1 in Münich, 1 in Düsseldorf). This network structure seemed to fit with the German view of regional decentralization.

From the previous experience at Cap Gemini Deutschland, the French managers had learned to avoid typical cultural clashes that may occur when French and

German managers are put together. Like the French, the German managers care about high wages,

> but above all, they care about the tangible manifestations of their status. You should not make mistakes in mentioning diplomas, in defining the function, in perquisites, such as cars...

> French managers assume power and modify their functions according to their skills and ambitions. On the other hand, German managers ask for precise definitions of their role. Areas and procedures have to be clearly defined. Once agreed upon, these rules are scrupulously followed...

> The French is a generalist, he needs polyvalence to feel happy at work. The German is by nature a specialist, he would feel insecure without compartments and divisions. (Roland, 1991, pp. 48–53).

In consequence it is very difficult to make French and Germans work together in teams. The French feel that the German lack flexibility and the German believe that the French should take care of their own work and not the work of their colleagues. In order to avoid cultural domination and to reconcile French and German managers, a Swedish top manager was chosen for SCS GmbH. Kaj Green had worked for Cap Gemini Sogeti for more than 10 years, and he had worked in France, in Germany and in Sweden.

First the values of the Group which more nearly corresponded to German culture were emphasized:

- The pride of working in a prestigious company, the leader in its market.
- The professionalism of the company.

Moreover, the decision processes of the Cap Gemini Sogeti Group seemed to correspond to the determination of German managers to preserve the autonomy of SCS:

- Negotiation of objectives.
- Centralized reporting.
- Decentralized operational management.

But national cultural differences are so deeply rooted that problems never are resolved definitively. For instance, the general manager of one of the subsidiaries of SCS mentioned that (notwithstanding his esteem for his French colleagues): 'During meetings the French have a tendency to group together, to speak French, or to practise a typically French humour that we (the Germans) do not understand. This sometimes creates an uneasy feeling' ('*A*' *pour Affaires Economiques*, 17 March 1991).

Openness

The case of a major French firm involved in the building materials sector illustrates what we believe is the correct attitude for buyers after a takeover.

The French firm took over a German firm in one of the new Eastern Länders in 1990. The stated objective was to 'implement synergies' (but actually it was mainly to transfer know-how to the acquired firm). The principles were the following:

- Be prudent and start with a thorough diagnosis, taking three perspectives: marketing, social and cultural.
- Avoid upsetting the local managers. Keep managers who are competent enough and motivated to improve (even if they had been members of the Communist Party).
- Achieve the 'coupling' of activities, investments and competences, instead of replacing them.
- Value former skills but improve them.
- Create opportunities for teams to meet, work together, organize common training sessions.

A seminar was organized in order to discuss the industrial and marketing strategy of the Group and the managers of several plants in East Germany, West Germany and France participated. German was the common language. After that, several exchanges of personnel were implemented: for periods of 6 to 12 weeks German technicians took up operational posts in France (and vice versa). In this case the buying firm typically took an *open* approach to the situation. It refused to take advantage of the asymmetrical power relationship and treated the East German partners as *equals* from whom lessons could be learnt. Such attitudes seem to be the first condition for transnational teams to work together.

Team dynamics

At the micro level, i.e. the level of a team, the risks of conflict could be dramatically reduced if firms paid attention to the psychological and sociological characteristics of the participants and the group. Too many firms still consider group dynamics as a 'black box' and hope that conflicts will be regulated automatically. This attitude is wrong and risky, because the failure of a first project may discourage the participants from joining another transnational team for a long time. A few guidelines are listed below.

- The individuals participating in a transnational team should know something about their own cognitive style, their own behaviour in a group, their biases related to their national or organizational culture. They should know something about group dynamics, and be aware of international cultural differences within the group.

- The individuals participating in a transnational group should be open-minded. They should tolerate diversity and be convinced that diversity is a source of creativity.
- The team should be composed according to the compatibility and complementarity of members, and one of the members should be able to play an integrative role.
- The firm's systems should support the priority given to *international team*work (in terms of reward systems, objectives, and training).
- The individuals should be *progressively* prepared to work in transnational teams, starting with international forums, then international training sessions, then short stays abroad, then participation in small mono-functional international projects, then participation in more diverse teams which include several functions and nationalities.

If these guidelines were followed, we believe transnational teams would be more effective and less stressful and that reciprocal learning would take place. Individuals would then be tempted by the experience, open themselves up and involve themselves.

In summary, implementing reciprocal learning between countries relies on the following principles:

1. Decisions should be based on thorough diagnosis (without assuming that everyone knows about cultural differences), and thorough preparation (without assuming that everyone knows how to work effectively in a team made up of diverse nationalities).
2. Firms can create openness by focusing on the potential technical synergies in a given profession. They should start with the easiest groups. They can for instance put together engineers from different countries who will soon discuss molecules or thermodynamics (depending on their common speciality or expertise).
3. Integration is based on the recognition that cultural or managerial models are relative, that no single model should be imposed, and that reciprocal learning is more effective. Modesty, curiosity, mutual respect and enthusiasm are the basic necessary attitudes. They should be demonstrated by both the top management and the individuals involved in a transnational team at the interface between organizations.

References

Albert, M. (1991), *Capitalisme contre capitalisme*, Paris: Seuil.
Amossy, R. (1991), *Les Idées reçues: Sémiologie du stéréotype*, Paris: Nathan.
Attali, J. (1991), *1492*, Paris: Fayard.

Belmont European Policy Centre (1992), *The New Treaty on European Union*, vol. 2, Brussels.

Centre d'Etudes Supérieures du Management (CESMA) (1990), 'La Mobilité des managers Européens', Rapport, Nouveaux Managers, Lyon.

de Rougemont, D. (1990), *28 siècles d'Europe*, Paris: Christian de Bartillat.

Duroselle, J. B. (1990), *L'Europe – histoire de ses peuples*, Paris: Perrin.

Féron, F. and A. Thoraval (eds.) (1992), *L'Etat de l'Europe*, Paris: Editions La Découverte.

IBM (1992), 'Human resources management; a global perspective', IBM report.

Kaelble, H. (1988), *Vers une Société Européenne, 1880–1990*, Paris: Belin.

Mermet, G. (1991), *Euroscopie: les Européens, qui sont-ils? Comment sont-ils?*, Paris: Larousse.

Minc, A. (1989), *La Grande Illusion*, Paris: Grasset.

Monod, J., P. Gyllenhammar and W. Dekker (1991), *Reshaping Europe*, Chapter 3: 'Human dimension', Brussels: European Round Table.

Morin, E. (1987), *Penser l'Europe*, Paris: Gallimard.

Morris, D. (1978), *La Clé des gestes*, Paris: Grasset.

Mutabazi, E., A. Klesta, Y. Altman and P. Poirson (1993), *Réussir à l'international: comment tirer parti des différences culturelles et managériales?*, Paris: Eyrolles.

Petit, M. (ed.) (1991), *L'Europe interculturelle: mythe ou réalité?*, Paris: Editions d'Organisation.

Price Waterhouse–Cranfield Project on International Strategic Human Resource Management (1991, 1992), London: Price Waterhouse.

Roland, M. (1991), 'Euromanagement: Allemagne mode d'emploi', *A pour Affaires économiques*, 17 March, pp. 48–53.

Scardigli, V. (ed.) (1993) *L'Europe de la diversité, la dynamique des identités régionales*, Paris: Editions CNRS.

Tylor, E. (1913), *Primitive Culture*, London: Murray.

CHAPTER 8
Integrating diversity: case studies

Tugrul Atamer, Pancho Nunes and Michel Berthelier

Internationalization patterns among firms differ and stem from two elements (Bartlett and Ghoshal, 1989), the first of which relates to the specific advantages of the firm such as geographical business locations, value chain configuration and subsidiaries' international role. Second, they stem from the characteristics of the particular industries in which the firm is active. Specific characteristics of local markets have a direct impact on international product policy. Strong pressures on costs lead to companies achieving cost economies through the integration of resources and capacities that are spread among the different countries.

In some industries, such as cheese or decorating paint, the heterogeneity of customers' tastes and preferences and differences in regulations compel firms which want to become international to give particular weight to the demands and characteristics of the local market. In other industries, customers' homogeneous behaviour and substantial scale economies allow firms which are becoming international to sell similar products throughout all main countries and then reap economies of integration by reducing the geographical dispersion of value chain activities as much as possible. This is the case for instance in the semi-conductor and civil aeronautic fields.

However, beyond industry characteristics and firms' specific advantages, firms' international strategies are also influenced by their geographical origin. According to Nonaka (1990), there are three internationalization logics and, depending on their origins, firms have adopted a development pattern that is either multinational, global, or multi-domestic.

In the past, American firms often adopted a multinational development by following the classical model of product international life cycle (Vernon, 1966). According to this model, the parent company transfers its knowledge to its foreign subsidiaries which, in turn, manufacture and sell, adapting to local needs and markets, products which were conceived in the United States. This knowledge transfer is deferred in time according to a hierarchical vision of the world economy, with the US being at the top of the hierarchy. Implementation of this strategy is based on headquarters maintaining very strict control over subsidiary units. It is a top–down process in which head office defines a world-wide strategy and plans its implementation, while subsidiaries execute the prescribed strategy. Even though the international life cycle model as it is summarized here appears to be over-simplified, it fairly describes the basic international strategy followed by most American firms until the 1980s.

Global logic is mostly fostered by Japanese companies. These based their world-wide expansion on the use of their domestic facilities to export intensively. All operations were conceived and organized to back up this strategy. The successful development of Japanese exports, up until the end of the 1980s, shows the effectiveness of this strategy. However, it has today reached its own limit. Japanese firms are now revising their development mode in order to reduce pressures from a growing number of foreign governments on international exchange conditions, and to cope with the high value of the yen and slow domestic growth rate.

Historically, a multi-domestic pattern has often been adopted by European firms. Products are conceived and developed in accordance with the demands of local markets. At the organizational level, it entails loose relationships between headquarters and foreign subsidiaries. These relationships are essentially financial, the parent company, in the end, having little control over its subsidiaries which on their side, adopt strategies that are tailored to the countries in which they operate. Today, this logic has also reached its limits and European multinational enterprises (MNEs) are being forced to revise their favourite international strategy in order to cope with challenges of integration.

The fact that each of the three internationalization logics described above is fostered by a particular geographical zone can be explained by several conditions that are external to the MNEs. A first condition concerns the historical context in which internationalization waves emerged. American firms initiated the first large wave of international investment in the 1950s, at a time when they were enjoying a very clear superiority over the rest of the world at technological and economical levels, and also when they represented the moral leadership of capitalism. As for Japanese firms, they started to become international in the late 1960s and early 1970s. The first industries involved were textiles and toys followed by steel, chemistry and shipbuilding (Dunning, 1993). At that time, Japanese firms benefited from clear comparative advantages (low labour costs) and received strong support from the MITI (Ministry of International Trade and Industry). This allowed them to attack labour intensive industries world-wide by means of an export-based strategy which generated high cash flows. European firms started most of their international investments as the reconstruction period was ending, i.e. in the mid-1960s. At that time, they invested in other European countries in order to escape from their own narrow domestic markets. They were then confronted with the fragmentation of European industry structures and compelled to adapt to market diversity by favouring a local response type of strategy.

Other conditions explain the link between the internationalization pattern and the geographical zone of origin. They concern the size of the domestic markets, the geography surrounding the country of origin, and finally the managers' cognitive maps which determine the way they perceive other countries and the world-wide economy. It is not in the scope of this chapter to illustrate in detail the contextual reasons which might explain the emergence of alternative internationalization patterns. However, it should be underlined that management of international diversity, which is a salient characteristic of European enterprises as highlighted by the Groupe ESC Lyon study for the ERT, directly coincides with the fact that European MNEs have adopted a multi-domestic pattern of internationalization. As one of the interviewed managers argued,

> When we had sufficiently dominated our home market, we naturally went abroad. In Europe, the size of a domestic market being quite limited, we quickly looked for growth by going international. We then transferred what we knew how to do in our own domestic market towards neighbouring countries. We rapidly noted that it did not work because of national differences. We then left our subsidiary to adapt on its own to local specificities.

However, when the number of countries managed by autonomous subsidiaries increases, when international revenues increase relative to domestic ones, and when competitive pressures from Japanese or American firms, or even from firms originating from low labour cost countries, get stronger, European companies realize that the multi-domestic configuration of their activities becomes a serious handicap. It is then necessary to integrate those activities in order to reap cost economies. They can ask themselves now to develop connections between subsidiaries in order either to reduce the global efficiency gap which exists when compared to competitors, or to build an international competitive advantage. Of course, the European MNEs' degree of integration varies depending on the firms' internationalization history and the industries' specificities. Nevertheless, it is worth noting that as far as their degree of integration is concerned, European companies are behind the Japanese and, to a lesser extent, American businesses. At any rate, this is the general feeling of the interviewed managers. As a result, developing and implementing integration while preserving some differentiation has become a major challenge for most European companies.

We have completed the study that was carried out jointly between Groupe ESC Lyon and the European Round Table with complementary interviews in 1993. This second round of interviews focused on what is at stake in the process of reconciling integration with differentiation. Six European MNEs belonging to diverse countries and industries were selected – Fiat, Hoffmann-La Roche, Lafarge Coppée, Petrofina, Pilkington and Unilever. In the case of Unilever, the first interview was complemented by document research. In the other cases, the first interview was complemented by one or two additional interviews with one or several members of the board of directors. We tried to obtain an historical view of the firm's internationalization process and to analyze the way they simultaneously manage the integration of their activities and the adaptation to local specificities. More precisely, we concentrated interviews on the moment when the need to integrate was acknowledged, the elements which led towards this integration, the adopted solutions, the difficulties encountered in implementing these solutions, and finally, the new challenges which were a direct result of the willingness to integrate.

1 Fostering integration to face diversity

Petrofina

Pressures towards integration are felt with different degrees of intensity depending on the varying weight of the local specificities that are at work within Petrofina's five basic activities, i.e. exploration-production, refining-distribution, lubricants, petrochemicals and paint. In semi-finished products such as petrochemicals, local specificities are of little importance. For some time now the necessity to reach a critical size at the production unit level has led Petrofina to centralize its production in Belgium and the United States.

The weight of local specificities increases when products are finished. For instance, in the motor-fuel business (10 years ago) Petrofina produced 25 different qualities, and it still produces as many today. The sensitivity to quality (local specificity) varies depending on the country, mainly because of the diversity in national laws. On the other hand, there is no objective reason why there are as many different qualities throughout Europe. Whatever country they live in, Europeans drive the same cars with the same engines. Only climatic conditions vary. Acknowledging this, Petrofina thinks that over the next five years markets will become more standardized, as far as product qualities are concerned.

In the past, within its finished products businesses, Petrofina gradually overcame the contradictions between the requirements of scale economies and market differences by the means of strongly integrated and centralized production operations while still maintaining differentiated and decentralized commercial structures. For example, in refining activities, European production site characteristics are no longer related to local consumption, but depend on the increased investments that are required in order to cope with stricter and stricter security and environmental regulations. The investment intensity, the improvement of transportation infrastructures, and the uniformity of qualities that can be anticipated in the next five years have already led Petrofina to favour efficiency, reorient its efforts towards production capacities for high octane gasolines, and optimize its investments by concentrating the main refining units in Anvers, Belgium. Petrofina has already adopted a distribution strategy which concentrates its network of outlets in regions where supply is integrated to refining centres, either directly or through exchanges with other oil companies, and where distribution costs are therefore quite low. Investment efforts begun in the late 1980s, and still in effect, are likely to solve most of the problems related to the integration of material flows. Through these efforts, Petrofina has been able to anticipate developments which are likely to push European markets in the oil industry towards a greater standardization.

In downstream activities such as lubricants and paint, local specificities are naturally more important than in petrochemicals or refining. However, several situations coexist within Petrofina. For example, in paint activities, Petrofina operates with a global vision in the marine paint niche, whereas in decorating paint it favours a local type of strategy in order to be responsive to differences in consumer needs and distribution networks. But even in decorating paint, increasing investments prevent Petrofina from dispersion. This trend is reinforced by the decrease in logistical costs which encourages the setting up of units whose production is no longer necessarily destined for local consumption.

Acknowledging these evolutions and relying on its integration experience, Petrofina has looked to apply, on a smaller scale, the optimization principles of its oil activities (petrochemicals or refining) to its paint activities. Therefore, at Petrofina, the European paint market is fed by six factories. Two large units, one in Amsterdam, Netherlands and one in Belfort, France are assigned for volume business markets. On the other hand, four smaller units feed country-specific businesses or produce speciality products. In all cases, factories are not related to the country where they are implanted in so far as they also make products that are sold in other markets than domestic ones. All of these optimization efforts have been realized in the last six years and follow a rationale of economies of production and logistical costs.

At Petrofina, all investments towards a greater integration of flows are made at the European level and will probably continue to grow in the coming years, especially in the paint businesses. However, Petrofina's American industrial and commercial operations are totally independent from European ones. Even though exchange relationships between subsidiaries are very dense and frequent within Europe, they are far less important and regular between Europe and America. This can be explained by the fact that a) unit optimization efforts are carried out at the continent level and b) the ratio of world market size to production unit critical size does not push towards a further world-wide integration (Atamer and Calori, 1993, p. 497).

To summarize, Petrofina's top executives do not think that the process of integration concerning their material flows raises any major problems at the European level. They feel the company has a high level of expertise that was acquired at the time when some of its activities such as petrochemicals or marine paint had to be integrated. The process of material flows integration therefore seems to be in control. The real challenge is somewhere else. As a result of technological evolution, the competitive environment is rapidly changing. Adapting to this evolving environment requires the quick development of all the firm's competencies. This major challenge raises, in turn, two essential questions for Petrofina. First, how to develop international career paths and learning processes which involve both technical and managerial skills, and second, how to develop, beyond local cultural specificities, a group mind-set and a feeling of belonging to Petrofina.

Unilever

Unilever has a long tradition of being international. Since the merger of Margarine Unie and Lever Brothers in 1930, the company has expanded internationally through export and local production. At first predominantly Dutch and British executives were expatriated in order to transfer knowledge from the headquarters to the newly created subsidiaries. However, Unilever has quite rapidly come to favour decentralization by giving local managers the responsibility for running subsidiaries.

An analysis of what happened in Unilever's food branch illustrates this. Until the mid-1960s Unilever operated with a country-specific management which was responsible for running and developing all businesses in its territory. In 1966, in order to cope with the need for rationalizing all supplies, the company adopted a new organization according to groups of products. Three profit centres were created in order better to manage the edible fats group, the frozen food and ice cream group, and the food and drinks group. After the mid-1970s, consumers' behaviour became much more sophisticated. For instance the awareness that one must be in good health and in good shape turned out to be a major trend with significant consequences for the food industry. The development of low calorie products and natural products became critical. As a result of this increasing sophistication Unilever felt the need to share the experience and knowledge about consumer research and new food-processing technologies that had been accumulated in the three product groups throughout the various countries. Consequently in 1988 Unilever reorganized the way its food branch was structured with the idea of building unity on top of diversity. In addition to the traditional 'Unileverization' of the decentralized units, a new formal structure and the creation of interpersonal networks have become the major cornerstones of this reorganization process.

Lafarge Coppée

Meeting the challenge of integrating international businesses has been a very different experience in Lafarge Coppée. The reasons are related to the business characteristics of the company, its internationalization history, and also its mode of development which relied extensively on acquisitions of foreign enterprises. Generally speaking, it was not until 1988 that Lafarge Coppée was confronted with a critical problem of interdependence between subsidiaries within its core businesses, i.e. cement, concrete and gravels, and plaster. Before this, Lafarge Coppée structured its operational units in such a way that countries could manage their own market and production because local specificities were perceived as being crucial for success. More precisely, differences in consumers' preferences and tastes, in logistical infrastructures and distribution, the need to benefit from close raw material supply, and the fact that the products were expensive to ship had shaped the structuring principles of Lafarge Coppée's operations. This picture still applies despite some exceptions, such as a sea-borne trade enterprise located in the Indian Ocean and a cement import–export subsidiary in the Mediterranean Sea. The former centralizes all shipments relating to the Indian Ocean while the latter links together and integrates several seaside cement units in order to even out Lafarge Coppée's production capacity in the Mediterranean.

In some activities that are not part of Lafarge Coppée's core businesses, the principle of a weak unit integration remains. For instance, the paint business is not very internationalized and is a juxtaposition of small autonomous enterprises operating in local markets without any significant integration.

In the calcium aluminate business which is one of Lafarge Coppée's speciality products, the company's organization is based on the global integration model. This business is actually a niche whose applications such as quick setting concrete for landing fields clearly concern global-type customers. Lafarge Coppée operates in 50 countries with marketing and research centrally coordinated from France. Integrated efforts in R & D are aimed at enlarging the speciality products range by developing new applications that are assigned to world-wide niches. Four highly coordinated factories feed the various world markets. Calcium aluminate constitutes one of the very few exceptions within the group organization: here the global model is adopted to exploit a world-wide high-value niche.

In core businesses, the idea of introducing a certain dose of integration to a structure which was historically founded upon the national differentiation principle, emerged in 1985. It came about under the pressures of rapid internationalization movements from major competitors and the need to cope with the cycles of the construction industry while monitoring the energy costs of each production unit.

For a long time, Lafarge Coppée has carried out half of its activities in France and the other half in North America. Indeed, the French cement manufacturer entered the American market quite early on, in 1956. At that time, the company's chairman intuitively felt that the colonial empire was going to collapse. He decided to take his company to Canada, even though Lafarge Coppée owned every cement unit in Maghreb. In 1958, Lafarge Coppée's presence on the American continent was extended by implantations in both Brazil and Canada. Relationships with subsidiaries were ruled through hierarchical coordination, and through expatriation or the parachuting down of managers to the subsidiaries. However, it was only in 1988 and 1989 that Lafarge Coppée became truly multinational by entering the Spanish, Austrian and Indian Ocean markets through the acquisitions of Asland and Cementia. Lafarge Coppée's internationalization speeded up further when they acquired several companies in the Eastern part of Germany, in Turkey, in Venezuela and in the ex-Republic of Czechoslovakia. These takeovers made Lafarge Coppée the second largest world producer behind the Swiss company Holderbank. With greater cost control essential, growing international competition, and the increasing weight of international operations, the company saw the need to develop interconnections between its different subsidiaries in the cement business.

Simultaneous to Lafarge Coppée's internationalization move in the cement business, the company faced a dramatic change in the structure of competition in its plaster sheet business. Whereas competition had traditionally been local and markets fragmented, a violent price war suddenly erupted in 1988 when a small group of German and British competitors unexpectedly adopted a European strategy. In a European market growing by 7 per cent a year, the German Knauf was the first to step out of its traditional national sanctuary. It attacked the British market where British Plasterboard (BPB) benefited from a monopoly position.

A new competitor, Redland, built plants in Britain and France. Lafarge Coppée in turn, took the offensive, first by exporting, then by buying Redland Plasterboard operations. A sheet of plaster is a heavy and inexpensive product. It cannot be efficiently transported. Intensification of international competition therefore requires the setting up of local production units. Newcomers cut prices in order to build a strong market position and use the full capacity of their plants. This is how the war that started between these three European competitors led to a price drop of 25 to 30 per cent in Europe between 1988 and 1990. Within two years, numerous enterprises disappeared. Three European leaders emerged and the European market suddenly became concentrated. Lafarge Coppée succeeded in reaching second position on the European market behind BPB, after having acquired the plaster division of Redland Plasterboard, a British enterprise. This deal brought into production units located in Britain, Germany, Norway and the Netherlands. The French company also added a plant in Italy. During this period, integration efforts were characterized by an international price policy that was tightly coordinated and technology transfers between countries that were designed to help set up efficient new plants.

However, in all of its core businesses, Lafarge Coppée considers that responding to competitive pressure does not necessarily entail a critical need to interconnect material flows between units. Rather, the problem of integration appeared in the form of two questions. First, how to take advantage of the sharing of experiences and expertise that was accumulated by units, some of which originate from past acquisitions, in order to organize a collective learning process. Second, how to create a common vision that is shared by units that have different histories and weak material and product interdependence.

Fiat

For a long time, Fiat remained an Italian company with a presence in other countries. Subsidiary managers were almost all Italian. This was particularly true for the automotive division. Today, the company is being confronted with the globalization of its markets, as in the case of the car business. Fiat's top management decided to internationalize further the management of subsidiaries. For the last two or three years, there has been a Frenchman at the head of the French subsidiary, a German in Germany, etc. Because of its history, Iveco (Fiat's truck manufacturing branch) has always had a more international management and possibilities for moving from one enterprise to another within Iveco have also been greater. Nowadays, Italian managers are a minority. However, as a group director said,

> It is not by having different passports that one makes a company
> become international. It is the mind-set which makes it. It is very
> difficult to make the French become more international because they
> belong to a very strong culture, and when you are too proud of your
> culture, you may become rigid. It is not the same with Germans. In

some way, it is more the same for the British because they belong to a very rich and strong culture and also they think they are international since they speak an international language!

In order to cope with this historical and cultural heritage, one of the key questions for Fiat has been expressed in the following way: 'Are there managers out there in the field who are ready to meet these [internationalization] challenges?' (Auteri and Tesio, 1990, p. 6). Thus, as for Petrofina and Lafarge Coppée, Fiat's main integration problem does not concern material flows, but rather human flows and the sharing of knowledge which has been accumulated in different countries. Developing managerial capabilities within the group is considered as a priority in order effectively to meet other global integration challenges. In this context, Fiat has set up the 'Internationalization Management Project' (IMP) with the following objective: 'To come up with answers at the corporate level as to how the management of the various companies of the group are to operate successfully within a business environment that is no longer limited by national boundaries, and which takes into account the progressive globalization of markets' (Auteri and Tesio, 1990, p. 6). In other words, it is a matter of organizing the foundations for global integration, i.e. exchanging human competencies, knowledge, expertise and information within the context of different national cultures and in conformity with the group's values. Fiat tries to consolidate a culture and a group mind-set which fosters professional behaviours and sensitivity to international contexts.

Hoffman-La Roche

'Our aim is to discover, produce and market goods and provide services which meet human and animal health needs in the areas of prevention, diagnosis, treatment and general well being.' This definition of the vocation of Hoffmann-La Roche is one of the 'Corporate Principles' which guide the activities of the chemical and pharmaceutical company. As is underlined by *Le Petit La Roche*, a small dictionary intended for friends and visitors: 'Our truly multinational character originates from the fact that neither illness nor medical science is limited by national boundaries.' About 0.5 per cent of the staff are employed in the headquarters which are located in Basel, Switzerland. The company's internationalization started right from its creation in 1896: Germany (1896), Italy (1900), France (1903), United States and Brazil (1905), Spain (1906), Great Britain (1908), Russia (from 1910 until 1918), Japan (1912).

Created in 1896, the German production unit located in Grenzach is both the company's oldest and its most important site in the European Community. La Roche started to delocalize its research and development activities as early as 1937 by creating a research centre in Welwyn Garden City in Great Britain and then a second one in Nutley, New Jersey (USA) in 1940. In 1968, the group established another fundamental research centre in Nutley, the Institute of Molecular Biology. Hoffmann-La Roche showed, in this way, that no activity is a priori limited to its native country borders. This Institute is equally a training centre for researchers of different nationalities and welcomes up to 80 academicians for a two-year period to attend its course in molecular biology. The first Japanese factory destined for the manufacturing of pharmaceuticals was set up in 1967 in Kamakura. It was completed three years later by an on-site research centre and a chemical factory located in Fukuroi. This strategy of commercial, manufacturing and research investments and implantations was completed by a strategy of take-overs in Switzerland – i.e. the Sauter Laboratories in Geneva (1958) – as well as other countries (Belgium, France, Britain, the US, etc.). One of the most important recent acquisitions concerned the Genentech company, located in San Francisco and specializing in genetics.

As a result of its continuous internationalization, Hoffmann-La Roche has today more than 40 per cent of its turnover and employs 45 per cent of its staff in Europe. Northern America employs more than 36 per cent of the staff and contributes more than 35 per cent of the group's total turnover.

The independence of individuals and units constitutes another founding principle of the group.

> Respect for the individual. We believe that the success of our company depends on the combined talents and performance of dedicated people. For this reason, we want:

- everyone in the organization to respect each other's rights and dignity;
- to help our people to develop their talents and make optimal use of their abilities and potential;
- to provide recognition based on performance and contribution to Roche's success;
- to encourage information-sharing and open dialogue.

Affirming and applying such a principle allows for diversity of behaviours and cultures. 'We would prefer to have thousands of very strong individual characters who work happily together rather than only one type of individual who is perfectly integrated into the system.' The 50 nationalities that are present at the Basel headquarters reinforce, on a daily basis, this cultural diversity.

At an organizational level, this principle is expressed through the large amount of autonomy which is given to the different company units, beginning with the four business divisions (Pharmaceuticals, Vitamins, Diagnostic Products, Scents). The objective of each division is to discover and implement solutions (especially in terms of organization and management) that can respond to the challenges and stakes which come up in each business. Belonging to the corporation does not mean conforming to a standard model. Respecting independence has also eased the integration within the group of small dynamic and innovative entities at the same time as preserving their substance and maintaining people and teams.

Pilkington

Created in 1826 in St Helens, England, Pilkington started its internationalization in the last quarter of the nineteenth century. At that time, internationalization was only a matter of export. Pilkington possessed a network of commercial depots and outlets in Europe (Italy, France, Spain, Holland and Germany), America (Canada, the US, and Latin America), Oceania (Australia and New Zealand) and Africa (Egypt and South Africa). This first important internationalization phase, which began early in the history of the company, was strongly affected by major events such as the growing self-sufficiency of the United States, strong competition from French and Belgian entrepreneurs at the end of the last century, the two world wars and the waves of decolonization. Pilkington's second important internationalization phase started after 1951 when sales offices and, above all, manufacturing units were set up in New Zealand (plant), India (plant), Mexico (plant), Singapore (commercial), Nigeria (commercial) and Sweden (plant). In the 1970s and even more in the 1980s, internationalization speeded up under the impact of numerous acquisitions carried out mainly in the US and Europe.

Since the 1950s, Pilkington has adopted three patterns for organizing its international operations. First, the company managed its international activities from the headquarters in a very centralized fashion, particularly when the group was, above all, a British company. Second, numerous acquisitions led Pilkington to adopt a quite decentralized management for most of its international businesses. The group was then typically organized like a collection of national entities which took care of their respective local markets with great autonomy, each developing specific competencies and resources.

Today, Pilkington is developing a new organizational logic. Achieving almost 85 per cent of its sales outside the United Kingdom in 1992 (76 per cent in 1989), the company felt the need to adopt a more effective and efficient organization in order to cope with strong environmental pressures. In fact, it has been confronted with several major evolutions since 1990:

- The growing sensitivity of core businesses (flat and safety glass) to economies of scale.
- The globalization of customers, especially in the automotive business.
- The globalization of competitors such as PPG (USA), Asahi (Japan) and Saint-Gobain (France).
- The recession in Pilkington's most important geographical markets (UK, Germany, Sweden, North America, Oceania) and the consequent recession in its main customers (car manufacturers and construction firms).
- The trend towards a higher homogeneity of certain needs, particularly in the construction industry (architectural glass for example).
- Falling world-wide prices for flat glass and insulation fibres.
- The rapid growth of capital intensity in order to respond to challenges concerning innovation and manufacturing efficiency.

In order to cope with the above pressures, Pilkington is trying to rationalize its production facilities, maintain its technological leadership over competitors and increase its presence in critical geographical zones. As a result, the company feels it is necessary to be more careful about the things that can and should be either centralized or decentralized. Decisions concerning centralization or decentralization are now made in reference to local or global forces which are at work on each element of the value chain, and to strategic objectives that are assigned to local subsidiaries on the global chessboard. In brief, Pilkington orients itself towards a more integrated organization. Actually, the integration problem is of particular concern only for intermediary activities, i.e. the ones that cannot be either totally centralized or totally decentralized, as in the case of Pilkington's R & D or production. Therefore, starting from a configuration that is historically and basically multi-domestic, the major challenge for the company is to organize the integration of its different units at the continent level (production) or the world level (R & D). Today, integration of material flows is well advanced at the European level and does not seem to raise major difficulties. Conversely, even if concrete actions have already been implemented, the integration of competencies, expertise, knowledge, and thus personnel, is not yet complete.

The above cases show that the integration problems encountered by European firms focus more and more on human resources and knowledge flows. More precisely, two elements appear critical in order to reinforce integration:

1. developing a corporate mind-set, and
2. creating and/or developing formal (structural) and informal (interpersonal) transversal networks.

These two dimensions are closely intertwined. However, in order to facilitate the following discussion, we have separated them in the next two sections.

2 Developing a corporate mind-set

European firms are today questioning themselves in an effort to discover what really makes up their identity. They are all the more eager to do so since numerous acquisitions have generally contributed to diluting the original corporate identity.

In the first section of this chapter we suggested that the firms in our study are not so much concerned with the integration of material and product flows as the integration of knowledge and human resources. Equally, it appeared that head office management was anxious to develop, among employees world-wide, a feeling that they belong to the same unified and visible group. At least two factors have given rise to this concern. The challenge of developing a corporate mind-set has strong internal implications in terms of motivation, responsibility, and managerial flexibility (multi-faceted or transferable individual managerial abilities). It is a critical element for people's involvement in the achievement of organizational goals and, in turn, the firm's international success. This challenge also has important external consequences which are related to the institution's image and credibility. At the key country level this credibility inspires a certain amount of confidence and stability in the minds of major partners such as states, investors, customers, suppliers, etc.

Before proceeding further, it should be noted that the managers we interviewed have used slightly different but equivalent expressions to name the same concept: corporate mind-set, corporate or group spirit, shared spirit, the feeling of belonging to a group or corporation. Hereafter, we shall consider these terms as synonyms.

The idea of a shared corporate mind-set is not a new one. In his time, Sun Tzu suggested that the most critical factor that leads an army to victory is influence on morale, which he defines as true harmony, and unity of mind that must exist between soldiers and their superiors. Today, the challenge remains and seems to be particularly crucial for European firms. Indeed, it is the very basis for the development of world knowledge integration and rationalization of the country-based units.

A corporate mind-set builds homogeneous perceptions and attitudes concerning the corporation's general mission and the processes that are used to achieve this mission. A corporate mind-set results in some shared behavioural norms and values which contribute in producing strategic unity *vis-à-vis* employees and stakeholders (Prahalad and Bettis, 1991; Ulrich and Lake, 1990). When a shared mind-set develops throughout all of the company's units and businesses, people inside and outside the firm experience strategic unity, i.e. they share a common understanding of what the organization's goals are and how to reach those goals (Ulrich and Lake, 1990, p. 55). In the end, this harmony should allow organizations to improve their competitive positions.

There is no one miracle solution to this challenge in so far as it directly affects various sensitivities and individual cultures. This is why the companies that we studied took a more or less wide set of measures, depending on their international maturity and their own specificities. However, the managers we interviewed are aware of the necessity to combine several concrete actions at different levels in order to achieve such integration. These different levels of intervention can be schematically represented by the combination of two factors (see Figure 8.1).

The first factor characterizes the vector of development of a shared mind-set, i.e. either information (Salancik and Pfeffer, 1978; Schwenk, 1986) or behaviour (O'Connor and Barrett, 1980; Staw and Ross, 1987). It is possible to strengthen a group mind-set by developing information flows at the world-wide level. The higher the clarity, consistency and recurrence of information flows, the higher the probability that a corporate mind-set will emerge and be shared. Such information flows should be both vertical (hierarchical) and horizontal. It is also possible to create shared mind-sets by reinforcing adequate individual and collective behaviours and creating integrating mechanisms which will stimulate those behaviours.

The second factor characterizes the content of the corporate mind-set. Here the traditional distinction concerning ends vs. means becomes handy. A shared mind-set

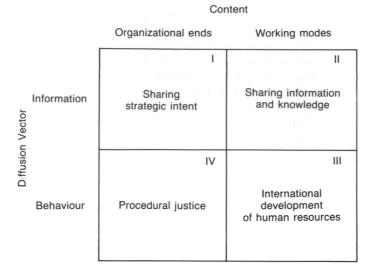

Figure 8.1   Developing a corporate mind-set

can be expressed by a clear and uniform understanding of the firm's goals. People are then expected to participate actively in the achievement of organizational goals. The content can also be established around the understanding of and adhesion to common working principles, i.e. common norms concerning work within the organization.

The crossing of the two factors generates four types of integrative mechanisms which are complementary: sharing strategic intent, sharing information and knowledge, international development of human resources, and procedural justice.

Sharing strategic intent

The managers we interviewed used different expressions to name the same concept: strategic vision, strategic intent, the mission of the company. Hereafter, we shall treat these expressions as being equivalent.

Companies develop a corporate mind-set through the intensification and formalization of information flows concerning corporate goals. The aim is to share the strategic vision as it is understood by the upper spheres of management and shareholders. This integrative mechanism is based on the premise that individual behaviours are related to the capacity of the human brain to treat, store and use information. Therefore, recurrent and consistent communication of the corporate strategy will shape managers' and employees' mental images of their firm so that individual energies will work, within each country and unit, towards the realization of common organizational goals.

According to an executive from Lafarge Coppée, 'Within the group, the first thing we try to share is a common vision of who we are. For instance, we are an industrial group which wants to remain independent and be international. It is sort of a definition of what we are and want to be.' According to Floris Maljers, Chairman of Unilever, a common vision is one of the fundamental ingredients in the preservation of Unilever's unity world-wide (Maljers, 1992). It fosters a unified philosophy of action across all the units of the Group.

> Once a year, each of the two chairmen addresses a meeting of 350 to 500 senior managers from all over the world ... After such meetings, every chairman of an operating unit and every manager of a department gets a copy of the main points and presents a similar review to the middle management in his or her own unit. (Maljers, 1992, p. 50).

Strengthening a common strategic vision is usually a top–down process. Pilkington executives carefully formulate the company's strategic intent. They want to avoid the gradual deterioration of the quality and clarity of the message as it goes down the hierarchy and distances itself geographically. The executives concentrate their efforts on explaining and communicating the strategic intent to an elite group of the top 50 managers of the company. The top management wants to create closer, more intense, and more frequent relations with these elite managers. The underlying assumption is that if the top managers perceive clearly the firm's strategy and if they adhere to it, they will, in turn, convince lower-level managers. In order to accomplish this, the Pilkington head office organizes short seminars, conferences, or meetings which bring together these top managers. The strategic vision needs to be clear and convincing, and must inspire managers' decisions and actions:

> The definition of strategy and our focusing of strategy ... provides more leadership because the people out in our business around the world – in Europe, in America, in Australia, in Brazil – understand clearly the strategic direction that the company has taken in ... Once people know where the company is going, then you get elements of leadership coming in and it's easier for the managers to lead because then they can communicate.

The paths used to communicate a strategic intent are well known. In the verbal fashion, one of the most common practices is the use of presentations during annual or bi-annual conferences in which executives and, more rarely, other employees are gathered. There are also training seminars during which members of the board of directors participate. For instance, at Hoffmann-La Roche or Pilkington, several Executive Committee members are charged with exposing, explaining and discussing the corporation's strategic intent during general management training seminars. The strategic vision can also be communicated in a written form such as booklets (Lafarge Coppée) or annual reports (Pilkington).

Sharing information and knowledge

In this case, firms use the information vector to influence work practices. Individuals are relatively passive in this process which is often based on comparisons. Comparing performance stimulates people-performance, in particular among low performers. The preoccupation with homogenizing work behaviours is not new. It exists in any company which grows fast or diversifies. The international dimension makes the task more difficult and calls for a more creative approach.

Internal publications are widely used in the purpose of sharing information. At Pilkington, divisional internal staff newspapers are designed to be a real source of information. They are organized with all of the traditional rubrics such as company news (businesses, organizational charts, innovations, etc.), the life of the personnel and the local communities where Pilkington is present, sports and hobbies, and games. The newspapers are published with the help of 35 Pilkington 'press correspondents' who work in different businesses or countries. Numerous pictures of the individuals and teams personalize the news and reinforce the feeling of proximity between the readers and actors.

At Fiat, various publications are circulated in order to widen the personnel's international horizon. Some publications are designed for particular readers such as head office executives, while others are made available to all employees. For example, *In Diretta* (live news) is a bulletin directed at executives and managers throughout the corporation. Bi-monthly editions are published in five languages (*In Diretta Internazionale*). *Fiat Quadri* and *Illustrato Fiat* are examples of other periodicals that regularly report on the countries where Fiat operates.

At Lafarge Coppée, three practices reinforce what the company calls technical doctrines. First, a few years ago, Lafarge Coppée created an internal *Who's Who* for all of its cement activities world-wide. An abstract of this *Who's Who* is available to all cement plants and makes it easy to find out where the sources of technical competence are located and thus contact, anywhere in the world, an engineer who has already dealt with a similar problem or situation. Making this informational tool available encourages engineers to exchange experiences, and thus stimulates an informal information network, and fosters the feeling of being part of an international group.

Second, every year, Lafarge Coppée sends to each plant manager a whole set of statistics concerning the performance of every factory and unit throughout the world. This informational device leads managers to self-regulate their behaviours since all statistical data is known by every manager. The less successful managers in the company try to understand what is wrong and imitate as much as possible the most efficient practices. The highest performers are encouraged to continue in their efforts. No formal or official sanctions are taken towards those performing less well. However, since the statistics are being widely diffused, low performers are challenged to improve.

Finally, each year, Lafarge Coppée awards a world-wide prize for the 'best case'. Each unit contributes and cases are circulated. This simple device reinforces the feeling that, in spite of geographic distance, the units are close to one another. For instance, it allows a Brazilian executive to contribute, indirectly but nominatively, to the resolution of a problem encountered by one of his British peers.

Even though the above practices concern only engineers, they stimulate the homogenization of work modes towards the best practice within Lafarge Coppée. Each engineer can share knowledge that has been accumulated within the group throughout the world. Such practices also speed up the transfer of technical knowledge. The personalization of the information inserted in the database reinforces the concrete character of the group's image.

Fiat has also set up a central information system. The manual (in five languages) defines the policies and guidelines on management development. The database assembles information concerning the individual skills of approximately 600 non-Italian managers and 3900 Italian managers. Moreover, it indexes information on the most critical management issues concerning foreign managers (Auteri and Tesio, 1990, p. 15):

● Selection and integration of new managers.
● Professional characteristics.
● Contract and remuneration problems.
● Education and training initiatives and assimilation.
● Image of the company.
● Relations with joint-ventures partners.

This central information system therefore helps to improve and harmonize the management of managers throughout the corporation world-wide.

In all of the above situations, information serves as the main vector for creating a shared mind-set. The use of comparisons promotes desired behaviours, while using examples fosters a more homogeneous conception about work modes, thanks to the voluntary alignment of low performers with high performers.

Strategic vision and sharing knowledge are based on data communication. Information transmitters endeavour to create a guiding framework for decision-making and action. However, the impact of such practices may remain superficial because receivers are relatively passive and the assimilation of information is uncertain. Alone, such practices are not sufficient for creating a solid and durable corporate mind-set. For this reason the companies we have studied are also looking at ways they can directly and personally involve personnel through actions.

International development of human resources

The companies we studied are looking to involve individuals in action. By doing so, they directly affect employees' work behaviours and methods. Since the objective is to influence behaviours several leverages are combined in order to win over inertia.

The main initiatives are concerned with training, international rotation of managers and managerial promotion systems.

Training

At Hoffmann-La Roche, particular attention is paid to managers training through an internal MBA type programme, which influences management behaviour. One of the essential objectives of Hoffmann-La Roche is to overcome the traditional vertical divisions by function, country or business. To reach this ambitious objective, managers need to become polyvalent and speak a common language (i.e. understand and share the same managerial concepts). Hoffmann-La Roche's high-level training homogenizes the managers' conceptual and theoretical knowledge. The training programme is considered as a unique opportunity in the career of a high-potential manager. It serves as a meeting place for discovering, learning about management concepts, and working inside a network. This approach shows there is a will to overcome cultural and professional divisions to facilitate the integration of mentalities within teams.

The programme demands full involvement from the participants, not only during, but also between the training periods. In fact, passing through this programme represents the recognition of a manager's potential and a career opportunity, and this ensures high motivation. Above all, it is an open door to corporate life and a genuine passport to a truly international management career. For example, a scientist working in Switzerland could acquire high managing responsibilities in Brazil. This is precisely the training's essential objective: to establish the basis for the development within the company of individuals with multi-faceted skills and rapidly permit the application of those skills in a different function and in a new country. In the last six years, about 1400 people, approximately a quarter of the managerial staff, have participated in this programme. As this proportion increases, Hoffmann-La Roche builds upon the foundations necessary for the development of the group mind-set.

At Fiat, the management training policy was revised in 1988 and today includes more international content. Conceived in collaboration with Isvor-Fiat, the group's training subsidiary, two important programmes are offered to directors and managers. Both programmes have taken on an international slant in both content and allocation methods with greater emphasis being given to European problems and a deeper analysis being made of the foreign business contexts of the Fiat companies. The management training course programme (CFD) took the group's future directors on visits to the group's headquarters situated abroad. In 1988, a model of the programme was held in Paris and Brussels and, in 1989, in London and again in Brussels. The Fiat management course (CFG) has widened the study of the Fiat business world from an Italian context to a European one; two days of the 20-day residential course at Marentino are dedicated to what is defined as Fiat's domestic market – Europe. The new initiatives in education and training concern the development of international awareness and the realization of completely new programmes aimed at developing intercultural sensitivity.

In addition to its language training programmes (Italian and English), Fiat has launched the 'Fiat Italian Briefing' and 'Country Briefings' (Auteri and Tesio, 1990, pp. 13–14). The former is a seminar for non-Italian managers (1200 out of 5000 Fiat executives) working in Fiat subsidiaries world-wide. The objective is to improve the practice of the Italian language and give a better understanding of Italy and the world of Fiat. The 'Italian Briefing' has contributed to integrating non-Italians into the group's culture. The 'Country Briefings' are held in each of the countries where Fiat operates and are intended for international managers. The goal is to facilitate an understanding of the major foreign cultural characteristics in which Fiat is involved and to provide a framework for successfully putting this understanding into practice. Finally, a seminar provides the managers with the necessary methods and tools to communicate effectively in front of an international audience. This seminar goes way beyond that of language training, as it includes both verbal and non-verbal intercultural communication techniques. Fiat has also developed 'professional' seminars directed towards fostering experience exchanges between countries, subsidiaries, and within professions: production engineers, cost controllers, product managers, human resources managers, etc. The main objective is to improve performance through reciprocal learning.

Pilkington has designed high-level training seminars for individuals who have a high potential and are already experienced in management. Usually, participants are between 30 and 45 years old, they are plant directors, functional managers (marketing, accounting, etc.) and sometimes general managers of small operations. Selected participants are expected to move up the hierarchy and take on multifunctional positions which require an ability to bring together disparate groups and functions. The content of the training relies heavily on case studies, whether internal or external, and essentially concerns strategic management (formulation and implementation). Up until recently, the training has been given by British business school professors. Now, head office has begun to diversify and Europeanize the group of teachers in order to increase the international content of the seminar.

Unilever has its own international management college located near London. The objective of training is clear: to succeed in the 'Unileverization' of all of its managers (Maljers, 1992, p. 47). Each year between 300 and 400 managers participate in the international training programme, in groups of 25 to 30 people of the same potential level. 'This shared experience creates an informal network of equals who know one another well and usually continue to meet and exchange experiences' (Maljers, 1992, p. 49). Unilever managers are directly and actively involved in a process which harmonizes management methods. As such, training contributes to the creation of a shared mind-set.

International rotation

International rotation facilitates the breaking down of divisions which stem from vertical progression. It also encourages a better knowledge of the group through diverse personal experiences and interpersonal relationships.

At Unilever, international rotation is organized according to two non-excluding patterns. The classical path consists of taking a position in another country. This allows for a deeper understanding of different nationalities in terms of culture and work methods. The second path consists of a system of temporary assignments which improves corporate cohesion. The principle is briefly described as follows.

> A manager can be placed for a short or long period in a head office department or subsidiary. In the early 1980s, when I was responsible for profits for a large group of companies, we had a staff of about 20 people. Of these, there were usually two bright young managers on temporary assignment from several of our far-flung companies. After a period of 6 to 12 months, they would move on to new positions – as marketing director in Brazil, for instance, or development manager in Turkey. When these managers return home, they are still part of the Unilever network. They know whom to call in case of need and what to expect. They also realize that their own ideas can make an important contribution to Unilever's overall progress. Exposure to another environment not only gives them more 'know-how' but also improves their 'know-who'. (Maljers, 1992, p. 49)

Lafarge Coppée also organizes international rotations, especially for its engineers. For example, in the cement business, engineers know at the beginning of their careers that they must change factories every three years. This develops a population of cement engineers that is relatively homogeneous in terms of experience. In fact, it is essential for Lafarge Coppée to create an accumulation of experiences because techniques and difficulties vary greatly from one factory to another. Here again, international rotations are clearly aimed at developing individuals' abilities through their experience of diverse situations.

Promotion and reward systems

Promotion and reward systems stimulate the alignment on desired working modes and behaviours. Two elements seem to be of major importance in the perspective of an international integration. In the first place, it is necessary to reduce the local managers' rigidity and focus on their local environment and offer them attractive international careers. Local managers should have a global understanding of the firm's challenges, and not try to defend their local interests at the expense of global efficiency. In the second place, reward systems should encourage information-sharing and transfers of know-how from each individual, not only to his or her subordinates, but also to his or her peers in other units of the group.

At Fiat, the Group Human Resources department recognizes the value of investing in an individual's international career. Following an internal study that was carried out in 1989, Fiat became aware that for the effective management of international operations people were at least as important as structures and systems.

Today, Fiat is able to identify several types of international posts which correspond to different types of environments (Auteri and Tesio, 1990, p. 10):

● Transnational positions; operating over the whole geographic area of the business without segmentation or limitations.
● Multinational positions; operating in the context of several countries defined by specific limitations.
● Open local positions; operating in the context of a single nation, with significant links, reference points and dependence on units outside the country, generally head office.
● Local positions; operating within the context of a single nation on the basis of locally determined variables, without significant interaction with other countries.

This classification of Fiat's managerial positions has shown that 40 per cent of them have an international scope, 75 per cent of which are located in Europe.

Reward system can promote the sharing of information and experiences. At Pilkington, two distinct situations coexist. First, in the task forces which were put into place by the Technology Management Board, the criteria of reward are based less upon traditional performance criteria than upon qualitative criteria such as international cooperation, team spirit and individual capabilities. The reward system that Pilkington has set up within task forces encourages cooperative group behaviour from participants. Using such a system, however, is limited to the task forces. As far as business units and functional units are concerned, the reward system is based essentially upon people's responsibilities and the performance and objectives of the unit.

The combination of international training programmes, rotations and promotions results in a mixing of people which is crucial for the reinforcement of a shared corporate mind-set.

Procedural justice

The challenge is to involve foreign unit managers in the process of strategic thinking aimed at achieving corporate goals.

Such approaches are developed in companies for whom world-wide integration is essential. The process is best described by the theory of procedural justice (Kim and Mauborgne, 1991, 1993). Briefly, procedural justice designates the equitable nature of strategy formulation processes *vis-à-vis* subsidiary managers. According to Kim and Mauborgne (1993, pp. 403–4), five elements contribute to procedural justice:

1. Head office management is knowledgeable about local situations of subsidiary units.

2. Two-way communication exists in the multinational's strategy-making process.
3. The head office is fairly consistent in making decisions across the subsidiary units.
4. Subsidiary units can legitimately challenge the strategic views of the head office.
5. Subsidiaries receive an account of the multinational's final strategic decisions.

At Hoffmann-La Roche, procedural justice is illustrated through two mechanisms. First, the group favours decision-making decentralization. For example, each division defines its own attitude, its own strategy, and its own management mode for its activities. This leads to a dissymmetry of the firm's organization depending on the characteristics of activities. The will for autonomy and decentralization also appears at the head office level, where the parent company functions in the same way as the other units. Therefore, the corporate head office must not infringe upon the managerial freedom and independence of each division (whose headquarters are also located in Switzerland). Also, the managerial freedom of country subsidiaries is substantial. For instance, the parent company's head of personnel does not have any hierarchical power over Hoffmann-La Roche France's head of personnel nor that of Italy's. The group recognizes that the local situation has a major impact on the success of the firm's operations, even in an environment where global forces are becoming stronger and stronger.

Second, the strategic thinking process involves local managers in an interactive and iterative fashion. At Hoffmann-La Roche, investments are decided upon and managed within the framework of a long-term plan which is organized by each business division. Each division elaborates its own business plan, then presents and defends it in front of the group's Executive Committee. After discussions and agreement on the business plan, investment programmes are included in the annual budgets which themselves are derived from the business plan. Within certain limits, the division has free choice. In the case of investments of over a certain amount, the divisions must get agreement from the Executive Committee.

In the same way, decisions concerning the location and implantation of the production units and the logistical centres belongs to the divisions. Here again, there is no absolute rule; diversity is accepted and flexibility is encouraged. In the pharmaceutical business, one can imagine that the production of an active substance would be highly concentrated in one or two sites for the entire world, while the manufacture of that substance into pills and capsules would be carried out at a regional level and the packaging at a local level.

According to the principles of procedural justice, putting the organization's functioning modes into question corresponds to a new and more global business vision. Marketing and R & D were the first two functions in which this process was developed while production, distribution and administrative activities followed the same evolution some years later.

The Hoffmann-La Roche case shows the involvement of managers in equitable procedures of strategic planning. These procedures help create a consensus concerning the firm's strategy, reinforce the feeling of belonging to a community of interests and to a group which recognizes the value of its managers. This feeling is all the more strong if competitors adopt a different style of management.

Summary

In the firms that we have studied, the creation and reinforcement of a company mind-set is based upon several integrating mechanisms:

- Sharing a strategic vision.
- Sharing information and knowledge.
- The international development of human resources.
- Procedural justice between the head office, the divisions and the subsidiaries.

The combination of such practices counterbalances centrifugal forces. However, the relative importance of those practices varies from one firm to another and depends on several factors:

- The competitive context in which the firm evolves may be more or less favourable to integration.
- The firm's international configuration.
- The firm's history and degree of international maturity.

The process of developing a corporate mind-set seems to follow three phases. In the first phase, the company tries to increase knowledge flows concerning work practices. In the second phase, strategic intent and international development of human resources are reinforced. During the third phase, the group redesigns the relationships between head office and subsidiary units according to the principles of procedural justice. Cutting corners could be problematic as the learning process has to be gradual.

These phases correspond to different levels of depth in the formation of a shared mind-set. At the first level, personnel have a more complete and concrete image of the company and their place within it. At the second level, a common philosophy, a common language, and a feeling of closeness, in spite of geographic distance, develop. Participation in shaping the group's strategy is based on knowledge and trust, and it emerges at a third level.

In the end, the question about which hierarchical levels are touched by the development of a corporate mind-set should be raised. It usually follows a trickle-down pattern, i.e. upper levels are first affected, then communication is progressively extended to a wider group of managers as it goes down the hierarchical levels. A complementary path consists in giving priority to solving key problems at any hierarchical level. The experience of the firms that we have studied shows that a top–down approach is insufficient if it is not combined with the development of transverse processes, formal and informal, deliberate and emergent networks.

3 Horizontal networks

The managers we met see reciprocal learning and the diffusion of knowledge as the major challenges in the integration process. The creation and development of formal transverse structures and networks is a necessary but not sufficient condition for reciprocal learning (see below). Formal horizontal networks create opportunities for meeting people and for the emergence of informal interpersonal networks which are just as important (see page 226). Horizontal networks are those that cut across divisions of function or geography, which involve interaction between all levels within the hierarchy.

Formal horizontal structures and networks

Reciprocal learning and knowledge-sharing are generally linked to one or several of the following objectives:

- To diffuse the experience of subsidiaries which have particular competencies within a particular value chain activity, with the aim of making the best use of existing resources and optimizing the efficiency of the entire international system.
- To define and develop new projects for the improvement of value chain activities by combining the knowledge and skills of the diverse geographical units. This process is particularly important in international firms which want to adopt a horizontal structure (White and Poynter, 1990). Known as the logic of resource redeployment, it requires the identification of common critical problems and a definition of common measures of performance.
- To share information, knowledge and skills which are located in different geographical units so as to generate innovations that respond to key market pressures. This is the logic of resource development.

In their world-wide resource integration process, the companies we have studied promote one, two, or more rarely, three integration logics, depending on their current priorities.

Lafarge Coppée is doing business in industries in which transportation costs are high, total costs are sensitive to volume, and in which there is little product innovation. Cement is one of the least expensive base products. As a result, a strong competitive position is founded upon efficient cost control, especially for energy costs. Therefore, it is logical that the diffusion of the unit's know-how concerning cost control and the setting up of joint programmes for improving efficiency have high priority.

Hoffmann-La Roche is doing business in industries of high added-value where product technologies evolve very rapidly. Priority is therefore given to the management of projects oriented towards resource optimization. One critical factor for developing resources is the management of multi-functional teams that are rich in diverse experiences.

Pilkington focuses on activities which have high added-value and at the same time require strong capital intensity. This strategy demands excellent control over production efficiency and a strong capacity for innovation. Under such conditions, Pilkington must organize the transfer of efficient solutions from the high performing sites towards the less efficient, using benchmarking methods. It must also put into place improvement programmes which establish the best practices at the European level. And lastly, it must continually consolidate the company's leadership in terms of product-process innovation.

Responses to all of these needs have relied heavily on the setting up of transverse structures. These include temporary task forces, permanent teams, interface roles such as project managers, permanent roles of horizontal integration, coordinating committees and the multiple hierarchies organized in a matrix form (Galbraith, 1973; Martinez and Jarillo, 1991). Such formal mechanisms develop experience-sharing and collective learning.

Lafarge Coppée

At Lafarge Coppée, in each business branch, there are functional units which foster and focus on experience-sharing between the various countries. These exchange structures were set up in the beginning of the 1980s and started to flourish in the 1990s. They were tried out within the cement branch before being transferred and adapted to other branches within the company.

In the cement industry, the techniques and difficulties are very different from one factory to another. The quarry, limestone, and all of cement's components are never identical. Such differences require important adaptations in the production process. In addition, factory histories within the group are also very diverse. For example, some factories were acquired twenty years ago, then transformed. Others were purchased much more recently. As a consequence, several engineering concepts coexist and form a complex ensemble at corporate level. Each unit had developed particular competencies and accumulated original experiences. In the past, there were no systematic exchanges between units, it all depended on the initiative of local managers. In the 1980s, under pressure for cost control, Lafarge Coppée began to organize exchanges in a more methodical manner.

The preliminary condition for any exchange between several dozen units was to have a common technical language and common premises concerning the manner of doing things well. Therefore, the 'Direction des Performances Cimentières' (DPC) was created with the mission to define technical doctrines. The wave of acquisitions in 1988 and 1989 in Spain, ex-Eastern Germany, Turkey, Czechoslovakia, etc., increased the need for a structure that could direct and focus on knowledge flows.

The current structure, formalized in 1990, was set up in order to obtain maximum synergy between subsidiaries, while preserving those local practices that fit with local specificities. This structure respects the firm's decentralized culture, the objective is to convince rather than to impose solutions on the unit. The search for consensus and the elaboration of solutions based on experiments conducted at low hierarchical levels are part of the corporate culture.

The new structure includes two functional integrating units: the DPC and the International Technical Centre (CTI). Their role is to organize the connections between subsidiaries, in terms of experience and knowledge. The DCP and the CTI cooperate closely and, in order to make this symbiosis more concrete, the same person heads both units. The two departments are directly attached to the Cement Committee which groups together five people including the Chairman of Lafarge Coppée and the Corporate Strategy Director. Within this structure, all countries are subsidiaries. In other words, Lafarge Coppée France does not play the role of a head office. The units are placed in a purely horizontal configuration.

Previously the technical centres were dispersed and quite independent. Now the aim of the CTI is to achieve economies of scale and knowledge transfers in research and technical studies. Three large units, Lafarge Coppée (France), Lafarge Corporation (USA) and Asland (Spain), also have their own technical centres, each of which have between 80 and 120 people. A country can have its own local technical centre once it has passed a threshold which is defined in terms of the number of factories, tonnage and market growth. Other subsidiaries have technical departments (not technical centres) comprised of about 20 people (located in Rio, Istambul and Munich). These departments are too small to have sufficient expertise. They are thus supervised, assisted and controlled by the CTI which is situated in l'Isle d'Abeau, France. Some other countries have no technical structure. In these cases, local technical management is taken care of by the CTI.

The CTI is a flexible structure that must constantly adapt itself to the evolution of subsidiaries. For example, a subsidiary could lose its technical centre and could give this function over to the CTI because it is situated in a declining market. Another subsidiary could create its own centre because it supplies a growing market where Lafarge Coppée has priority development projects.

The DPC is responsible for federating all of the technical practices by establishing technical doctrines. Its objective is not to define normative policies in a centralized manner. It is aimed at *inspiring* the cement technical community. The DPC leads discussion sessions in which the heads of each country take part and *together* they elaborate the technical doctrines which are finally agreed upon as 'beliefs' as to the correct way of doing things concerning processes and products.

The second goal of the DPC is defined as 'to be the guardian and the authority for the firm's techniques and cement technologies'. Here, the objective is to coordinate research efforts and technical practices, and to supervise the consistency of investments. The DPC ensures that there are no technical areas, in particular new techniques, which have been inadvertently ignored. On the other hand, it prevents the duplication of research projects. The DPC is consulted on all significant investments so that all investments integrate the best technical knowledge.

The third role of the DPC is to set up a common policy concerning standards. It starts by elaborating common technical definitions based on the data provided by the units. Technical definitions are then published in a manual and diffused throughout the corporation, by the Cement Know-How Centre (CKHC). The CKHC also circulates annual performance indicators which are used for the self-evaluation of each unit.

The fourth objective is to create and feed a central 'memory' of knowledge, know-how, and experiences accessible to everyone. A database, called the 'Cement Who's Who', contains individual résumés and technical profiles. Access to this database is limited to authorized hierarchy. Another database, managed by the CKHC, supplies a list of all major equipment with their characteristics. The records of each factory's annual performance are also included. Finally, each year, the CKHC collects concrete cases which describe resolutions of problems, tests and new practices. Cases are circulated among all engineers in all countries. In order to motivate the staff, a competition is held every year which awards a study trip to the person presenting the best case.

In brief, at Lafarge Coppée, the horizontal sharing of knowledge is organized to fulfil four objectives: establish common premises, a common language, criteria for common measurements and a collective memory.

Pilkington

To manage the challenge of integrating knowledge, Pilkington has adopted a twofold approach. On the one hand, it sets up formal horizontal structures which must create a favourable framework for taking initiatives, for innovating, and for fostering international awareness. On the other hand, it leaves the coast clear for all informal initiatives as long as they do not come into conflict with the above objectives and as long as they do not interfere with formal efforts of integration. Two significant examples show how Pilkington has succeeded in reinforcing transversal structures:

1. The new matrix organization of the company's European operations.
2. The creation of the Technology Management Board.

The matrix organization of European operations

Until recently, Pilkington's European production system was typical of a multi-domestic configuration in which most of the factories supplied their national market. For example, British factories tended to supply Great Britain, German factories did the same for Germany, Austria and Switzerland, etc. Then the company decided to adopt a pan-European organization along business lines in the flat and safety glass operations. The matrix structure has been effective since 1 April 1993 and has three objectives. First, to establish an organization which aims at achieving strong product leadership throughout Europe, second, to optimize the group's resource allocation and improve efficiency, and finally, to develop national management structures that conform to local laws and practices. In short, the company wants to encourage managers to develop a pan-European vision of their markets and competitive forces.

The new structure comprises four business lines, Automotive Original Equipment, Automotive Glass Replacement, Building Products, and Special Glasses, each line having its own Executive Manager. The Building Products line is itself divided into two regions, Northern Europe (Great Britain, Finland, Sweden, Norway, Poland, France and Spain) and Central Europe (Germany, Austria, Switzerland, Benelux and Italy). The whole is coordinated by a Chief Executive Europe who has every business line manager and country manager under his responsibility. The country managers are in charge of institutional communication, public relations, and legal matters concerning accounting and personnel relations. There is no subordination relationship between business line managers and country managers. Middle managers report to one or the other as required.

Setting up the new structure has not been easy and took about 18 months to become fully operational. Business line managers had to be selected carefully: some are British, others German or Finnish. Today, each is responsible for all the industrial subsidiaries in their entire geographical area and they can adopt the production configuration of their choice in order to improve efficiency significantly. Each subsidiary unit becomes specialized in a certain number of products and supplies the whole European territory. Thus, the new matrix structure fosters the rationalization of Pilkington's entire European production system and strongly encourages the adoption of a European strategy and management.

The Technology Management Board

Created in 1991, the Technology Management Board (TMB) is a world-wide horizontal structure which organizes transfers of knowledge, know-how and expertise in R & D between research centres, businesses and countries. The TMB is a response to competitive pressures (growing capital intensity and critical size in R & D), it supports the focalization strategy on high added-value activities within core businesses, and contributes to the development of horizontal technological synergies.

During the 1980s, the configuration of R & D activities was multi-domestic. For example, there were R & D centres in the UK, Germany and the US, each covering substantially all the company's products and processes. The need to integrate accumulated experience and knowledge, and rationalize R & D activities world-wide led to the creation of the TMB. This board receives support from the marketing function and is composed principally of the Executive Director responsible for technology and the senior technical executives from around the world. The TMB's objectives are the following:

● to create centres of technological excellence.

- to develop the R & D teams' sensitivity to market signals.
- to establish formal communication networks world-wide.
- to avoid redundant duplication of R & D efforts across the R & D centres which are located in England, Germany and the United States.
- to transfer technology effectively and efficiently around the world.

The TMB determines the priorities for both R & D programmes and investments. It also shares R & D objectives among the three research centres and names project managers for each major technological area.

All of the TMB's concrete substance comes from the numerous international task forces that it establishes. These task forces mainly include engineers involved in international programmes. Engineers are selected according to their skills and experience, national origin, and human qualities such as their ability to cooperate and work in groups. Aside from engineers, Pilkington also tries to include marketing specialists in the task forces. This is more difficult since those people must also be able to understand the many technological aspects of the topic at hand. Marketing personnel therefore need a double, high-level experience. However, the inclusion of marketing skills in the work team is seen as necessary in order to take into account market constraints. Participants in task forces are free to manage their team according to objectives that are assigned by the TMB. Their obligation is related to results, and not to means.

The creation of the TMB leads to the specialization of each technical centre in specific and well-defined products or scientific areas. Thus, British people specialize on R & D areas that are different from the specializations of their German or American colleagues. The TMB also leads to the development of the company's capability to spot a technology which has been developed within one unit and transfer it rapidly to another unit, business or country where a similar need has emerged. However, the integration process by the TMB is not yet complete since it will take another two years before the system is totally operational. Human and cultural constraints impede a quicker implementation. From a human point of view, Pilkington must solve several problems concerning the international movement of researchers or managers. Movement is necessary in order to transfer skills and knowledge from one centre to another according to the achievement of current programmes and individual constraints. From a cultural point of view, Pilkington must cope with the psychological resistance of the users of new technologies: development engineers working in other units or marketers in other countries. According to a Pilkington's executive:

> There may be a distrust of somebody doing a programme for you because people often only trust the output of units that they know, that are close to them or that they can see. And now, what is happening in Pilkington is the R & D output, in Germany, for instance is getting sent to the USA for use in the USA. And the American may say 'I am not sure about this'. There may be a sort of natural mistrust that comes in.

What you have to do is to build in mechanisms that overcome that distrust. One of them is to have more multicultural teams of people.

Task forces should help to eliminate some of the mistrust and resistance towards outputs coming from other units. This is one of the critical conditions of success for horizontal structures which are designed to integrate and develop knowledge. Through such formal structures and international task forces, Lafarge Coppée and Pilkington are also creating opportunities for the emergence of informal networks.

Interpersonal networks

Most interviewed executives emphasized the necessity for creating interpersonal and transnational networks among managers and technical staff in order to foster knowledge transfers and reciprocal learning between subsidiary units. To cope with an environment which has become increasingly complex, horizontal structures alone are no longer sufficient to ensure rapid and intense knowledge flows (even when supported by a shared corporate mind-set). Interpersonal networks facilitate exchanges between individuals who are geographically distant but yet feel close to one another. This feeling of closeness is based on the sharing of common professional or extra-professional values, mutual credibility and respect, and emotional factors such as mutual trust, good-companionship and friendship. Unilever views interpersonal networks as a way to ensure world-wide corporate unity. 'In practice, this network – as represented by both the company's formal structure and the informal exchanges between managers – may well be one of the ingredients in the glue that holds Unilever together' (Maljers, 1992, p. 50).

Interpersonal networks seem to have two functions

First, they support and improve the functioning of formal networks that are set up around permanent or temporary projects or problems. According to a Lafarge Coppée executive,

> It is not obvious that people who come from fifteen different countries have the same understanding of things in order to share experience... It is necessary that people see where their interest is and understand that sharing experience is going to make them progress... They also need to know each other, speak a common language and spend time together.

Research concerning the functioning of intercultural teams has illustrated their difficulties in working effectively (Adler, 1986). Cultural diversity makes the functioning of these teams more difficult since participants interpret situations, act and communicate differently. As a consequence, errors of perception, interpretation, evaluation and communication multiply. This complex, uncertain and ambiguous context can increase individuals' stress and confusion. However, if such problems are avoided, a multi-cultural group offers a high potential for creativity and performance thanks to the confrontation of various experiences and interpretations.

Therefore, in order for the horizontal and transnational structures to work effectively, it is important to create relationships based on trust and a common language – in short, a sort of 'sub-culture' which is common to all members of the network.

> By what means? Precisely by recognizing the existence of clearly identified networks within the enterprise, by running these in a way which is entirely transparent to the respective hierarchies of their different members, by creating subcultures which are not only strong but clearly compatible with the general culture of the enterprise. Such 'functional' subcultures can, moreover, help to attenuate those differences of a national origin which often appear in the various components of a global group and which act as a brake on the development of a real culture within the enterprise. (Feneuille, 1990, pp. 299–300).

The second function of interpersonal networks is to create autonomous networks of informal exchanges. These networks work non-stop all year long and outside the formal organization which is often bureaucratic. By reducing the number of intermediaries and by stimulating the use of temporary *ad hoc* structures, they serve to decrease hierarchical coordination costs. These temporary exchange networks are created and dissolved depending on the problems being encountered. As argued by Unilever's Chairman, 'While our network may seem disorderly, it does work. Formal systems of information transfer certainly exist, but sometimes it is simply much faster for a product manager in Brazil, for example, to fax a rough sketch of a new information to her opposite number in Italy' (Maljers, 1992, p. 50).

At Lafarge Coppée, the head of the DPC (Direction des Performances Cimentières) also emphasizes this function of interpersonal networks. He argues that the DPC triggers a process of development of interpersonal networks beyond national borders. This has been achieved through the availability of comparative statistics on performance and the creation of the central cement *Who's Who*.

> We provide plant managers with the means to assess themselves through comparative performance data. It is then up to them to phone, send faxes and organize exchanges or visits. The *Who's Who* only constitutes a databank on expertise [within the corporation]. Unit managers can look up those persons who probably experience problems that they encounter, and organize exchanges with them.

By accelerating information flows, informal networks increase the ability of the organization to react when facing a complex and turbulent environment. 'Lafarge Coppée has experimented successfully with a type of organization which, by establishing links across traditional hierarchical barriers and encouraging involvement and initiative, is most likely to give the enterprise the flexibility and adaptability it needs to face the uncertain world of the nineties' (Feneuille, 1990, p. 296).

Before one can take advantage of the use of transnational interpersonal networks, two major questions need to be considered:

1. How can the development of interpersonal networks be stimulated?
2. How can they be directed in such a way that they remain in harmony with the formal structure and bring solutions to the firm's most important problems?

In reality, companies have brought more answers to the first question than to the second. This is certainly due to the very nature of interpersonal networks which are on the invisible side of organizations. When studying the development of transnational informal networks, it becomes more fruitful to analyze the circumstances which foster the emergence of such networks, since the company cannot really control the process. Four facilitating practices were usually mentioned by interviewed executives:

1. Putting the right people together into formal networks (task forces).
2. Rotation of managers.
3. Training.
4. Conferences and meetings.

Task forces

The practice most currently used to stimulate the emergence of informal interpersonal networks is the setting up of formal networks, i.e. international task forces or teams to exchange ideas or information about problems that concern a function or an activity. The objective of these teams is to bring together geographically distant people who are facing technically similar problems. In spite of national cultural differences, there is a high probability that a functional subculture emerges since individuals speak the same technical language and have similar concerns. At the same time, the probability of directing these subcultural networks into conformity with the corporate culture is high because participants are selected according to well-defined competences. Under these conditions, it usually follows that interpersonal networks are contained within the limits of the formal network. However, since each individual in the group has their own network, they may share some of their relationships with other members of the formal group. As a result the frontiers of the group network may stretch. On the other hand, working together in a temporary group is not sufficient to guarantee that interpersonal relationships will survive the life of the group.

As already seen above, Lafarge Coppée has set up different forms of transnational horizontal networks, such as the technical community which is led by the CTI and which is comprised of plant managers and the technical centre heads, the work teams which are created around action plans and the permanent theme groups which are led by specialist leaders from the DPC. Meetings provide the opportunity for informal interpersonal relationships to develop both during and outside work time.

Petrofina favours long-term project teams. For example, when the company decided to implement a software common to all production and sales units, an enormous amount of work was required to adapt the software to each country's local requirement. A team of 30 people coming from each country subsidiary of Petrofina was set up. After being trained, the members of this team started to travel around. They helped the different local units to adapt and implement the new software. The work lasted for three years. The experiment was felt to be particularly stimulating for the network members. After the formal network dissolved, former members showed a unique ability and motivation to communicate, thanks to their common experience and the knowledge which they acquired about all subsidiaries that were involved in the implementation.

Unilever uses committees, temporary *ad hoc* groups, and permanent groups that are set up around key problems. For example, the ice cream snacks market grows rapidly and requires rapid innovation. In order to follow the market's growth and generate innovation, Unilever decided to create a strategy team chaired by a marketing director of the United Kingdom and consisting of five other people who work in marketing departments in three other countries, Italy, Germany and Holland. This team advises the food division's corporate head office and has authority over the implementation of strategy.

Today, Pilkington uses task forces quite intensively in order to create networks, especially within the context of the Technology Management Board. These task forces are composed of people who possess various expertise and experiences and come from different units within the company. The objectives of these work groups are generally ambitious and tight in terms of deadlines. These programmes are not loose projects. They require a lot of work, energy and personal involvement. Participants feel that they are sharing a strong and memorable experience. Moreover, the planning of meetings and, more generally, the team management are totally under the team's control. Team members travel a lot and work in very different places. Under these conditions, socialization opportunities are many and allow for the creation of more informal relationships. Finally, the severe selection process and the international visibility among the personnel reinforce the feeling of belonging to a unique network of individuals who participate in such task forces.

Rotation of managers

All the executives we interviewed emphasized the important role of internal rotations within the process of integration.

Manager rotation is, by definition, a source for the development of inter-personal networks. At Petrofina, increasing the number of national, international or transcontinental rotations within the company is a major objective. Networks of interpersonal relationships that are created during long stays (three to four years on average) in different units or countries remain strong after the departure of the manager. They feed subsequent exchanges of experience and advice. Such networks, in turn, expand and reinforce themselves. As noted by an executive of Petrofina:

> It is a self-generating process. The more top managers work in several countries, the more knowledgeable they become about the company and its needs, and the more they suggest ideas. The head of a subsidiary unit who had part of his career in another country and who made some friends there will be happy to send some of his assistants to this country.

Unilever considers that a manager who has lived through several rotations not only possesses more know-how, but also improves his or her know-who which allows him or her actively to use interpersonal networks.

In this area, Hoffmann-La Roche has set up an innovative decentralized system which lets individual initiatives emerge. In order to foster organizational flexibility and transverseness, Hoffmann-La Roche has allowed a free employment market within the entire corporation. Each unit head and manager is free in their internal recruitment policy and in the orientation of their own career path. Each manager can propose a new position to any competent person, no matter where this person is working within the company. Thus, this internal market works in the same way as an external employment market (supposedly efficient). However, some limits have been set up in order to avoid too frequent rotation. For instance, it is being discouraged to 'headhunt' internally people who have been in a position for less than three years. On the other hand, any manager holding the same post for more than five years has the right to ask for a move within the company.

The way in which this particularly dynamic internal market operates is directly linked to the corporate human resource policy. It essentially rests on two factors: succession and personal development. The succession plan concerns each post. It is elaborated by each manager for his or her immediate subordinates. For each position, two elements are defined: a) the incumbent's profile and personal development wishes and b) a list of potential replacements (identified and approached candidates, or candidates who have been considered but not yet approached). The personal development plan contains the person's management dimensions (strengths), résumé of educational background and experience, as well as his or her preferences concerning the geographical areas where he or she wishes to work. A fundamental operating rule completes and underpins this system – each manager knows all candidates who are likely to join his or her team but does not know what posts the present team members are candidates for.

Therefore, since no barriers exist between divisions, countries, or functions, the internal employment market naturally encourages various transverse career paths. An engineer from an R & D department in Switzerland may very well join the marketing team of another division in the United States.

This management system is very demanding of people, especially of those who have the highest positions in the hierarchy. First, it forces managers to anticipate the succession of their team members, who can leave at any time in order to take on other responsibilities within the corporation, and second, it forces managers to improve their leadership in order to avoid a high turnover among team members and to attract good candidates. By facilitating transverse professional paths, Hoffmann-La Roche's internal market also limits power games which are often at work within vertical systems.

The system is very decentralized since succession plans are established by each manager for his or her closest team members and not by a corporate human resources director. The role of human resources directors within the company is to advise and to provoke encounters in order to facilitate the elaboration of succession plans and personal development projects. Indeed the system of a free internal employment market encourages managers to develop their own interpersonal network within the company.

By responding to pressures for an interdisciplinary and transversal approach to professions and activities, the internal employment market fosters and facilitates bridges between the different units. It contributes to loyalty to the company and to a feeling of 'belonging' to Hoffmann-La Roche. The flexibility and openness of the system also facilitates the integration of newly acquired enterprises within the corporation. Integration is crucial since the development of firms that are involved in innovative businesses such as pharmaceuticals often relies upon acquisitions of and partnerships with small high-tech firms. In such take-overs, what is at stake for the acquiring company is the maintenance and even improvement in the level of expertise and technical performance of the acquired firm, while succeeding in reaching a critical size. Synergies can be achieved by drawing on the acquiring company's resources and international network. They are also facilitated and stimulated in a system of job rotation that is open, flexible and respectful of individuals.

Exchange opportunities: training and meetings

Training programmes create favourable conditions for meeting other people who come from different countries or functions. They also create opportunities for the emergence of networks and interpersonal relationships. However, depending on their objectives, training programmes do not always create opportunities to develop extra-professional exchanges. Thus, socialization often appears as a sub-product of those training programmes which are usually designed to reach specific (technical) goals. Nevertheless, some companies such as Hoffmann-La Roche and Unilever explicitly attribute a prevailing socialization role to their seminars. According to a Hoffmann-La Roche executive:

> Designed for top managers who have a few years of experience within
> the company, the MBA-type programme is a key element not only in
> the human resources management but also in Hoffmann-La Roche's
> organizational adaptation capability ... The programme is
> simultaneously a place for meeting people, discovering, and learning
> management concepts as well as working through networks.

The Chairman of Unilever is even more explicit on this subject: 'Every trainee becomes part of a group of 25 to 30 people recruited for similar managerial positions. This shared experience creates an informal network of equals who know one another well and usually continue to meet and exchange experiences' (Maljers, 1992, p. 49).

Annual meetings and conferences are aimed at reinforcing the company's identity as well as stimulating interpersonal networks. Regarding this point, all interviewed executives agreed. Generally, creating and reinforcing networks takes place on the 'periphery' of meetings which gather between 200 and 300 people who are usually senior and top managers. By 'periphery', we mean the meals, evenings and drinks which are all moments when people gather in small groups and have exchanges. Methods used to organize those meetings are improving and are beginning explicitly to include ways and means of creating and developing networks. The 'open space' formula is typical of the willingness to create networks during meetings. In such sessions, participants organize themselves in order to express and exchange ideas. The principle is based on the village food market model. People who feel passionate about a subject or an idea, display their topics on a board. Then participants list their names under one or several topics that are of particular interest to them. When registrations are closed, people form groups on their own and create workshops. The foundations of interpersonal networks are thus put down around common interests.

Interpersonal networks emerge around task forces, rotation, encounters during training seminars and meetings, but also thanks to numerous personal initiatives. They are informal and invisible, and constitute an essential force in the dynamics of reciprocal learning and of transverse knowledge flows. In addition, interpersonal networks are sometimes the origin of formal networks which are created deliberately. The loop between deliberate and emergent processes is thus completed.

Because of their very nature, interpersonal networks cannot be controlled by head offices. Furthermore, the question concerning the way these networks can be linked to priorities held by top executives has not been clearly answered. It can only be assumed that there is harmony as soon as the formal and the informal feed each other and a shared mind-set exists (cf. section 2).

4 Comments and perspectives

Sharing a corporate mind-set and developing horizontal networks are two dimensions that cannot be dissociated from each other in the integration process. Both reinforce knowledge flows and reciprocal learning. Most of the deliberate integrative mechanisms, the international organization (procedural justice, transverse structures, etc.) and the international management of human resources (training, rotation, promotion, exchange meetings, etc.), contribute to the development of a corporate mind-set *and* horizontal networks.

It seems that European firms increasingly control organizational matters and the bases of international human resources management. However, according to the managers that we interviewed, the international management of human resources must respond to even more ambitious challenges:

- Enlarge the company's reservoir of technical experts.
- Combine a top-down approach with a bottom-up approach for manager recruitment.
- Balance cultural influences in training activities.
- Develop a reservoir of transnational managers.
- Internationalize head office teams.

What distinguishes the competency of one company from another is the critical expertise of the people within it. Maintaining and developing expertise is a condition for long-term success. Geographical dispersion sometimes makes the systematic identification of critical experts, whether they be inside or outside the company, difficult. Geographical dispersion can also hinder the international spread of competencies through internal training programmes. These are priority challenges for human resources departments.

Corporate head offices are usually involved in the recruitment of top managers such as country managers, area managers, or subsidiary unit managers, while the recruitment of subsidiaries' senior managers is often delegated to subsidiary units which can be tempted to act according to their local interests. Recruitment policies should be harmonized. It is not a question of centralizing the manager hiring process but rather of opening up the internal employment market and encouraging concerted efforts between head office and units.

Training programmes for managers are still too often influenced by the culture of the dominant country. Training sessions usually take place in the country where the headquarters are located. They generally use the training resources of the headquarters' country. Such practices have the advantage of creating a larger unity within the corporation but the risk is that they develop and favour a national model that then becomes dominant. As suggested by Adler and Bartholomew (1992), a truly world-wide integration should take into account sensitivities from all countries. For example, a manager training programme should be conceived by a multinational team and delivered by teaching staff from different countries.

The identification of high potential managers, their international career path, and the development of their transnational skills are often biased by the head office model. The model of the 'bi-cultural' manager (country of origin and head office country) should be seen as a first step. A transnational manager should have experience from several subsidiary units and should have participated in at least one important *multi*national project. Being aware of the material constraints of successive expatriations, the passing from being bi-cultural to multi-cultural is a great challenge.

Finally, in most international companies, the composition of the executive committees shows that the presence of nationals from the headquarters' country is predominant. Under such conditions, is it possible truly to integrate international diversities? The managers that we interviewed are convinced of the need to internationalize top management teams. International businesses originating from small European countries often set the example in this matter.

References

Adler, N. J. (1986), *International Dimensions of Organizational Behavior*, Boston, Mass.: Kent Publishing Company.

Adler, N. J. and S. Bartholomew (1992), 'Managing globally competent people', *Academy of Management Executive*, 6, 3, pp. 52–65.

Atamer, T. and R. Calori (1993), *Diagnostic et décisions stratégiques*, Paris: Dunod.

Auteri, E. and V. Tesio (1990), 'The internationalization of management at Fiat', *Journal of Management Development*, 9(6), pp. 6–16.

Bartlett, C. A. and S. Ghoshal (1989), *Managing Across Borders, The Transnational Solution*, Boston, Mass.: Harvard Business School Press.

Dunning, J. H. (1993), *The Globalization of Business*, New York: Routledge.

Feneuille, S. (1990), 'A network organization to meet the challenges of complexity', *European Management Journal*, 8(3), pp. 296–301.

Galbraith, J. (1973), *Designing Complex Organizations*, Reading, Mass.: Addison-Wesley.

Kim, W. C. and R. A. Mauborgne (1991), 'Implementing global strategies: the role of procedural justice', *Strategic Management Journal*, 12, pp. 125–43.

Kim, W. C. and R. A. Mauborgne (1993), 'Procedural justice, attitudes, and subsidiary top management compliance with multinationals' corporate strategic decisions', *Academy of Management Journal*, 36(3), pp. 502–26.

Maljers, F. A. (1992), 'Inside Unilever: the evolving transnational company', *Harvard Business Review*, September–October, pp. 46–51.

Martinez, J. I., and J. C. Jarillo (1991), 'Coordination demands of international strategies', *Journal of International Business Studies*, pp. 429–45.

Nonaka, I. (1990), 'Managing globalization as a self-renewing process: experiences of Japanese MNCs', in Bartlett, C. A., Y. Doz, and G. Hedlund (eds), *Managing The Global Firm*, New York: Routledge, pp. 69–94.

O'Connor, E. J. and G. V. Barrett. (1980), 'Informational cues and individual differences as determinants of subjective perceptions of task enrichment', *Academy of Management Journal*, 23(4), pp. 697–716.

Prahalad, C. K. and R. A. Bettis (1991), 'The dominant logic: a new linkage between diversity and performance', *Strategic Management Journal*, 7, pp. 485–501.

Salancik, G. R. and J. Pfeffer (1978), 'A social information processing approach to job attitudes and task design', *Administrative Science Quarterly*, 23, pp. 224–53.

Schwenk, C. R. (1986), 'Information, cognitive biases, and commitment to a course of action', *Academy of Management Executive*, 2, pp. 298–310.

Staw, B. M. and J. Ross (1987), 'Understanding escalation situations: antecedents, prototypes, and solutions', in Staw, B. M. and L. L. Cummings (eds), *Research in Organizational Behavior*, vol. 9, Greenwich, Conn.: JAI Press.

Ulrich, D. and D. Lake (1990), *Organizational Capability – Competing From The Inside Out*, New York: John Wiley & Sons.

Vernon, R. (1966), 'International investment and international trade in the product cycle', *Quarterly Journal of Economics*, 80, pp. 190–207.

White, R. E. and T. A. Poynter (1990), 'Organizing for world-wide advantage', in Bartlett, C. A., Y. Doz and G. Hedlund (eds), *Managing the Global Firm*, New York: Routledge, pp. 95–113.

CHAPTER 9

Changes in management education and development: a European perspective

Bruno Dufour

The directors interviewed in the Group ESC Lyon study for the European Round Table agreed upon two priorities: increasing 'people involvement' and the need for 'reciprocal learning' in Europe (cf. Chapter 3). Management education and development have a significant role in taking up these challenges. Directors themselves suggested several ways in which management education could be improved. The first part of this chapter is based on their views. In the second part their ideas are developed and the perspective of universities and business schools is added.

In recent years companies and business schools have already taken major steps to make their programmes more international in an effort to increase diversity. However, the changes and improvements are still uneven, and the best practices in management development still need to be communicated and expanded within the business and educational community.

1 Top managers' views on the future of management education and development

If one accepts that the main challenges are to learn from the best practices abroad and involving people within the organization, the ideal manager profile in Table 9.1 is not surprising; some would say: 'we know that'. The problem is that many schools in Europe still do not recruit their students according to these aptitudes, and many still concentrate on teaching techniques rather than on developing people. Many firms continue to recruit managers on their technical competencies and diplomas rather than on their aptitude to learn and to involve people. Reward systems often suffer from the same biases – individual evaluation primarily based on performance, while team evaluation including behavioural criteria is underdeveloped. In other words, practices often lag behind the principles and most educational institutions and international firms do not follow the example of the leading European organizations.

Table 9.1   Towards an ideal profile for the European manager.

ABILITY TO INVOLVE PEOPLE
- communication skills (listening, consulting, explaining, dialogue)
- skills in psychology (understanding people, cultural differences)
- capacity to work in teams (multi-national, multi-level, multi-cultural)
- capacity to coordinate, to create enthusiasm and to motivate

INTERNATIONAL SKILLS
- international experience
- competence in several languages (3 minimum)
- geographical mobility
- global thinking

FLEXIBILITY
- aptitude to manage change
- aptitude to manage diversity
- tolerance to ambiguity and uncertainty
- capacity to learn (self-evaluation, openness)

INTUITION
- intuition
- creativity, ability to innovate

BROAD VISION
- aptitude to have a general view of a situation (combining several disciplines, considering the historical context, and taking a systemic approach)
- deep understanding (sociological, philosophical, ethical)

Senior managers should ask themselves the questions:

- What do we do to develop these abilities in concrete terms?
- What do others do in concrete terms?
- What could we do, in concrete terms, to bring about improvement at all levels in the company?

Examination of current practices in management education and development leads to four areas of recommendations which will be reviewed separately but which are intimately linked as shown in Figure 9.1.

To achieve improvement in management education and development it is essential to develop close cooperation between schools and firms which should share the tasks of education and development more than they do at present. Individual member state governments and the EC should back up these efforts. It is also important to acknowledge that learning comes both from experience on the job and from the 'classroom' – giving managers opportunities to learn on the job is at least as important as organizing training and development sessions.

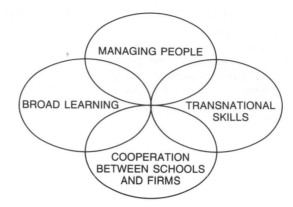

Figure 9.1 Paths for management education and development

Managing people

Developing managers' skills in this area requires efforts in four main directions.

Developing education and training in human relations and in psychology

In the majority of management schools, the study of psychology and sociology are still underdeveloped. Students seldom have the opportunity to assess their personal styles in relationship with others, to study motivation, power relationships, or to practise their skills in group dynamics and in negotiation. In addition students need feedback from psychologists on their performance (behaviour) in these areas. The present situation in engineering schools and universities is even more unsatisfactory, with priority still given to 'hard' sciences. The balance needs to change, and quickly.

More and more firms are realizing this need. Managers (who have been basically trained in the illusion that technical competence is *the* key to success and that implementation will smoothly follow decisions) need complementary training in psychology, sociology, group dynamics and negotiation as early as possible in their career.

> You have to develop skills in human relations, in negotiation, I don't mean commercial negotiation, I mean internal negotiation, negotiation with stakeholders and with peers. Young managers are not trained in this domain, sometimes they are not even aware of the crucial importance of negotiation and human relations.

> In our training programmes, we give more and more importance to psychology, how people 'function', how they learn, what motivates them. Even for professionals, top people in their domain, R & D

engineers, they have to unfreeze their sensitivity to these aspects if they want to be able to communicate and to be effective.

We make more and more effort on attitudes, on personal behaviour, in line with the culture of our company.

Developing teamwork and communication skills

Again this is a matter of behaviour, the basis is to learn to listen to others, then to develop teamwork skills. Teamwork and group evaluation should become systematic in management schools and in engineering schools. Team-training should be encompassed in companies' in-house training programmes. 'In the past an engineer could stay happily in his laboratory and make great discoveries. Today you need to mix different specialities and you need to communicate with other laboratories abroad. So they need to communicate, they need to be effective in a team.'

Developing cross-cultural awareness and understanding

Management schools and engineering schools need to include more knowledge of different cultures and countries in their programmes. The work done in basic education should be reinforced and supported by educational European TV channels. Education by TV is not necessarily didactic: 'An entertainment TV programme in Italy is very different from an entertainment programme in Germany or in England. You can learn a lot when comparing them.'

The teachers' role is to help students understand and interpret cultural differences. In addition, management schools and engineering schools could transform their foreign course teaching by combining language, history and culture. Moreover, they should give priority to periods of training within foreign universities and firms.

A few years ago the European Round Table launched the EUROJOB programme. Firms in the network can swap managers between countries for a period of about three months to work on a specific project. Three months gives enough time to understand a foreign business culture and to learn from it. On the other hand it is short enough not to raise all the problems of longer-term expatriation. Moreover, the EUROJOB system can prepare a manager for future expatriation. The system provides an excellent way to go beyond the mere taste of a foreign culture; but how many European managers have gone through something like EUROJOB? Such practices should be more widely spread.

The universal introduction of personal development plans for managers

In Europe the system of personal development plans for managers is still limited to a few 'blue chip' companies and to the upper levels in the hierarchy.

> I think that the most important innovation would be the universal introduction of personal development plans for managers. It is much easier to have people design their own personal development plan. Then the people have to know what is available in the 'cafeteria', and they have got to have personal counseling.

Personal development also means having the opportunity to refresh one's mind.

> You can contribute to managers' development by taking your people out of the organization and sending them to a business school or saying take three months sabbatical, go and write a novel if you like, go and read philosophy if you want, or whatever else it may be, so that you refresh your mind and can look at yourself and then look at the organization from the outside in.

Senior managers should be in charge of management development. 'I personally address, in management development, about the top 250–300 people. I don't know all of them. But I know the ones that matter, and I keep an eye on them . . . Of course I don't do it myself, but we have a management development department that is also handled by the top.'

The challenge in European firms is to complement top–down approaches and to extend the principle of management development to lower levels in the hierarchy by involving middle managers, who have the skills to help their subordinates in their own personal development.

Transnational skills

Management schools and universities, engineering schools and universities should become more international.

Learning foreign languages

Learning foreign languages is a basic requirement which should start at primary school and gradually intensify so that graduates master *at least* three languages (including their native tongue). Graduate schools complement education by providing intensive learning for individuals who have not reached a high enough level and by offering opportunities for in-company internships abroad.

Transnational training

Transnational training means studying outside one's own country:

● Practical experience in a foreign company (from one month to one year).
● Attending courses in a foreign school (from one semester to one year).
● Business studies in a foreign school.

EC programmes such as Erasmus or Tempus help to finance training abroad. Given its high diversity concentrated in a small geographical area, Europe provides such opportunities much better than do the United States and Japan.

> These young people, they should travel around. They should see new university environments, new business school environments. You meet them with open eyes and you broaden your base as you see their thirsts and appetites grow. And I think that is the future for European business schools and universities, they will have this diversity which will make it much richer, which is something very valuable compared with Japan or with the USA.

As students move across borders in such educational and business exchanges the student bodies will become more international. Such cross-fertilization is already underway in European business schools but is less developed in engineering schools. However, the relative proportion of foreigners from other European countries is still too low to allow truly effective cross-cultural fertilization (the threshold is estimated at around one-third of foreigners in a class).

It is also crucial that faculties of European schools and universities become more international. This can be done by giving teachers experience in foreign universities and/or companies (sabbatical periods and/or teachers' exchanges, for periods between one month and one year) and by the recruitment of foreign faculty members. Sabbaticals and exchanges do occur in Europe but they are costly and therefore their development is limited.

The recruitment of students and of professors abroad represents a tremendous effort for most schools and universities. As a result, agreements, alliances and networks between schools from different country bases are developing. Some institutions regret that the links are not more selective and stronger between partners in a network: everybody has agreements with everybody, but such agreements are too volatile or superficial to really co-develop programmes or engage in long-term intangible investments.

In this perspective, companies and the EC should encourage the creation of multilateral *joint ventures* between schools from different European countries. For instance one joint venture already exists at the graduate level in management – the Ecole des Affaires de Paris. There is certainly a need for a new European programme (at the level of the best MBA graduates and executives) developed and realized by a joint venture created by management educational institutions from different European countries (the UK, Germany, France, Italy, Spain, Belgium, the Netherlands, Sweden and one of the Eastern European countries). By working as an integrated network the joint venture would compete with INSEAD and IMD, and provide the combined diversity of skills and cultures from the participating organizations. Companies could also be involved in this initiative. The same kind of school in joint venture could be created between engineering schools and universities and provide some management skills together with scientific and technical knowledge at the highest level.

In addition, joint products should be offered to companies, designed and realized by *ad hoc* networks of schools from diverse European origins: for instance development programmes of 2–3 weeks for executives on managing a European business, or tailor-made programmes for international companies in Europe, co-developed with the companies themselves. Some management schools are now launching joint programmes for executives, for instance three to five schools from three to five European countries share the development of the programme, the promotion, the delivery and the risks.

Developing transnational skills can also be done by companies themselves without the help of management schools. The first step is to structure training sessions which mix managers from different countries. Such a policy is more costly (in terms of travelling expenses) but it enhances the level of international experience. A second step is to use systems like the EUROJOB designed and launched by the European Round Table: three-month periods abroad for managers, in a job corresponding to their position, in a foreign partner company.

Selecting foreign countries

Training students, teachers and managers abroad should be carried out in places and countries from which we can learn. The present practice of sending European students and teachers to the United States should be balanced with more intra-European experiences, in particular towards Germany (in collaboration with German institutions), and with experiences in Japan or other Asian countries.

> Teachers should learn to integrate foreign models, not only the US model. During the last 20 years the international training of teachers was too much directed towards the United States. It would be useful to have teachers who understand the Japanese model. Teachers should also study firms in Germany more than in the US. Take Saint Gall, the prestigious school of management in Switzerland, the French schools do not seem to be very eager to collaborate with Saint Gall... They should establish stronger links with German universities and schools.

Europeans should stop copying American schools and start learning from other sources. Germany and Japan are successful enough to attract students, teachers and managers.

> The Japanese have studied us and they have studied the Americans, and you can see the results. We have not studied the Japanese carefully enough. What is dangerous is this 'Japan bashing' that you see in the States and in France: 'they are unfair', 'they are dumping', 'they never open their market'...
>
> When it comes to developing your business, it is much more important to try to understand why the others are successful... We have made this agreement with Mitsubishi, we have been heavily

criticized in France. We think it will be a very good school, and that we will learn.

The MBA model has not been successful in Germany either within firms or within German universities. To some extent, this is a result of incompatibilities between the value system on which MBAs are built and the Germanic value system. There is in fact no reason to align management education in Europe on the US MBA standard (which, by the way, is now criticized by the Americans themselves).

On the one hand North American authors dominate the market of management books (with their global perspective), on the other hand many books are focused on single country experiences (taking a domestic perspective). The number of truly European books integrating European diversity (and taking a transnational perspective) should increase.

Europeans need case studies which deal with issues faced by European firms and which present concrete issues:

> Many case studies are too far from reality, we changed them for concrete case studies, everyday problems in firms. For instance, the case study of a group of Swedish forestry firms having to solve a problem of inventories. A serious situation where you have to work in groups and reach concrete propositions to make to the top management ... The case studies that we know from the United States always address issues from the point of view of the US top manager, but the young European managers are not US CEOs!

In addition case studies comparing practices in several European companies in a given sector would be of particular interest, 'for instance, take the beer industry: comparing Kronenbourg, Heineken, Interbrew and Carlsberg with each other'. Such case studies help to bring understanding of the diversity of market structures and cultures in Europe, and to highlight current integration mechanisms.

Exchanging students, teachers and managers requires some harmonization of educational systems in Europe, so that a person can switch more easily from one system to the other during his or her studies and can accommodate to new conditions in short periods of time. By harmonization the directors we interviewed do not mean homogenization, they see the benefit of maintaining diversity but at the same time creating compatible systems. They place responsibility for this on educational institutions and governments (see section 2).

Broad learning

Developing a broad knowledge – understanding and learning – should *complement* the specialized technical knowledge of managers.

Diversity and interdisciplinary approach

Learning from diversity and interdisciplinarity are the bases of a broad understanding. The European and world-wide business environment is still diverse, such
diversity requires cognitive variety (according to Ashby's law of 'Requisite Variety'),
moreover diversity is a source of learning. Schools and companies should seize the
opportunity to learn from diversity, make diverse cultural work groups rather than
narrow groups and allow individuals to confront their schemas to new contexts
abroad. 'Since 1967, I have been sending our managers to other European countries,
whether to learn a language or to understand the culture of other countries, in the
perspective of our integration in the EC. From 1960 we thought Portugal would join
the EC, then we anticipated and got prepared.'

Students' and managers' work groups should be interdisciplinary, mix different
functions on issue analysis and problem-solving. Such combinations develop
individual skills and later improve the communication between individuals and
functions in the firm. In this domain, double education should be encouraged, in
particular engineering and management. The success of multi-functional teams
depends on people who can play integrative roles in teams and who have been
prepared for that, both in schools and firms.

Understanding the context

Broad understanding means developing the capacity to understand the historical
context and the sociological context of a situation, beyond technical and economic
aspects. It is a must for effective dialogue with stakeholders. Management education
in Europe should be a combination of generic basic knowledge, techniques and
humanities.

> I think that the education and training of managers should go deeper
> into basic sciences which develop understanding. More psychology and
> sociology and less personnel management, more economics and less
> accounting... It may be a caricature but I believe that managers need to
> understand situations better and not only to apply techniques. There are
> techniques, many of which are universal, but you have to understand
> the context in which they can be applied.

> In order to make interfunctional teams to work, you need a common
> denominator between the people, a good level of general culture. The
> level of general culture (scientific and liberal arts) could be higher than
> it is today when young people come out of schools and universities...
> The other day, the friend of one of my sons asked me 'what do you
> think I should take at the university, what area, in order to succeed in
> the business world?' I said 'You are still at the beginning, take
> philosophy.' I think philosophy helps you the most in understanding
> who you are dealing with, why the things are moving in a given

direction. 'Then later on when you graduate you can fill your head with technical know-how.'

The big companies are well equipped today, they can provide the technical training but what they cannot provide in-house is a general culture.

A broad understanding of issues is a necessity for managing uncertainties and change and for identifying problems, while specific techniques are used to solve the problems.

Learning to learn

Managers have to develop their skills in managing change and to learn to deal with uncertainty and ambiguity. 'What you really need in order to manage change is a capacity to think and to adapt yourself... The techniques are not everlasting, they also change and improve all the time.' Managers have to learn to deal with complexity, to go beyond dilemmas and reconcile forces and logics such as: short term/long term, economic/social, etc., which are the essence of management. Education should develop intuition in order to survive complexity, fight inhibitions and come out with innovative solutions. The broader the base of knowledge and of understanding, the higher the place given to intuition relative to techniques.

A broad understanding requires and develops an aptitude to learn which may be the ultimate skill for an individual:

Managers or simply people must learn to learn. It is fundamental. No one learns once for ever in his or her life any more. You have to learn lifelong and in consequence you must learn to learn. You still teach someone a speciality but you also have to teach this person how to learn something else in the future. It means that you give a broader knowledge, a broader culture.

Lifelong learning implies that schools and firms have to share responsibility for the education, training and personal development of managers, and consequently should cooperate more and more with each other.

Cooperation between schools and firms

During the last twenty years many schools, universities and firms have built cooperative links together. The idea of cooperation is not a revolution but cooperation has to become more systematic and should be strengthened.

Reciprocal learning

Cooperation starts with better reciprocal information on respective needs. Organizations such as the European Foundation for Management Development (EFMD) at the European level and national associations can help in this respect.

Cooperation in research and development is already significant between firms and engineering schools, it could be improved in the field of research on management and pedagogy. In this case, firms should increase their support for schools and universities through foundations (as the North Americans have been doing for decades); on the other hand, schools can help companies in getting the best from different practices (benchmarking). Companies should offer students more opportunities for in-company training periods based on practical experience, and should encourage their managers to lecture in universities in order to link theories with experience. For their part, schools should offer better training opportunities for managers in the form of part-time programmes and distance-learning.

As lifelong learning becomes more and more important, the challenge is to step from a supplier–client relationship to multiple partnerships which co-develop, and/or co-realize training programmes.

Base training on experience

Training students and managers should be based increasingly on experience. In-company periods abroad organized by schools (internships) and firms (for instance the EUROJOB system) should be developed systematically and should use the network of each institution and a broader system of exchange at the European level (that will facilitate access for those schools and firms which do not have a large enough network of their own).

The content of training has to become more pragmatic, building on concrete everyday issues both in students' education and in lifelong learning programmes. The pragmatic orientation does not mean a technical or specialized orientation, it should be compatible with broad learning as described in the preceding section. Jobs should provide experience for managers who are learning lifelong. Job definitions should contain opportunities to learn through responsibility for projects, participation in multi-functional teams and through international rotation. This should be the responsibility of the hierarchy and of human resources and organization departments. Also, this orientation requires more management involvement in training.

Lifelong learning

While schools provide basic education – general culture, skills in human relations, broad bases in sciences and some technical knowledge in order to start a career – in-house training should provide complementary technical training and complementary management skills as the career develops. However, in order to achieve this balance and complementary nature between the two, and a smooth transition, concrete experiences should be incorporated into education and broad learning should be incorporated into in-house training. In this perspective in-house training should use some outside resources:

> We as a company are great believers in in-house training. We have very extensive in-house training programmes for all levels. From the factory

floor up to the board, we have general courses and specific courses, from general management to refining sunflower-seed oil and anything in between. A lot of it is in-house, but for in-house courses we also use a lot of outside resources.

Outside resources can bring expertise in a given domain and can also contribute to the development of *jointly* designed programmes. In this case cooperation between schools and firms takes the form of pedagogical engineering or design for the firms which have their own 'internal university'. Cooperation between schools and firms also helps to mix geographical origins of the participants and of the faculty, by creating diversity in the class and by getting the best from the best practices outside the firm.

In our study, the directors who expressed their views on the future development of management education belong to big international firms. These perspectives are not necessarily shared among the whole business community. The heads of small entrepreneurial local firms may not share exactly the same priorities. For instance, one may hypothesize that entrepreneurs would expect schools to instil entrepreneurial spirit and skills, and attach more importance to basic technical skills which often are still missing in their firms. However, small entrepreneurial firms do not escape the turbulence of international business, and many of them seize opportunities of international development. In this context the guidelines outlined by their counterparts in big international firms probably hold true.

2 Business schools and firms take up the challenge

An historical perspective shows that the business community and the educational community have been too distant from each other for several generations. Business schools were often founded by managers, but, in the past, academic priorities tended to separate schools and firms (Locke, 1989). For instance, the Gordon and Howell report (1959), recommended strengthening the rigour and academic standards in American business education in order to come closer to a scientific approach to management.

The strength of the relationships between the two spheres varies in each country (or geographical zones) according to different philosophies of business education, but it mainly varies according to the economic situation and to the status of the educational institutions: private or state-owned. In periods of economic recession most firms reduce their financial contribution to education and their expenses in management development programmes (however, a few firms seem to react the opposite way by increasing their demands on management training). Until recently state universities in Europe were less dependent on business to finance their activity, and as a result they felt free to follow a more academic route. On the other hand, private business schools tended to strengthen their relationships with business, to establish contractual links, and develop products in a more cooperative manner, sometimes neglecting academic standards.

During the last few years such differences have started to blur. Most educational institutions have tried to increase their resources by developing their activities in management development ('formation continue'). Also, after a first phase of dissemination of knowledge and techniques (mainly elaborated in the US), many European business schools started to invest in research and development and to create more *specific* knowledge in order to improve the quality and the differentiation of their products. In so doing, schools and firms got into closer contact and increased their exchanges. As firms began to consider training as a strategic weapon, exchanges turned into cooperation. The development of new information technologies (Levy, 1990) in a new 'Knowledge Economy' strengthened the links between the two spheres.

Now, business education has become more like a high-technology service. As in most service activities, the increased interactions between the 'suppliers' and the 'clients' have led to cooperation and co-production, for instance in the form of consortium MBA or qualification of in-house company programmes. The resulting networks and the processes may look 'chaotic', but they form the context in which the joint study between the Group ESC Lyon and the European Round Table was undertaken. The results of the study should help in thinking about adaptations.

More than a science, management is a practice, an application of basic disciplines: micro and macro economy, sociology, organization and psychology, including symbolic representations such as accounting and information systems. Being a practice, management should be partly dependent upon culture. Indeed, the results of the above-mentioned study show that, in Europe, the common characteristics of management (people orientation, negotiation, managing international diversity, cf. Chapter 2), and the main challenges (enhancing people involvement and reciprocal learning, cf. Chapter 3) all refer to the management and development of human resources.

Techniques have become more and more universal but people are still shaped by their cultural environment. The same methods, techniques and tools will often be applied differently depending on the cultural context. Everyday work with multi-cultural groups of students and managers demonstrates how decision-making and behaviour are diverse. Management education itself is diverse across European countries, at least as diverse as management practices in firms (cf. Chapter 1). Voltaire wrote 'L'ennui naquit un jour de l'uniformité', the future convergence of management systems across Europe could mean homogenization (and boredom?), but it could also mean the integration of diversity – which may be less boring but will be complex to implement.

Homogeneity vs. integrated diversity in European business education

Paradoxically the trend towards the homogenization of business education in Europe started with the transfer of the American model. During the 1960s planes full of European teachers were sent to the United States to learn their job, they came back with an MBA (Master of Business Administration) or a PhD (Philosophy Doctorate), or a DBA (Doctorate in Business Administration). The United Kingdom, France, the Netherlands and Scandinavia were particularly active in making the transfer. Germany has never been so attracted by the MBA system. Italy and Spain came to it much later.

Should the MBA model inspire a further homogenization of business education across Europe? There is more and more suspicion about such a scenario. First, the Americans themselves came to question their own educative system (see for instance Porter and McKibbin, 1988). The MBA model has been described as too analytical, too instrumental, too individualistic, focused on 'hard' aspects of management, neglecting cultural aspects and personal development. It naturally carries what are seen as the dominant values and constraints of American firms: financial performance, short termism, and managers' mobility. The low attractiveness of this approach to German firms and German universities is no longer surprising. In Germany (as well as in some other places and firms in Europe), social responsibility, long-term thinking, loyalty to a firm and a profession are some of the values which are incompatible with the strict MBA format. Moreover, if managing people, and broad learning are seen as priorities, European schools have to invent something else. Indeed, a closer look at the MBA programmes which were launched in Europe shows that adaptations had to be made soon after the system was adopted.

If we assume that the MBA model is not the best to homogenize business education across Europe, we address the second and actually more basic question: do we need, in fact, to homogenize anything?

A 'Diplom-Kaufman' in Germany, an English MBA, an Italian 'Laurea', a Spanish 'Carrera' and a French diploma from the Grandes Ecoles, are all different from each other. To some extent each of these qualifications fits with the specific nature of the business system in which it is embedded. As several business systems still coexist in Europe, eliminating the diversity of business education is both utopian and risky. Moreover, directors in companies which recruit graduates do not ask for the homogenization of curriculae, they expect reciprocal learning, that is to say, learning from the best practices abroad. In this perspective diversity generates curiosity, and paradoxically attracts students, teachers and scholars abroad. Wherever they go they will learn new ways of doing things, new ways to communicate, they will learn to deal with international diversity and develop transnational skills – precisely what top executives expect from younger managers. Instead of isolating communities from each other, diversity gives opportunities to bring people together and to learn from others. As far as business education is concerned, European diversity should be seen as an asset.

Heads of educational institutions and CEOs who are accustomed to dealing with diversity will not consider differences as an unbearable constraint, but it does raise the issue of the compatibility and equivalence of diplomas. In order to exchange students and teachers, and to deliver double or multiple diplomas, European institutions need to compare and assess their programmes. They also need to identify corresponding levels of qualification. At present the structure of business education consists of three levels after the 'Baccalauréat', or 'post-Maturity', or 'post-Abitur':

1. The undergraduate level, three to four years (depending on the country) after the baccalauréat, without professional experience.
2. The graduate level, five to six years (depending on the country) after the baccalauréat, which may include some professional experience, and which includes two years of graduate training.
3. The postgraduate level, with two possible diverging branches: specialization (mainly for graduates who already have a professional experience) or a research orientation (doctorate).

Moreover, in line with this general structure, most of the programmes of European educational institutions should go through a process of qualification. On this question two philosophies coexist:

1. The detailed accreditation of programmes in line with standards which help in assessing the correspondence between professional qualifications and the content of training programmes (this is the method the NCVQ and the ASB have chosen in the UK, see next section).
2. A process of accreditation of educational institutions (more than programmes) in a long-term perspective.

It could be risky to reduce the evaluation to rigid standards, the recent evolution of the American Assembly of Collegiate Schools of Business shows that the second route is the best. Moreover, it gives more responsibility to the institutions which have to organize the qualification process.

The qualification of the institutions involved in business education is much dependent on cultural contingencies. So the accreditation and quality assessment should be done first at the country level. Some organizations already take care of qualifications: ASFOR in Italy, AEEADA in Spain, Chapitre des Ecoles de Management in France. The only way to facilitate international exchanges and networks and guarantee some consistency is to provide a European umbrella. The European Foundation for Management Development could coordinate the qualification processes across European countries and also stimulate networking. Indeed this would be done according to the principle of 'subsidiarity'. Finally, a system at the international level – International Recognition of Management Education Norms – would facilitate and stimulate exchanges and networks at the world level. The whole system would provide the minimum harmonization necessary to develop reciprocal learning.

The models for qualification are not yet designed, moreover each country is free to elaborate its own. However, faced with the need to exchange with foreign partners, schools may be pushed to align themselves with the following general criteria:

- Openness to a broad culture beyond management techniques (languages, history, sciences).
- Research in order to innovate, renew programmes and produce new pedagogical material.
- International networks which are the bases of students' and teachers' exchanges, and international contents of the programmes.
- Qualitative development of the faculty.
- Cooperation with firms.

Some harmonization (not homogenization) may result from the process of qualification of business education programmes.

The common characteristics of management across Europe: an orientation towards people, managing international diversity, negotiation, and balancing between extremes, indicate directions that European schools cannot neglect. If they all follow the 'market signals': develop managerial skills (managing people), and transnational skills, broaden the scope and cooperate with business, European business schools may well look more alike by the beginning of the next century.

However, the existence of some shared priorities and the increased harmonization will certainly preserve some diversity, enough diversity to stimulate and regenerate intra-European networks. In this perspective intra-European networks between business schools should develop in order to balance the 'transatlantic' networks which have developed since the 1970s. There is no doubt that strengthening the networks with Eastern Europe and Asia will also be crucial in a global economy. As they add new partners and firms into the existing networks, the heads of European business schools will no doubt agree that education is becoming a more and more complex activity.

Firms and schools: management development

As lifelong learning develops, the relationship between schools and firms tends to change. The management development market (or 'formation continue des cadres' as the French call it) is being restructured. The present heterogeneity of the market is a result of past practices: companies had difficulties in formulating their demands, and educational institutions tended to sell the products in which they had skills without taking much care of the needs of their clients.

The new market demands

The management development market is extremely fragmented. For instance, in France, 25 000 suppliers operate, among which are a few big private organizations, many small ones and thousands of individuals. Moreover, new businesses have mushroomed over recent years. In the Rhône-Alpes region, about 200 private or public organizations now sell about 700 different management training programmes! Some suppliers work on marginal costs and many others with no overhead costs. As a result competition is getting stiffer especially since the economic recession which started in 1990. Companies are becoming more and more confused by such a proliferation of products, they rely on the reputation and image of the educational institution in order to minimize the risks. Then, in order to minimize the cost, some firms negotiate directly with the experts they identified, professionals call it 'cherry-picking'. However, in most European countries 'at the top of the pyramid' the best educational institutions attract the biggest international clients and maintain their differentiation.

At the end of the 1980s more and more firms started to consider training as a strategic intangible investment and to define and coordinate their demand, whereas, in the past, individual choice was most frequent. The economic recession has since 1990 accelerated these changes. One result is that under the pressure of greater efficiency, managers tend to prefer shorter programmes.

Companies are also buying fewer and fewer 'off the shelf' training programmes, looking for custom-made seminars which require intensive preparation and pedagogical engineering. As the managers' job becomes less specialized, inter-functional skills and problem-solving become training priorities. As a result, custom-made seminars on implementing strategies or strengthening corporate culture are becoming more and more popular. Looking for solutions to *their* particular problem, some firms tend to encourage educational institutions to develop new products adapted to their particular *sector* (for instance, banking or computer services, etc.). Seminars especially designed for one sector may provide very concrete 'benchmarking' to the participants. In brief, firms now expect management development to contribute to the improvement of their effectiveness and the implementation of their strategies.

In a few years qualification norms will probably be in use. Clients are already indicating such an evolution. For instance, in the United Kingdom, the government created a National Council for Vocational Qualifications (NCVQ), where firms participated in the development of a catalogue of managers' jobs and standards of competences required, in order to guide the adaptation of educational programmes.

The internationalization of markets creates new needs in the area of management development. More and more firms ask for seminars to have an international content and international faculty, and even suggest international joint ventures between their suppliers. Finally, quality is not high enough, firms expect improvements in quality, both of the core service (content, methods, teaching material) and of peripheral services (information, accommodation, etc.).

How should educational institutions respond?

First, schools realize the importance of management development both as a financial resource *and* as the best way to understand the needs of their clients—partners, which can also inspire the content and design of (more basic) higher education programmes (diplomas). Listening to clients is now a necessity and it suggests that four market segments are forming:

1. The most advanced educational institutions can supply international/multi-cultural programmes (open and/or company-specific) on issues of strategy implementation and international management, to international clients.
2. At the national level schools can offer short seminars focused on one crucial *issue* (for instance, managing a crisis, or managing a network, etc.); these can be specific to a company, specific to a sector, or open.
3. For companies in their region, business schools can provide more basic training, both integrative and oriented towards improving functional skills, sometimes through longer programmes which can lead to a diploma. In this category distance learning could help to enlarge the zone of influence.
4. For companies which are developing in-house training, schools can provide pedagogical engineering or 'facilities management'.

To do any of this suppliers will have to adapt their products. For instance, the British business schools had to adapt themselves to the standards defined by the NCVQ. The Association of Business Schools (ABS) created a group – the Management Verification Consortium – whose role is now to assess the quality of the programmes and to give a label when the programme fulfils the standards of the NCVQ. Also, the ABS provides training for the personnel at the interface between schools and firms.

Second, some sort of total quality management should be implanted so as to improve the level of quality and reliability of the service to companies.

Designing custom-made products requires that teachers involve themselves in negotiations and sales. Monitoring the multiple relationships with a given client demands new marketing skills, and a new organization in which people can coordinate their actions. The use of new technologies in distance learning will require both new skills and organizational adaptation. Schools need to become more 'professional', and to look more and more like service firms, interacting with their clients. All principles and methods of business-to-business marketing should be applied, and these activities should be managed by individuals with credibility with the faculty, in addition to negotiation and managerial skills.

As schools behave more like service providers, the relationship with companies will improve. Given the long-term intangible character of management development, supplier–client relationships will often turn into cooperation and partnership. Here the frontiers between management development ('formation continue') and higher education ('enseignement supérieur') are no longer relevant – partnerships combine the two activities.

Partnerships

Developing partnerships between firms and schools requires a new way of organizing and raises the question of how business education is financed. The result is an innovative approach aimed at bringing education and business closer together.

The director of education

Partnerships between schools and businesses are made up of multiple (multi-point) interactions: pedagogical engineering, management development programmes, applied research, managers coming to teach in higher education programmes, in-company training periods for students, selective recruitment, funding, etc. In order to manage the complexity of such networks of interactions, some innovative firms have created a particular job dedicated to managing the company's relationships with universities and schools: the 'Director of Education'.

The job can be part of the human resource division (or any other similar headquarters' unit reporting directly to top management). The director should work with managers in different operational and functional units of the company who interact or may interact with educational institutions. The 'Director of Education' needs to have a holistic view of the company and a good knowledge of educational institutions in order to optimize relationships between the two spheres. He or she works in coordination with the senior management development unit when there is one. By creating this position companies can improve recruitment, search for external expertise, develop joint research projects, and participate in the engineering of management development programmes.

Partnerships between schools and businesses are not a luxury that only large companies can afford. Large firms can work on developing an international network while smaller firms work at a national or even regional level.

Money and influence

Private business schools already receive some funding from the business community. However, this represents a small percentage of their budget and any recession in the market of management development creates tensions. Universities also need extra financial resources. Sweden has an objective to privatize some universities, a new private university has been created near Paris, etc. Business should be more and more involved in financing higher education *and* in controlling the evolution of the institutions.

In most European countries there is no co-financing of higher education, although several social groups benefit from it: the state and the local communities, the firms, the students and their families. When public education dominates, the state is by far the most important contributor to the budget. On the other hand, in some countries (for instance France) where private business schools operate, the students (and their families) are by far the major contributors together with local firms – 'Chambres de Commerce et d'Industrie' – and firms pay a 'taxe d'apprentissage'. However levying a tax does not lead to companies feeling involved in or committed to the system.

We suggest that:

- there should be a better balance between the three sources financing business education: state/region, companies, and students;
- companies should be involved directly in financing business schools and should be given some influence on the orientation of education.

If higher education is strategic for a country and the business community, then companies should not delegate its destiny to the state. Senior managers and 'Directors of Education' should participate on the governing bodies of the universities and influence decisions so as to improve the adaptation to the labour market. On the other hand governments should modify tax systems in order to balance the contribution from the students: for instance tax exemptions on the amounts that families spend on higher education, special loans at low interest rates for students. Value Added Tax refunding could help modernize universities, tax exemption on the funds that firms give to educational institutions could stimulate the involvement of the business community.

Given the diversity of education systems across countries and the even greater diversity of tax systems, it will be hard to promote a European approach to the problem, however combined efforts are needed to create consistency across borders. Framing the relationships between firms and schools is not enough; besides joint management development projects, an innovative approach by *sector of activity* could also stimulate partnerships.

A new approach by sector

By sector we mean groups of activities such as: chemicals, automobiles, food, banking, health care, tourism, etc. Each sector is characterized by a specific set of structures, a specific history and culture, a specific mix of critical success factors. Firms often prefer to adapt management development seminars to their sector and its specific characteristics. For an educational institution, a way to get closer to firms and stimulate partnerships is to develop expertise and pedagogical material in one or a few sectors. This creates a third dimension in a matrix made of:

- Programmes (undergraduate, graduate, doctoral, management development, etc.).
- Disciplines (business policy, marketing, finance, management, etc.).
- Sectors in which the school has expertise.

Expertise would be spread across the departments which are organized by discipline. A leader would organize the transverse task force of experts in a given sector. The task force would be in charge of doing research, developing teaching material, designing and conducting seminars which are specific to the sector. Sector-specific seminars could be offered in any of the programmes of the institution.

As soon as a firm and a school share a common interest in a given sector, the opportunity for a partnership increases and partnerships become more effective:

- Co-development of teaching material.
- Participation of managers in education programmes.
- Teaching engineering of management development programmes.
- Financial participation under the form of Foundations or Chairs.
- Participation of the corresponding professional association on the governing body of the school.
- Recruitment of graduates.

In order to avoid the risk of over specialization of the students, only a small percentage of the total programme would be dedicated to sector-specific approaches (say 25 per cent in graduate programmes). Also, a given school would have to select a few industries in which it can develop an expertise. In the selected areas, no doubt the school would be closer to its business environment, not only to the bigger firms in the industry but also the small businesses and start-ups in search of young managers who understand the dynamics of their sector.

3 Concluding comments: a typical European challenge

Much of what we have written on developing the relationships between schools and companies in Europe could hold true for North America. In concluding this chapter we want to underline the issues which we see as specifically European in nature.

European business systems are still diverse, the class and the faculty must reflect that level of diversity. To do this European universities and schools will have to strengthen their European *networks* in order to develop truly European high-quality programmes. New demands and new partners from the East will increase the complexity of networking. The cooperative networks need to become more effective than in the past when everybody was 'flirting' with everybody. Schools need to *select* a few partners for long-term in-depth collaboration. Taking this step from a domestic scope to an international scope is unique in the history of business education.

Both the cultural diversity and the characteristics of management in Europe (people orientation, negotiation, managing diversity) call for an *opening-up* of business education, from 'hard' management techniques to 'soft' managerial skills, and to basic sciences and humanities, in brief from the US MBA model of the 1970s to a European concept for the 1990s and beyond.

By a European concept we do not mean a homogeneous education system, indeed some diversity should be preserved. However, as the qualification of business education programmes and institutions will take place, some harmonization will be achieved. Top managers believe that the European concept should be based on four characteristics: managing people, transnational skills, broad learning, and cooperation between schools and firms. It is to be hoped that the heads of universities and business schools in Europe share this view, and that all parties work together to improve the transition and strengthen the synergies between higher education and management development in the perspective of lifelong learning.

References

Gordon, R. A. and J. J. Howell (1959), *Higher Education for Business*, Report, Ford Foundation.

Levy, P. (1990), *Les Technologies de l'Intelligence*, Paris: Editions La Découverte.

Locke, R. (1989, *Management and Higher Education Since 1940, The Influence of America and Japan on West Germany, Great Britain, and France*, Cambridge: Cambridge University Press.

Porter, L. W. and L. E. Mckibbin (1988), *Management Education and Development, Drift or Thrust into the 21st Century?*, AACSB-EFMD, Prentice Hall.

Conclusion

CHAPTER 10
Towards a European model of management

Philippe de Woot

The construction of the new Europe represents a major challenge for our businesses. It means a fundamental transformation of their environment and the expansion of their perspectives and horizons to the continent. The creation of a common market of 350 million consumers has propelled European business into the process of breaking new ground in terms of dimension, complexity and time frame. It is a new experience affecting many businesses, with all of them undergoing the process at more or less the same time and encountering comparable problems and opportunities. Nobody doubts that this is both influencing their management models and reinforcing the points they have in common.

1 A new international dynamics

European integration is a *dynamic* process which affects all of society, and is in turn influenced by the participants as they create and react to the rules of the game. It is a process which is only just beginning and is destined to expand and develop. There is consequently scope for 'proactive' initiatives that will orient its evolution towards increasing European competitiveness.

It is clear that the vision of Europe and the European policies of firms are a strong influence on the structure of the currently emerging management model. The construction of Europe is accelerating this creative process: what we observe today as common features – an orientation towards people, negotiation, managing international diversity and managing between extremes – could be the first signs and ingredients of a genuine European management model that would distinguish us more clearly from the Americans and Japanese.

The European management model is not a substitute for national models. It simply adds a new dimension to them, a common way of being European. National management systems will doubtless remain strong, and this is no bad thing, since diversity, as we shall see later, is Europe's greatest strength.

We should not expect management practices to be totally homogenized within this dynamic of integration. In the past, we have tended to believe too strongly in a universal model and have attempted to imitate the American or the Japanese. But culture is stronger than methods. However reasonable it may be to consider methods as universal, it is equally necessary to recognize that leadership (the government of men) is dependent on the history and culture of a country. Each civilization has its own way of organizing the relationships of power and authority between individuals.

This holds equally true for each of the countries of Europe. However, a common dimension can be seen taking shape which transcends the individual countries because it is born out of the shared experience of integration and derived from the historical values of a long-established civilization.

Within this dynamic perspective, the emergence of a more European model will make us more aware of our strengths and weaknesses. That awareness, paired with reciprocal learning, will help us to develop our strongest points and correct our shortcomings more rapidly. To achieve this, today's managers are prepared to enrich European practice with the most interesting elements of American or Japanese management. The sole important criterion is that these should be compatible with our cultures, and that we should be able to adapt them accordingly.

Does this new dynamic enhance our performance and competitiveness at an international level? The evidence suggests a positive answer. The harmonization of management philosophies and practices and the harmonization of the socio-political culture (in which management practices are embedded) are powerful factors of development. We need look no further for proof of this than the dynamism and influence of the American and Japanese models, despite their great differences from each other. The key question is not whether the model emerging in Europe will be better or worse than other models. The essential point is that it should be better adapted to *our* values, *our* attitudes and *our* culture, and that it should give more cohesion to our competitive strategies.

Complementarity between economic activity and the socio-cultural environment is a central element in competitive efficiency. Europe is a *young* continent, still in the full flood of self-creation. For this process of integration to be successful, a specific model is required that will enable it to deploy all of its potential and dynamism. Europe today is the largest trader in the world. If it is to become once more – as Lester Thurow believes – the dominant economy, there is no reason for it to use a management model that is not its own.

European integration and the management model that this implies will considerably strengthen the competitiveness of our businesses. By crossing the threshold into the continental dimension, our companies are entering a creative competitive process. Recent research has shown this for high-technology businesses (de Woot, 1988). The result is likely to apply to the full spectrum of economic activity.

Creating competitiveness

The firm increases its performance and its competitiveness when it integrates itself into a cumulative process of development in which it is simultaneously the driving force (the subject) and the result (the object). This process is stronger than the enterprise alone, since it includes the commercial, technological and political environments, which have a decisive influence on a business's chances of success. Yet the process itself is also strongly influenced by the firm: by seizing opportunities and constantly readjusting the competitive stakes through its strategic initiatives, the firm is a driving – and often innovative – force.

Such a process creates competitiveness. Enhanced competitiveness is based on the following elements (Figure 10.1):

1. *Long-term perspectives and large-scale opportunities.* Long-term perspectives and large-scale opportunities justify the risk involved in new technological developments and large-scale investments; these perspectives can be catalyzed by large open markets, rapidly growing demand, and by certain large-scale public projects. When domestic markets are relatively small, an international scope is the only way to create large-scale opportunities.
2. *An expanded strategic capacity.* The creation of sufficient strategic capacity enables the business to act on a global scale in the key sectors.

   ● Improved strategic methods and processes of anticipation enabling more far-reaching and daring strategic choices.
   ● Development of the key resources of progress: people (skills, management, internationalization, etc.), technological expertise, relationships, finance.

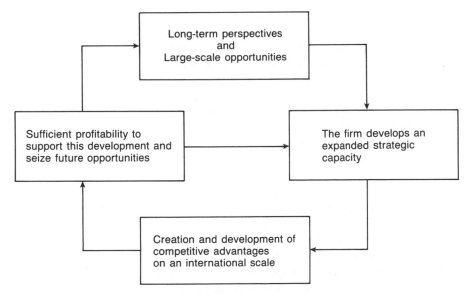

Figure 10.1 The process of creating competitiveness

- Expansion of functions to the international dimension, either independently or via alliances and cooperative actions (the creation of a global distribution network is particularly important in this respect).
- Strengthening of the capacity for innovation and change by better integration of R & D in competitive strategies, and by a growing mastery of complex structures.

3. *Creating competitive advantages on an international scale.* Creating competitive advantages on an international scale, arising out of the increased strategic capacity give companies:

- the option of playing on the differences between countries and exploiting their respective comparative advantages, at the same time as adapting more rapidly to their evolution;
- the ability to apply economies of scale to the business world-wide, bringing cost advantage that can be decisive in many activities (the experience curve becomes a key competitive weapon here).

4. *Sufficient profitability to seize opportunities.* Sufficient synergies between activities and resources enable the optimization of strategic investments, such as R & D, marketing, organization, administration, etc.

Sufficient profitability is necessary to cover development and internationalization costs, as well as the risks inherent in such a strategy. It goes without saying that the profitability of current operations (a healthy base) must be constantly monitored and maintained at the level required by strategic needs. Turnaround is on an ongoing basis, rather than as a reaction to crisis. Profitability also enables a company to seize the opportunities opened up by the business environment, which in turn allows the profit level to be raised to a level consistent with longer-term future perspectives. The 'virtuous circle' is thus closed and the dynamic becomes a process of creating competitiveness. Schematically, this is shown in Figure 10.1.

A European strategy will contribute to the creation of a large common market, to its integration and to the reinforcement of our competitiveness. A European management model will improve the implementation of European strategies.

Business has less chance of success when it cannot insert itself into such a virtuous circle. Its prospects diminish still more when it is trapped in *a process of destructing competitiveness*. This may appear a paradox, and there are those who will argue that a firm will do all in its power to escape this form of 'vicious circle'. This view assumes that business has full liberty of action and can escape its environment. This is not always the case.

A process of destructing competitiveness can be represented schematically as in Figure 10.2. Today, the main weakness of some of our companies is that they have yet to initiate the process of creating competitiveness. Any company that allows

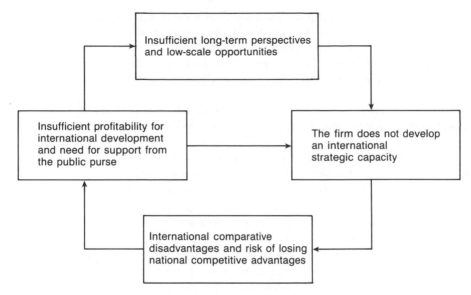

Figure 10.2 The process of destroying competitiveness

itself to be locked into a destructive process and does not react rapidly and vigorously by adopting a more European and international perspective will effectively be sealing its own fate.

Is it possible to 'skip' the European stage and raise the stakes directly to the global dimension? That is another question. It is worth noting, however, that the majority of global successes are based on a powerful position in the domestic market. The European dynamic may therefore represent a useful step on the way to conquering global markets, and could well further strengthen the international positions which a company already holds.

The emergence of a European management model thus represents a potent means of making the Single European market a company's domestic market, and should help firms to exploit the new dynamics.

2 Diversity, openness and integration

Diversity is a feature of Europe and its greatest originality. Yet it is a diversity that contains a powerful ingredient and overlay of unity. Edgard Morin (1987) gives the following definitions of Europe:

'Everything that simplifies Europe with idealization, abstraction or reduction, mutilates it.'

'Europe is complex (complex: that which is woven together ...).'
'To assemble is to bring together the widest range of diversities ...'
'Combine contrasts so that they are inseparable.'
'The European Gordian knot, a pluralistic and contradictory unity.'
'Think the one in the many, the many in the one...'

Europe is a diversity, certainly, but one permeated with periods of political or spiritual unity: the Roman Empire, the Christian Middle Ages, the Enlightenment and the current European integration. These times of relative unity have left their legacy in the collective memory of Europeans. They remind us that, beyond our differences, there are also shared values and a common civilization.

Europe is also openness and curiosity. The sea was for Europe a source of adventure and enterprise, 'an opening, a prolongation, a nourishing placenta', Morin (1987) notes that in Europe there is one kilometre of coastline for every 290 square kilometres of land, while in Africa the ratio is one for every 1420 square kilometres. Europe was the continent of great navigators, explorers, merchants, colonizers and – sadly – of conquerors too. Since the Middle Ages a long commercial tradition has made possible 'long-distance trading' operations, the 'rapid currents' and 'high points' (added value) of global exchange have been progressively seized (Braudel, 1979).

If there is a common unifying thread in the European management model, it is its diversity. The European model is by definition multi-faceted. Is this a strength or a weakness for our competitiveness? Whenever we have pushed our differences to the point of confrontation and rejection, it has proved a weakness and often a disaster. When we have tried to accept our differences and enrich ourselves by them, it has resulted in progress. And this historical experience is valid for business too.

The positive aspect of diversity is the adoption of an attitude of *openness, curiosity and a tolerance of differences*. An ethnic and linguistic patchwork, a mosaic of states, regions and cultures, borders which are open, but which are nonetheless everywhere – Europe has created for our businesses an 'assault course' for growth, expansion and the conquest of the international dimension. In a small country, selling to a customer 100 km away from the factory may already mean exporting, and as a general rule in a foreign language, another culture and with different marketing messages. Learning and accepting differences has been the standard means of development for businesses which have adopted and accepted this open way of operating. It has also been their strength.

Lawrence and Lorsch (1982) have shown that the ability to manage diversity could be a key to performance in a complex environment. They have emphasized the need to differentiate company structures in line with the environment. This theory can be applied to the phenomena of internationalization and globalization. The strategic, commercial, cultural and geo-political environments of our businesses are diverse, and differentiation is becoming a key to long-term business success. In so far as the European management model contains this dimension, it holds a considerable potential advantage. This still has to be exploited, however. But Lawrence and Lorsch have also shown the necessity of integrating mechanisms. Managing diversity successfully requires more than recognition and acceptance of differences. Sufficiently *powerful integrating mechanisms* also have to be put in place to avoid confrontation or schism.

The emergence of a European model is a factor of integration. When we strengthen a shared vision of management, we create a powerful integrating mechanism at a European level. If the European management model succeeds in provoking a degree of convergence on some fundamental concepts, it will fulfil its integrative role. For this reason it is important to reflect collectively on the following themes:

- Our concept of competitiveness and the importance of motivating people (see sections 3 and 4).
- The responsibilities of business in its dialogue with diverse stakeholders: government authorities, unions, educational institutions, etc.
- The purpose of business (its *raison d'être*) and the values that underlie its legitimacy (see section 5).

Sharing the same concepts is necessary, but it is still not enough. Methods of integration are also required which are more specific and customized to the individual company. Research in this area has shown the importance of conflict management to reduce the tensions that are the constant by-product of diversity. The way we manage conflict transforms our differences into either opportunities or threats. Confrontation between adults is based on the recognition of differences as a source of enrichment and progress. This depends on a creative dialogue and an active will to communicate (to communicate = to place in the common domain). All conflict management based on dissimulation, aggression, intimidation or simple compromise can only impoverish our diversity and transform it into a threat.

Many companies build their development on the traditional skill of Europeans at managing diversity, as evidenced by international strategies, management mobility, multi-cultural teams, alliances, joint ventures and cooperations. European diversity, however, can have negative aspects if managers view it as a dangerous confrontation, and if behaviour and management methods are not adapted to the situation. The strategy of 'national champions' derives from this weakness and leads to trapping the firm into the process of destructing competitiveness, described above.

One of the greatest errors for a European company would be to reject openness and to adhere to purely national models. Such an attitude would result in rapid alienation from the new European and global environment. The challenge is to build *unity in diversity*.

3 Combining individual talents

Leadership and collective qualities

Many managers in Europe attach great importance to personal qualities, character and natural authority – in short, to everything that cannot be learned at university or the great seats of learning. An example is authority or leadership. This essential management feature comprises both talent and character. Everybody involved in proactive work knows that the best managers owe at least part of their authority to their innate qualities. This is a constant factor in human history.

Baudelaire suggested a definition of talent when he asked his friends: 'Have you ever asked yourselves what you have inside you that was not acquired by education, work or money?' What is this if not the gifts bestowed on us by the Gods who watch over our cradles, our 'charisma', the part of us that is innate? This side of us can be developed and enhanced, but over its origins we have no control. Speaking of the Grand Condé, the Cardinal de Retz said: 'The Prince was born a captain, and that has only ever happened to Caesar and Spinola.' It is an interesting starting point, but it is also disturbing, since it means that charisma transcends analysis and cannot be taught. It is, however, at the heart of the matter, and all those who have spoken of it mention a series of innate qualities derived from nature in much the same way as human nature participates in the animal world. Moreover, most of the metaphors we use are of this type: people speak of being eagle-eyed, having the heart of a lion, being as cunning as a fox, and so on. Said Cardinal de Richelieu: 'You must sleep like a lion, never closing your eyes, which must remain constantly alert.' Livy described Fabius Maximus thus: 'An immutable constancy, the magnanimity of a lion.'

This then is an essential ingredient of management – and Europeans emphasize it with relish. It is an ingredient that is also dangerous, however, since it can compromise the collective efforts essential to a successful company. If too much importance is attached to talent, character and personal dynamism, there is a risk that those who should be participating in the game – although perhaps less gifted – will be excluded from it. There can be a tendency to believe ourselves superior to those around us, and a great temptation to overcentralize power or over-personalize management. An anecdote serves to illustrate the point. A manager was asked what gave him the greatest pleasure in his work. He replied: 'It is the problems that have no solution, the ones my colleagues have already torn their hair out over; because that's when they need divine inspiration and they come to me.'

Talent, God-given gifts and charisma all exist, and are at the heart of skilled professional management. But when they are not counterbalanced by collective qualities and methods that encourage broad participation, they can be dangerous and lead to all the perversities of excessive centralization, feudal rivalries and Byzantine behaviour.

This insistence on highlighting our more charismatic qualities is likely to go hand-in-hand with a certain scepticism towards oversophisticated management methods, overdetailed procedures or overprecise planning. Paradoxically, this scepticism could be an advantage in the contemporary atmosphere of instability. The famous 'management gap' between the United States and Europe, long considered one of our weaknesses, could be transformed into an advantage if it contributed to rebalancing the principal tasks of management by contributing to faster reaction times, greater flexibility and enhanced staff motivation in a turbulent and uncertain world.

Strategic development

Uncertainty has become the central element of competitiveness and business conduct. In a world that is defined by turbulence, surprise and a lack of continuity, predictions are increasingly erroneous and therefore dangerous. This turbulence is being caused particularly by:

- The acceleration of technological progress.
- The globalization of competition.
- The restructuring of capitalism on a global scale.
- The slowing-down of growth.
- The political changes in Eastern Europe.
- The high growth rates of the Asian countries.
- The large imbalances in the global economy: deficits for some, surpluses for others, the indebtedness of developing countries and unemployment in Europe.

This type of environment confirms the scepticism of Alphonse Allais: 'God, but it's hard making predictions! ... especially about the future.' Or Paul Valéry: 'The future, sadly, is not what it used to be.'

In a world where prediction is becoming less reliable, decision-making and management models are evolving. When we consider that virtually all long-term management tools are centred upon prediction, it becomes easier to understand the need to modify the approach and to question five-year plans. Successful companies are organizing to become progressively 'ready-for-anything'. They are equipping themselves to be able to seize unexpected opportunities and retreat rapidly from bad risks. In more concrete terms of methods and structures, this evolution centres around three principal axes:

1. The improvement of strategic analysis and thinking in terms of scenarios.
2. The anticipated development of additional capabilities in key resources.
3. Increased speed of action and reaction.

The concept of planning gives way to strategic development, which is a key factor of dynamism and success.

Strategic development has much in common with ancient wisdom when it comes to strategic action, focusing on creative preparation and rapid intervention.

> You know only too well, Athenians, what contributed most to Philip's success: it was above all his constant presence and readiness to act before we did. He mastered an army that was at all times under his control and was able to anticipate his wishes ... We, by contrast, react only to news of an event in tumult and turmoil. And what is the result? We arrive when the die is already cast. Therefore all our resources are dissipated in pure waste. (Demosthenes)

> We must be attentive and available, not for what will be, but for what might be. (Gracian)

> As far as the future is concerned, what is important is not to predict, but to make possible. (Saint-Exupéry)

Strategic development requires talent but it also requires *participative* methods, in order to enhance creativity and speed up action.

Talent and participative methods

The European tendency towards a more intuitive approach based on judgement and experience can undoubtedly contribute to fast reactions to the unexpected and to discontinuities. Its main advantage is that it does not constrain the future or decisions to a formal plan or too rigid an analysis. 'System D', 'muddling through' or 'combinazione' are useful at times of turbulence and discontinuity, but they need to be complemented. If this European tendency makes decision-making the prerogative of a small minority of talented individuals, it becomes a great weakness because it then tends to discourage the collectivity that is so necessary to the development of our competitiveness.

Collectivity is based on methods and approaches that harness participation. It derives from a state of mind at least as much as from management tools or information systems. When the first American walked on the moon, the press, radio and television interviewed the Director of NASA, James Webb. He did not paraphrase Neil Armstrong by saying: 'One small step for NASA, one giant leap for mankind.' Nor did he intone the American national anthem, which would have been the inclination of more than one European. He simply said: 'The power of method. A method that enabled ordinary men to do an extraordinary thing.' And they were

400 000 ordinary men, 20 000 businesses and 200 universities. Who can fail to perceive a genuine philosophy there? What counts is the balance between, on the one hand, talent, character and the innate conviction of managers, and on the other hand, the methods, processes and delegation of authority that help to include the largest possible number of people in the collective participation process. The temptation of a Europe that has been feudal for so long is to still believe exclusively in personal power. Today, individual talent is no longer enough. To win the battles of the future, what will be required is professional application and more methods that encourage participation.

Balthazar Gracian, the great Jesuit who spoke out in favour of personal talent, character and strong individuality, nonetheless recognized the huge importance of method: 'Applied mediocrity goes much further than unapplied excellence.' Nietzsche, the inventor of the Superman, wrote in one of his essays: 'Power is method.'

Universities and business schools teach method more than behaviour and the development of personal talents, but they are also conscious that, by pushing method too far they run the risk of falling into the trap of technocracy and bureaucracy. In the current climate of turbulence, method is a support, a tool, but never a substitute for individual quality. *Everything resides in balance*, and maintaining it is a subtle art. It is the aspect of management which will always transcend quantitative approaches.

Recent research (de Woot 1988; de Woot and Desclee, 1984) has shown that the most efficient managers are those who succeed in establishing an adequate balance between their personal talents and professional management methods. This balance is difficult to achieve and often precarious. It varies from one culture to another. The challenge for Europeans is to find *the right balance between leadership, management methods, and participation.*

4 'People make the difference'

One of the most visible aspects of the European model is its focus on people: people orientation and internal social responsibilities are described in terms of negotiation, discussion and dialogue (Groupe ESC Lyon study for the European Round Table, 1993). The need to inform, persuade and motivate returns like a leitmotif throughout the interviews with company directors.

People orientation

People count: 'People make the difference' concluded Olivier Lecerf (1991) after directing Groupe Lafarge for 15 years. In terms of education, the expectations of large European companies are moving in the same direction: increasingly they are looking towards the behavioural sciences, communication and teamwork (Groupe ESC Lyon study for the European Round Table, 1993).

Since World War II, European business has passed through two huge cultural upheavals:

1. It has had to create a climate of confidence after 150 years of class struggle, and persuade its social partners and personnel that the development of business and pursuit of profit are socially acceptable objectives.
2. It has had to move from a centralized, hierarchical structure with an often feudal atmosphere, to organizations which are more open and participation-oriented. Companies have discovered that strategic success also depends on attitudes and culture, which are difficult to change, they evolve slowly. It is often in this area that traditional companies have found most difficulty. Most firms, however, have succeeded in this transformation to openness and have realized that the atmosphere of the 'law of the jungle' and 'court intrigue' discouraged initiative and creativity. In the feudal environment, energies were diverted from external strategy to the struggle for internal power. Relationships were often appalling: 'Court friendships, fox loyalties and wolf societies' (Chamfort).

It is in this way that the most successful companies have progressively refined their leadership concepts and practices. Their directors' definitions of leadership vary enormously, which shows the richness and intangible nature of this quality. An interesting and modest definition is put forward by Shell: 'Leadership is a natural, unforced ability to inspire people. The influence which emanates from a good leader is unspecifiable, but it cannot be effective unless it is combined with natural drive and a fundamental respect for, as well as a genuine interest in people.' At the centre of this definition are people, and this complements one of the deepest currents of European culture.

People and competitiveness

Will this orientation towards people reinforce the competitiveness of European companies? Without doubt, provided it can be successfully combined with strategic development and competitive action. Recent research (Bocconi and UCL, 1993) emphasizes the growing importance of motivating all staff in implementing winning strategies. As shown in Figure 10.3 the change process and the learning process are based upon structures, people and leadership.

In the current atmosphere of turbulence, every winning strategy is constantly threatened, either by discontinuity and surprises from the external environment, or

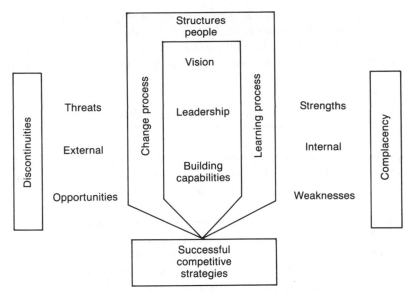

Figure 10.3 People and competitiveness

by self-satisfaction (nothing fails like success). To respond to these threats, managers should examine their company before it is overtaken by crisis. They can do this by putting in place permanent processes for learning and changing, which require all staff to adopt dynamic and creative behaviour. The efficiency of these processes appears to depend on the quality of leadership at all levels of the business, on a shared vision of the firm's future and on the development of collective know-how.

It is easy to see the vital importance of attitude and employee participation in this type of operation. In so far as the European model favours dialogue, information and participation, and then combines these with strategy, it will contribute to the creation of new conditions for long-term success and increase the competitiveness of our companies. If, conversely, this type of approach were to degenerate into interminable negotiations, defensive protection of the existing structure, or excessive caution unrelated to the competitive environment, it would slide rapidly towards a loss of our competitive advantages.

5 Social responsibilities

Europeans have asked themselves many questions regarding the purpose of business and its social responsibilities. They have never fully adopted the simplistic approach of Milton Friedman, who claims that the only social responsibility of business is to make money. Europe has never really believed that the pursuit of individual well-being alone would necessarily be to the common good, nor that an 'invisible hand' establishes 'naturally' the most harmonious balance between all interests present.

Responsibilities and ethics

Permeated by a powerful socialist current for a century and a half, Europe has often chosen intervention by the public powers to correct the disfunctioning of the market (e.g. the labour market), to establish solidarity among citizens and to protect the weak.

Business has also entered into this dialogue and into cooperation with its social partners and the political powers. The search for a consensus on the priorities of the common good and the general interest is part of the normal function of European managers, who often help seek them together via professional associations. Cooperation and public responsibility are a key element in the European model and have been for a long time, even if in certain cases and at certain times individual behaviour has not always lived up to this description.

Today, the evolution of competition and the development of corporate strategic power have given rise to new problems and new stakes. They reinforce the social responsibilities of the company and the demand for ethical behaviour. The globalization of competition and the need for a 'triadic' (Europe/United States/Asia) approach often constrains a business to master considerable strategic capability. Power grows out of the creation of the key resources required to develop it: international teams, technologies, information, networks, relationships, etc. In this perspective, private power becomes more important and more international.

The acceleration of technological progress continues apace: research and development is a major competitive weapon. In many areas, firms decide on the extent and orientation of technological progress. This not only refers to the volume of research, but also to the combination and cross-hatching of disciplines. This can lead to the emergence of extremely rich and sometimes innovative new avenues.

The increased role of finance in restructuring global capitalism is a further example. Without wishing to separate too rigidly the worlds of finance and business, it is reasonable to ask if their respective objectives are sufficiently close and their approaches as complementary as some would claim. In certain cases, the splitting up of a business for short-term profit can undermine its long-term development by destroying its subtle networks and barely perceptible synergies which contain within them potential for progress. The stock market does not always accurately reflect the long-term calculated risks taken by entrepreneurs. Given the sums at stake, the intervention of financiers can have a considerable effect. Today there are some $30 billion in LBO (Leverage Buy-Out) funds; using a factor of 10, this makes $300 billion potentially available for this type of investment in financial manoeuvres whose industrial objectives are not always visible. If we add to that the scandals and 'rackets', reported in the media it is easy to understand why many people ask serious questions about the objectives of such enterprises.

There are also the 'mega-problems' which can affect a company, either because the company is their cause, or because it can contribute to their solution. Of particular note here are the environmental accidents at Seveso, Bhopal, Three Mile Island, Alaska, etc. We could also mention the development of the Third World and of the countries of Eastern Europe. Can and should the immense know-how of our companies be used to tackle causes of this scope?

Finally, if a company is defined as a society of people involved in relationships of authority, cooperation and exchange, the scale of the ethical questions posed by the conduct of an organization can be seen in clear relief. Which method should be used for exercising power? Which personnel development policy should be implemented? How should redundancies be managed? Can the economic imperative and the aspirations of staff be harmonized? How can conflicts of interest be resolved? And so on.

Innovation: for what? for whom?

The creation of a large European market forces us to deal with these problems at a European level. It is essential for our management model to be based on a shared concept of the purpose of business and the values that confer societal legitimacy upon it.

To achieve this, we have to take as a starting point the specific function of business: what it alone fulfils and what distinguishes it from other organizations. It is clear that the concept of profit is inadequate to deal with these questions, even if it constitutes an essential motor and a condition of survival.

When studying the functions, performance and strategies of firms, research has confirmed Schumpeter's hypothesis: it is innovation that explains their development and survival. If we observe firms over a long period, we can see that none survives without constantly renewing its products, procedures, markets and methods. It is through innovation that companies create and disseminate technological, economic and social progress.

The dynamic enterprise takes the risk and makes the effort involved in this progress. It develops within itself the characteristics of Schumpeter's entrepreneur: a vision of possible progress, a sufficient taste for risk to take the initiative and implement it, an authority and power of action sufficient to carry it through to its conclusion. In this way, it systematizes creativity and engages in a dynamic process of change. Entrepreneurship in this sense consists essentially of changing an existing order. If we place this function in an environment of (open) international competition and add the various public incentives, we already have the fundamentals of the mechanism for creating economic and technological progress. In this context, a central concept can be proposed which describes the specific function of business: economic and technological creativity.

It is reasonable to suggest that, among the great civilizations, the West has constantly favoured this type of progress and raised pursuit of it to a fundamental and worthy level. Looking at the great myths at the root of our culture, one sees rapidly that they devote considerable space to economic and technological progress. Is not the meaning of the myth of Prometheus precisely this? Taking the risk of progress, robbing the Gods of 'fire, the father of all arts, the endless path ...', Prometheus embodies and symbolizes the qualities and spirit of the entrepreneur. 'One day, in the sacred fennel stem I hid the spark ... I have transmitted you, O liberating Fire, O source of creation, Master of all arts, path without end which opens itself up to man ...' (Aeschylus). Around this central figure other Gods or heroes embody the function of economic progress: Vulcan, the engineer; Ulysses and Jason the creators of markets; and even Icarus, the hero of the ill-considered risk and abortive progress – Icarus ... the Concorde!

The West has retained and gradually developed this belief in the potential and utility of material progress. Whether by the admiration it devotes to distant adventures and great discoveries, like those of Marco Polo, Christopher Columbus or Magellan, or by the will to define itself ceaselessly as an urban society inclined to international changes, open to the sea and all the freedoms that implies. A thread running through our evolution in the West is that of the merchant cities, wheeler-dealing and free: Athens, Alexandria, Byzantium, Venice, Bruges, Antwerp, Amsterdam, London, New York, etc.

This was the evolution of a movement, of a tension leading to change, of an incessant questioning of the existing order, of an adherence to a rapid evolution which people accepted and occasionally believed they controlled. 'Whoever points his sail to the breath of the earth, a new wind will arise which will always force him to take the highest sea' (Teilhard de Chardin, 1958). Is not one of the characteristics of the West that it has often accepted the course of the highest sea, be it in trade, the arts, institutions, knowledge or thought? André Malraux, meditating on the extraordinary capacity for self-renewal of Western artistic creativity, defined this as 'the art of the great navigators.' Is this collective attitude not symbolized in the motto of the Hanseatic League: 'Navigare necesse est'?

For two centuries in the field of economics, the most active force was business. And its creative function was for a long time part of a general spirit which led all of society towards a different future. We could say that business was more than a simple societal phenomenon. In the West it was a fact of civilization. But can we define the purpose of business as economic and technological progress? Can it be an end in itself, or must it be subordinated to the imperatives of the general interest?

Today, we notice more clearly the limits, costs and dangers of unbridled technological progress. We also see that this can be only a means, and not an end in itself. It is interesting to note that in Western myths all the heroes who are catalysts of material progress are doomed. This underlines the ambivalence of this type of progress.

Technological progress renders the threat of nuclear war possible. It does not prevent thousands of humans dying from hunger, and it does not by itself resolve social inequalities. In his pride, Prometheus, 'the saviour of man', proclaims: 'I have eradicated the anguish of death.' Today we all know that Prometheus must be subordinated to a political order that is superior to him and provides him with orientation. This orientation can only be given by investing progress with purpose. We have to transcend the too exclusively financial, economic and technological approach in order to arrive at our social, political and spiritual values.

The European management model will both reflect and shape the shared values of the whole of European society.

References

Braudel, F. (1979), *Capitalisme et civilisation matérielle*, Paris: Armand Collin.
de Woot, P. (1988), *Les Entreprises de haute technologique de l'Europe*, Paris: Economica.
de Woot, P. and X. Desclee (1984), *Le Management stratégique des groupes industriels*, Paris: Economica.
Groupe ESC Lyon study for the European Round Table (1993), 'The characteristics of management in Europe, paths for the development of managers', Report, January.
Lawrence, P. R. and J. W. Lorsch (1982), *Organizational Environment*, New York: Irwin.
Lecerf, O. (1991), *Au risque de gagner*, Paris: Editions de Fallois.
Morin, E. (1987), *Penser l'Europe*, Paris: Gallimard.
SDA Bocconi and Université Catholique de Louvain (1993), 'The emerging characteristics of companies in search of the competitive edge', working paper.
Teilhard de Chardin, P. (1958), *Le Phénomène Humain*, Paris: Seuil.

Index